AN AFRICAN VILLAGE-BOY IN AOTEAROA NEW ZEALAND

Dr. Kudakwashe Nomore Tuwe

Publisher: Dr. Kudakwashe Nomore Tuwe

Cover design by: Catherine Chidawanyika

Prepared for Publication by:	WordWyze Publishing Ltd http://wordwyze.nz colleen@wordwyze.nz

A catalogue record for this book is available from the National Library of New Zealand.

First printing in New Zealand by YourBooks.co.nz (2024)

Paperback ISBN: 978-0-473-70926-6

Dedication

This book is dedicated to my dear wife Annette who has been a key supporter in my journey as documented in this book.

Annette's bona fide love and unwavering support in our 31 years of marriage is a true testimony. She stood with me through thick and thin.

If I were to re-start my life, I would choose her over and over again. Many thanks to her for the hundreds of hours invested in editing this book.

You took this project as your very own.

May the good Lord continue to bless you, my sweetheart – bone of my bone and flesh of my flesh. ♡

Contents

Foreword

I remember very well the first time I met Dr Kudakwashe Nomore Tuwe – way back in 2006 in Auckland, New Zealand. I had been in the country for less than two months. When we were introduced, he hugged me in a display of carefree exuberance. He was extremely friendly, courteous, and very knowledgeable. In the years since our relationship has grown and we have become firm friends. Today, as I write this foreword to his captivating autobiography, I share words that I always hoped—and in many ways knew—I would have the chance to write.

This autobiography provides a concise, easy-to-understand overview of Tuwe's life in both his native country Zimbabwe and his adopted home Aotearoa New Zealand (NZ). The text is chockfull of fascinating details and insights—who would have known that Tuwe is a surviving twin? Or that at one time he nearly crossed into neighbouring Mozambique to train as a Freedom Fighter? And that he lived with Tongan and Samoan families in his newly adopted home, NZ? Each chapter depicts his life from his more difficult childhood years growing up in the rural village-areas in segregated Rhodesia (now independent Zimbabwe) to the time he emigrated to NZ and the challenges he later faced. For clarity, there are several beautiful photographs showing Tuwe and the significant people he interacted with in his world (family, friends plus several NZ prominent people like former Prime Ministers Helen Clark, John Key and Jacinda Ardern; and the former Mayors of NZ cities). The book captures in vivid details of his work experience in Zimbabwe plus his struggles in securing employment in NZ. Other chapters illustrate his journey in academia, his pursuit of further education culminating in a PhD. There are some sentimental sections where he talks about his journey to find love and his work in communities; other sections highlight his principles and cathartic experiences. A recurring theme in the book is his strong Christian beliefs and studious habits. The stories in this book can help readers understand the lives of other new Kiwis who come from different backgrounds and how their cultures are similar in some ways to other cultures. One takeaway from the book is that one needs courage and determination to pursue one's dream.

Dr Abraham Simbarashe Chawanji – *Researcher, Fonterra Research & Dev Centre NZ*

Endorsements

1. In this Book, Dr Tuwe has recounted the story that I 100% relate to, not only because of the family connections or having been raised around the same neighbouring villages, but for the hunger for knowledge, believing in oneself and rejection of the notion that the circumstances of one's birth is the determinant of how much one can achieve. As most can appreciate, the village life offers very different cultural dynamic to the city life not to mention foreign lands like Aotearoa New Zealand, yet in this book Tuwe demonstrates how he maintained his character and humanity whilst positively contributing to the various cultures and excelling in his endeavours, winning at work and also winning at home. I endorse this book which will teach you about how an African village-boy who navigated all obstacles and challenges and finally settled well in a far-off indigenous land. He also triumphed over adversity, and held on to the importance of knowing one's history and background and how to achieve balanced success whilst maintaining one's faith. I think Dr Tuwe is perhaps the most accomplished and successful of my very extended family and I am proud of this book and proud of him.
Denys Denya {BAcc, ACIS, FCA(Z), MBA, AMP (Harvard)}
Executive Vice President, African Export and Import Bank, Cairo, Egypt

2. Dr Kudakwashe Nomore Tuwe is my *muzukuru* (nephew). Tuwe's maternal grandmother was a sister to my late father. As mentioned by Tuwe in his interesting book, his father was raised and looked after by my parents. I have known Tuwe all his life. He grew up in my village; under very challenging circumstances but due to focus, tenacity and determination, he managed to make breakthroughs in life. His humble, but hardworking life, is serving in our extended family and village as an inspirational testimony, especially for the youth. I'm so proud of my *muzukuru*, Dr Tuwe, for all his life-achievements. To know more about his challenging but interesting biography, I kindly invite you to dig-in, in this book. Thanks.
Mike Byton Musaka – Senator (Senate of Zimbabwe)

3. *"An African Village-Boy in Aotearoa New Zealand"* by Dr Kudakwashe Tuwe is full of optimism and hope. Despite the challenges encountered by many migrants to Aotearoa New Zealand, Tuwe shows us that, by virtue of family, community and friends, we can eventually reach the top of our academic mountain. The perseverance, humour and camaraderie that embody Tuwe are illustrated in the chapters of this book.
Dr Camille Nakhid, Professor - School of Social Sciences and Public Policy. Auckland University of Technology, Auckland, NZ

4. An outgoing, resilient and determined young man is how I remember the start of Dr Kudakwashe Tuwe's career in the banking sector in 1986. I was his ever-first manager at Zimbank, in KweKwe, Zimbabwe. These qualities are evident in how far he has come in life and the achievements attained academically, in his career and as a family man. Tuwe's life story is a lesson in daring to dream and knowing that it does not matter how life has treated you in the past, it is about how much work you are willing to put in to

get to where you want to be. It is also just as important, that Tuwe's life should serve as an inspiration to the many Zimbabwean young people leaving the country in huge numbers seeking a better and more rewarding life across borders and seas. Regards and best readings as you 'dig-in' in this exciting and empowering real Life-Story of Dr Tuwe.

***Gordon G Savanhu**, Senior Bank Executive, Harare Zimbabwe*

5. Dr Kudakwashe Tuwe and I both come from the African continent. Tuwe's journey is an inspiration to many migrants in NZ. I employed Tuwe as the Regional Engagement Manager – Central Region in the then Office of Ethnic Communities (now the Ministry for Ethnic Communities) in 2020. He inspired the panel with his passion for ethnic communities and being the voice for those communities. I just knew he will connect, engage, and understand the migrant journey in NZ because Tuwe brought his own lived-experience as an ethnic migrant in NZ. Tuwe's book is not only appropriate to those who are currently going through difficult situations, but also for everyone who would like to succeed in life. It shows personal focus and determination despite facing challenging moments on arrival in NZ. The book serves as a source of inspiration to reach your goals and never give up.

    ***Anusha Guler**, Former Deputy Chief Executive – Community & Partnerships: Ministry for Ethnic Communities, NZ*

6. I am Dr Tuwe and Annette's eldest and only daughter. Growing up in our beautiful indigenous country Zimbabwe, we were surrounded by a loving and vibrant community that embodied the meaning of Ubuntu (all for one and one for all). When we moved to NZ, it was important to our parents that we stayed connected to our roots and culture, to nurture a sense of belongingness. At home in NZ

baba (dad) and amai (mum), always encouraged us to speak in Shona (our vernacular language).

Baba exposed us to Black literature, historical influences like Dr Martin Luther King Jnr, President Nelson Rolihlahla "Madiba" Mandela, Professor Ngugi wa Thiongo, Professor Chinua Achebe and content about varying liberation movements around the globe. I'll never forget when he introduced me to Chinua Achebe's literature by practically handing me over Chinua Achebe's international bestseller novel *"Things Fall Apart"*. What a life transforming moment that was for me as a teenager who was going through an intense identity crisis. Although we have our differences (as any father and daughter do), over the years we have always bonded over books, politics, social justice, human rights and our desire for social transformation. As you'll witness in reading this book, his life is a testimony that touches on themes of the richness of African culture, colonialism, independence, migration and living in a settler colony and all the challenges and experiences that come with that. From him, I have learnt the importance of centring my values as a compass for how I show up in the world and that no matter what people say or think, the truth and justice come first.

Makanaka Tuwe, PhD Candidate (Tuwe's Daughter)

7. Every day I see people doing great things in the world and nothing beats the joy to see this simple village-boy who grew up in a rural area become a PhD holder. Tuwe is my *muzukuru* - his mum is my dad's sister. I have watched Tuwe overcome one hurdle after another to become probably the most distinguished in his huge family, among his peers and friends in the village, and to do all this with so much fun and positivity has just been amazing. I have known Tuwe all his life and have seen how he has approached life with such a passion, such tenacity and desire to conquer the world.

Well done my *muzukuru* on demonstrating how nothing is impossible to him who is daring and I don't doubt that many will find this book a joy to read.

Timon Simbarashe Nyatsambo; MD - Financial Services, South Africa

8. I have known Dr Kudakwashe Nomore Tuwe since he was a boy growing up in our rural village in Mhondoro-Ngezi, Zimbabwe. Tuwe's mother is my father's sister. Therefore, in my Shona African culture, Tuwe is my son (*chana chaTete*). From these humble beginnings, Tuwe has risen to the heights of success in life. His success stems from his hard work, focus and determination inspired by his love for God from a very early age. I recommend this book to anyone who is motivated by real-life stories.

Beauty Mabasa (Nee Nyatsambo) - Pastor Global Life Ministries, Harare. Zimbabwe

9. Dr Tuwe's recounting of growing up in abject poverty, struggling through education and eventually rising to attain a doctoral degree and working in senior positions, is a testimony that God honours hard work, humility and tenacity. I believe that this book will help you appreciate the fact that God has no favourites and that He had created you with full potential to fulfil your destiny. Dr. Tuwe did not allow his background to limit him. See you at the top because that's where you belong!

Friday Fumbilwa, JP, Senior Minister, El- Shaddai Worship Centre, Auckland NZ

10. I first met Dr. Kudakwashe Nomore Tuwe (Dr NKT), more than two decades ago, when he was my Sunday School Teacher at Torwood Baptist Church, in Redcliff, KweKwe Zimbabwe. He

had a passion to help the youth. Somehow, I knew straight away that I had finally met my life-mentor and friend. I was inspired seeing Dr NKT rising in his career-path in Zimbabwe, from humble beginnings. When he moved to NZ, through hardworking and divine blessings, he rose from being a Toilet Cleaner to Senior Managerial positions. This is the Dr NKT I know. I hereby "Endorse" this Book. It is indeed a must-read.
Saul Phiri, Leeds, UK

11. As a teenager while seeking answers to pressing life issues in the mid-eighties Dr Tuwe was placed by God in my life in time to give the adequate response. I observed him close up and from a distance. He never uttered a word or shared with me any scripture to lead me to Christ but his life spoke louder than words. What made him to be what he was then and years following is the fascinating uplifting narrative of sheer determination, grace and resilience. This book unpacks that and more.
Fanwell Nyoni - Administration Manager, Harare, Zimbabwe. (Former High School Classmate and Friend)

Acknowledgements

Firstly, I would like to sincerely thank the Lord for granting me life and blessing me throughout my difficult and challenging childhood.

Secondly, I am grateful to the following individuals for the pivotal role they played in my life and this project:

Agatha Tuhwe (My dear mother) – I am what I am because of my mother. She sacrificed all she had for me and my siblings. May the Lord continue to bless her.

Dr Abraham Simbarashe Chawanji – Dr Chawanji was instrumental in editing this book from its draft form. This is why I gave him the opportunity to write the "Foreword". Thank you, Dr Chawanji.

Annette Tuwe – As I mentioned in my dedication section, my wife Annette did a great job of editing the final manuscript. She spent many sleepless nights working on this book-project. Thanks, my sweetheart.

Makanaka Tuwe – Thanks to my daughter Makanaka for developing and creating our Tuwe Dzinza Family-Tree.

Colleen Kaluza of Wordwyze Publishing – Thanks to Colleen Kaluza for helping me to publish this book.

Cathrine Chidawanyika – Thanks to Cathy for designing the Book Cover.

Chapter One:
I Am a Twin

The Village-Twins Are Born

"*Makorokoto* and *Amhlope*". These were the only two utterances which seem to have enveloped and dominated the entire village, at that particular time and moment. These utterances simply mean '*Congratulations*' in Shona and Ndebele (respectively) which are the main two vernacular languages in my country, Zimbabwe.

Zimbabwe is geographically located in Southern Africa. We share boarders with South Africa, Mozambique, Zambia and Botswana.

In addition to the aforementioned congratulatory utterances, some excited villagers were overheard saying "*they are twin-boys again.*" A second set of twin-boys was born, to Agatha Kanda and Simon Mutsau Tuhwe (Tuwe), in a grass-thatched hut. The glad tidings spread like wild fire within the entire village and there was spontaneous joy, unspeakable celebration and ululation.

The old ladies were immediately seen walking in a single-file, displaying their '*kudengezera*' skills, carrying presents for the newly born-twins. *Kudengezera* is a Shona word which describes the art of skilfully carrying something, for example a bucket of water on one's head, balancing it without the support of hands - yet the bucket would not fall over. They were singing joyous traditional songs as they marched in a long queue leading to my *amai*'s (mother) grass-thatched and cow-dung floored hut.

The birthday presents were in the form of home-made mealie-meal, home-grown vegetables and other precious African traditional gifts. This was the herald and announcement of the arrival and birth of the twin-boys. The twin-boys were my fraternal brother Anyway Tendai Tuwe and I, Kudakwashe Nomore Tuwe. This was in the mid-1960s in the heart of Mhondoro-Ngezi, within the Mashonaland West Province in the then Rhodesia (now independent Zimbabwe). Mhondoro-Ngezi is about 132 kms southwest of Harare, the capital city, and 130 kms east of my district town of Kadoma. My village is popularly known as Madhondo. My village *Sabhuku* (Headman) is Muchemwa and my *Mambo* (Chief) is Benhura. See Zimbabwe and Africa maps below.

This is the genesis of the story of my life: I was born in a relatively poor Zimbabwean family to Agatha Kanda and Simon Mutsau Tuhwe. Although materially poor, we were rich in culture and traditional values. In my vernacular language (Shona), *amai* means mother and *baba* is father. I will be using these words interchangeably.

For the avoidance of doubt, my proper surname should be spelt as 'Tuhwe', but unfortunately at the time of getting my birth certificate there was a spelling mistake. 'Tuhwe' was written as 'Tuwe'. This contamination of my original surname was mainly due to the fact that most of the clerical staff at the then District Administrator (DA)'s office, who issued identification documents (IDs) was mostly manned by the British nationals, our colonial masters, who had no clue of our local languages and spellings. This is the tragedy of colonisation. However; half of my family is known as Tuhwe and the other as Tuwe. Therefore, in this context, Tuhwe and Tuwe are one and the same.

My *amai* is always reminding me that the Lord loves me so much. A story is told that one day when my *amai* was working in a field, a few kilometres from the village, my twin brother and I were asleep under a tree (enjoying the shadow) and I suddenly started crying uncontrollably. My voice changed, my eyes drowned in their sockets, my entire body immediately turned greenish in colour. I was lifeless. She immediately took me back to the village, where I was pronounced half-dead. They called my *amai's* elder cousin-sister (*Mbuya* Rina Musaka) who prayed for me. Slowly, I woke up from the land of the dead and they later discovered that my intestines were almost popping out of my lower-stomach. There was a big lump protruding ready to burst. I was rushed to Gatooma (now Kadoma) General Hospital for an emergency major operation. Up to this day, the operation-scars are distinctive and visible. Kadoma is my district town, 130 kms west of my village. The dust road was in a terrible state. Up to this day, it is not tarred. Thank God I survived the operation.

Later in years, when my mother took me and my twin brother, to our local village Methodist Church for baptism, she told *Mufundisi* (Pastor) that my name was Nomore, thus, '*no more children again, because I have suffered enough*'. My twin brother was named Anyway, meaning, '*whatever happens in life, I care less...*' Mufundisi vehemently rejected both names as he believed in the power and influence of names in the life of the name-carrier. He therefore gave us both new Shona names, with a Christian meaning. I was renamed *Kudakwashe. Kudakwashe* means '*The Will of the Lord*'. My twin-brother Anyway was renamed Tendai which means '*Thankful*'. This was the origin of my official name (Kudakwashe). I love it.

However, those who are well acquainted with my roots and my early childhood village-life, know me as Nomore. If I hear anyone calling me 'Nomore', I straight away know that they really know me and my roots. Please see the first photo page for maps of Zimbabwe and the African continent.

'Vahosi' the 'Greater House' and My Siblings

I was born in a polygamy set-up (*barika*) which means my father had more than one wife. Traditionally, as the senior and first wife in a polygamy set-up, my *amai*'s household was referred to as *'Vahosi'* meaning the *'Greater-House'*. *Amai* had seven biological sons, in a naturally unique way, thus, singles followed by a set of twins. The seven boys were born in the following order: Peter (single), Maxwell (Bhuru) and Michael/Mike (Tsuro), first set of twins, Paul (single), Anyway and Kudakwashe Nomore (me), the second and last set of twins and lastly Tapiwa Ignatius (single). Since my *amai* had no biological baby-girl of her own, she adopted a newly born pretty baby-girl from her younger sister, Agnes Kanda. The baby-girl's name is Grace. From the day that Grace joined our household, up to now, she is our only baby-sister in my *amai's* greater-house. When asked how many siblings I have from my mother's side, I always say 'eight' - without thinking. Not many people know that she is not my mother's biological daughter. In our Zimbabwean African tradition, this is normal and accepted practice. One does not require any adoption documentation.

The report has it that, at birth, Maxwell was nicknamed 'Bhuru' (bull) because he was *'as fat as a traditional African village bull-cow'*, while Mike was nicknamed 'Tsuro' (hare) because he was *'as clever as a wild-hare'*. His tiny eyes were all-over and his big ears always 'stood-up', ready to capture every single gossip of the village.

For the avoidance of confusion, we later relocated to Sanyati, from Mhondoro, in 1993, soon after my wedding. Sanyati is about 212 kms west of Mhondoro-Ngezi, but within the same Mashonaland West Province. My maternal grandparents (Kufonya and Lydia Kanda) also relocated to Sanyati with us and our new homesteads (in Sanyati) are only about three kilometres apart.

The Old Zimbabwean Culture on Twins

I am told that in the olden days (especially before the mid-1920s) it was traditionally a taboo and culturally unacceptable to give birth to twins and let them live. It was considered a mystery, a natural abominable event, and culturally intolerable. One of the twins had to be killed. Within a Zimbabwean cultural context, Norbet Mafumhe Mutasa presented an explicit narration and fascinating account on twins in his intriguing novel titled '*Mapatya*' (Mutasa, 1978). In my Zimbabwean Shona language, '*Mapatya*' means 'Twins'.

Based on the stories I have heard, some of the ways of killing the twins implemented in those olden days in Zimbabwe were brutal and barbaric (Mutasa,1978). This included pouring red-hot ashes in the mouth of the innocent newly-born baby and then tightly closing its mouth. The resultant effect would be 'cooked' internal organs, including the throat and intestines. Again, I am informed that if the twins were a boy and a girl, they would normally sacrifice the girl-child since the boy was regarded as a family name-bearer who would later advance and biologically promote the family lineage and heritage. In the event of being both boys, they would preserve the '*first one to see the sun*', thus the first one to be born, who would be deemed the elder one, and kill the younger one.

Not only in Zimbabwe was this traditional and cultural practice happening, but in other parts of Africa such as South Africa, Zambia, Kenya, Nigeria, Rwanda, Burundi and Uganda (Verbal Communication, 11 October 2019).

In our case, I was the younger twin - I was born last. If we were born in the 1920s, I would have been one of the statistics, thus, dead and gone. In simple terms, I would have been brutally killed. I was therefore blessed and fortunate to be born outside the parameters of those dark and dangerous cultural days (1920s).

I am forever grateful to the Lord, the Creator of heaven and the earth for saving my life. Indeed, I concur with the Biblical prophet Jeremiah who proclaimed that *"I knew you before you were formed in your mother's womb"*. I thank God that I am still alive. As a result of this miraculous preservation of my life, I have therefore purposely decided to humbly seek to please both God and the human race by doing good and getting involved in effective service to my family, my local community, my country and the global community of nations.

While I am still too far from reaching the apex of my community contribution, I have started, in a small way, by writing on the importance of African cultural practices and traditions as well as the significance of using African Oral Tradition of Storytelling as an internationally accepted research methodology (Tuwe, 2016).

In addition, I have written two theses, (i) Master of Philosophy (MPhil) on *"Challenges of Health Promotion for African Communities in New Zealand"* (Tuwe, 2012) and (ii) PhD on *"Employment Challenges for African Communities in New Zealand"* (Tuwe, 2018). I have also contributed a book-chapter titled *'Ziva Kwawakabva/Yazi Odabuka Khona/Remember Your Roots' (ZRSLT, Forthcoming, 2024)*.

Based on the evidence gathered so far, these publications have had a positive impact, especially on Africans in the diaspora, thus, people of African descent living outside of the African continent. In addition, I hope this book (you are reading now), will also have a meaningful contribution to the community development within an African context and African flavour.

My Twin and Our Childhood Village-Boys

Growing up as fraternal twins in our village, Anyway and I were very close to each other. We profoundly loved each other and deeply cared for each other. We always played together – as depicted in the photo below. We never fought, as far as I can remember. Yes, we had our own disagreements and arguments, just like any other small children, but we resolved them in a civil and harmonious way. Thanks to our *amai*, who taught us to genuinely respect and love each other.

Apart from my twin brother being my closest friend, we were blessed to have two close friends in our village who were of the same age-bracket as us. These two were not only close friends but close relatives whom we referred to as family members, within the context of our African culture. Within the Euro-centric culture, these would be referred to as extended family. However, within the African cultural vocabulary, there is nothing called *'individualistic, nuclear family or extended family'*. We are family. The natural and umbrella Shona word is *'mhuri'*(family).

The names of these two close special friends and relatives of ours were Lloyd Mutizwa popularly known in our village as Chikuru Musaka and Taurai Matonga who was also known as Taurai Gumbeze. I was related to Chikuru from both my father and mum's side. From a cultural standpoint, I called him *'babamunini'* (meaning 'my small father'). Taurai was my *'muzukuru/muzaya'* (nephew). The four of us were always together, both in doing good and naughty deeds. We were partners in crime. At one time, all four of us played for our formidable junior soccer team at Muchemwa Primary School. My twin brother Anyway was one of the most gifted footballers in the village and the surrounding areas. He played centre striker (number 9) and rarely missed the goalpost. Chikuru was left-legged and hence he played the far-left wing (number 11). He was one of the greatest assets in our team. Taurai was the best goalkeeper in the entire Mhondoro-Ngezi region. He was nicknamed *'Katsi, the Cat'* because of his ball-catching skills. I played the far-right wing (number 7). Out of the four aforementioned "soccer stars", I was the least skilled and talented. I think my close association with these three great soccer players immensely contributed and influenced my entrance and acceptance into this arduous team. I couldn't have made it on my own.

The saddest news is that my dear twin brother and my two close childhood village-friends have now passed-on. They all died at a very young and tender age. I am the only one left. At times, when I think and reflect on those great and interesting olden days, I feel lonely and miss my trio best comrades, in particular my twin brother. However, I feel indebted and grateful to the Lord, for His sufficient grace. As for my twin brother, he peacefully passed-on in his sleep in December 1990, in my flat, in a town called Redcliff, in KweKwe, Zimbabwe. I was working for Zimbabwe Iron and Steel Ltd (Ziscosteel) and my twin was staying with me. Due to our umbilical closeness, from birth, his death shattered and shocked me to the core. It was devastating, to say the least. Had it not been for the abundant and sufficient grace of God and the unwavering support I got from my local churches (Torwood/Peniel Baptist Church), work colleagues from Ziscosteel and the Torwood/Redcliff community at large, I may have not survived. Some of the youth from Torwood/Peniel Baptist Church accompanied me to Mhondoro-Ngezi (about 100 kms) for the burial of my dear twin-brother. I am forever grateful. From my former employer (Ziscosteel), the assistance was huge, especially from my former boss, Mrs Anna-Mercy Mashingaidze.

As for Lloyd, he later worked in South Africa but passed-on in Zimbabwe in the early 2000s. Taurai had joined the Zimbabwe National Army and then died in a town called Chiredzi in the early 1990s. I dearly miss my trio-youthful connections. May their dear souls rest in everlasting peace - MHSRIEP 🙏.

Growing Up in the Village

Apart from the abovementioned tight-close team of the four village-boys, everyone in our village was somehow connected to each other. People cared and looked after each other. Within the context of our African culture, they say *"It takes a village to raise a child"*. If a child was seen misbehaving, any elder in the village would institute instant discipline. There was no need to seek prior approval from their parents. If the naughty child made a mistake of reporting the incident to his/her parents, he/she would be further chastised and forced to go and apologise to the disciplining elder for misbehaving. The whole practice and tradition were meant to indoctrinate and inculcate the village-child that the village was a united single-entity and family. It was all about the importance of unity and oneness in the village. This is based on the African philosophical concept called Ubuntu (Mandela, 1994; Tuwe, 2018). This is the equivalence of the Biblical principle of *'being thy brother's keeper'*. Ubuntu means *"I am what I am because of you"* (Mandela, 1994, p.10, Johann, 2006, p.15; Tuwe, 2018, p.14). In my mother-tongue (Shona), Ubuntu is interpreted as '*Munhu, munhu nekuda kwevanhu'* which means '*a person is a person because of other people'* and *"I am human because I belong to the human-community and human-race; and I view and treat others accordingly"* (Chavunduka, 1978, p. 25; Tuwe, 2018, p. 97). According to Tutu and Tutu (2014, p. 148), Ubuntu means, *"I am incomplete without you"*. The entire concept is centred on people and humanity (Carson, 1998; Mandela, 1994; Tuwe, 2018).

Since my *amai's* household had the highest number of boys in the village, our homestead was used as the 'village-stadium' for soccer games. The balls were made of old cloth-rags bound in plastics. Most village-boys would congregate at our homestead mostly on weekends to participate in soccer while girls would grace the events by supporting and cheering their boyfriends. That was during the day. At night, all youth would rotate different village-homes to dance to the tantalising African traditional songs and drums (Tuwe, 2018).

In between songs and dance, the youth would sit around a fire and listen to thought-provoking traditional stories from the elders (Ngugi, 1965; 1986; 1998; Tuwe, 2018). Before reading and writing was developed in ancient Africa, Africans used oral storytelling as a way of transmitting their history, heritage, knowledge, experiences, thoughts, aspirations, dreams, beliefs, values, fears and feelings from one generation to the next (Achebe, 1987; Cannarozzi, 1999; Ngugi wa Thiong'o, 1967, 1986; Tuwe, 2018). Among others, these stories were about the many gods and goddesses worshipped by our ancestors in the valleys and mountains, and some were about our heroes and heroines, and leaders and kings who fought and won great wars and battles (Ngugi wa Thiong'o, 1964; Tuwe, 2018). Stories were also about the evils of colonisation and how the African ways of knowing were invalidated and side-lined (Achebe, 1959; Ngugi wa Thiong'o, 2000; Tuwe, 2018). There was no written language, so stories were transmitted orally. This kept African history alive (Ngugi wa Thiong'o, 1982; Tuwe, 2018). Apart from traditional underpinning teachings, the oral stories were pregnant and punctuated with political propaganda and African activism and awakening (Tuwe, 2018). The main reason for this indoctrination was that our country was still called Rhodesia and under the oppressive minority white regime of Prime Minister Ian Douglas Smith.

Most of these activities would take place under the bright moon and the shining stars of the night-sky. There was no electricity and no water-taps in our villages. We drew water from dug-wells and nearby river-streams and oases. There were no tarred roads. The food was fresh and healthy, mostly organic and traditional. For most village-families, especially mine, we normally had *Mahewu* for breakfast. Within the context of my Zimbabwean culture, traditional *Mahewu* (Shona) and *Amahewu* (Ndebele) is a nutritious non-alcoholic home-brewed drink made of thin, slightly fermented maize-meal porridge or left-overs of sadza. Sadza is Zimbabwe's main traditional staple food made out of white maize mealie-meal. It's rich in starch and carbohydrates. Mahewu is often mixed with yeast or *rapoko* for fermentation process. Due to non-affordability, most of the time we had it with no sugar. The taste is not that good without sugar; it's sour and bitter. This is not similar to the current, luxurious, modernised commercially-packaged *mahewu* known as '*Pfuko*', which is in the form of an instant ready-mix. Far from it. Due to poverty and lack of economic independence, coupled with colonial marginalisation and political oppression, most villagers only drank tea on Christmas Day. The majority could not afford it. My family was one of those. My *amai* had to do piece-jobs in other people's fields for us to have tea and bread on Christmas Day. The good thing in my village was that even those who could not afford, like my family, the other village-members generously shared with them. On Christmas Day, everyone was free to visit and eat from any household. No one took offence. Again, this was the implementation of Ubuntu at its best.

For lunch and dinner, we normally had sadza with vegetables. Cooking oil and meat were luxuries. If we did not have mahewu in the morning, we had sadza three times per day, thus, for breakfast, lunch and dinner. Life was tough.

As little village boys one of our main duties was to look after cattle and other animals such as goats, sheep, pigs and donkeys for our parents. For those households who did not have boys, the community members would freely help.

Apart from some of the aforementioned economic challenges, life in the village was lively, vibrant and interesting. You could feel the bona fide love and sense of unity and purpose in the air. Such was the spirit and culture of my Madhondo village. I miss it dearly. At times I still dream playing in the village, with my childhood friends.

This is the story of my life:
An African village-boy from Madhondo in Mhondoro-Ngezi, Zimbabwe.

Chapter Two:
My Dzinza (Genealogy) –
My Family-Tree

My Dzinza (Genealogy/Whakapapa)

The following is my brief *Dzinza*. In my mother tongue (Shona), *dzinza* simply means genealogy. In Ndebele, this is known as *Usendo*. In Māori (the indigenous people of Aotearoa New Zealand) it is called *Whakapapa*. These days, the dzinza/genealogy concept is normally presented in a diagrammatical way, in the form of a "Family-Tree". Please see my Dzinza/ Family-Tree in the 'Photo Section' further on.

My Amai (Mother): Agatha Tuwe (nee Kanda)

My *amai* Agatha Tuhwe (nee Kanda) is the eldest daughter of Paul Kufonya Kanda and Nyanya Lydia Kanda (nee Denya). She turned 89 on the 9th of September, 2023. I thank the Lord for granting her a long, healthy life despite the many challenges and abuses she went through in her marriage. Hers was a heavily polygamous marriage setup as mentioned before. She was the first and senior wife (Vahosi) of my father's three official wives. At one time, in addition to the three official wives in the village, my baba had several extra marital affairs in cities and towns in which he had lived and worked.

My siblings and I were fortunate and blessed that our dear *amai* did not abandon us regardless of the hardships she faced in her marriage. The challenges started in the very early days of her marriage. In my view, (and confirmed by her), the main reason why she sacrificed for us is that she was raised in a solid and functional Christian family who had strong traditional principles. Her life-values and upbringing were based on her Christian faith and African traditional extended-family beliefs. Her parents were committed Christians. My maternal grandfather was a devoted para-priest (conducting church services) in a local Anglican Church as well as a Village-Headman. My maternal grandmother was a disciplinarian and firm believer in our African traditions and culture. From an African cultural perspective, a responsible and cultured woman does not turn her back on her children and return to her parents' village no matter how tough it was.

My *amai* was one of the very first young girls in her village to have a proper Christian Church-wedding; after all important African traditional marriage rituals were completed. In those olden days, it brought joy, happiness and respect to one's family if a daughter got married like that. Most of her younger sisters had no choice but to follow suit. They, too, had weddings that had huge gatherings in the village to the upliftment and happiness of both my maternal grandparents.

When my parents were wedded in 1954, my *amai* was around 20 years and my baba 22. Baba was doing well in his Police Officer-job and was always getting promoted. *Amai* was a stay-at-home mum and did not have a circular job. In my view, this was a fulltime-busy job. Initially, they were a very happy young couple. However, this happiness did not last long because my baba married more wives as well as got involved in other extra marital relationships.

Since my baba was now a husband of many wives and a father of several children, it was no longer financially viable for him to support his suddenly large family. My mother, who has never been formally employed, single-handedly provided for my siblings and I from her earnings as a subsistence farmer. She would work in other people's fields in order for us to have food on the table and to go to school. She did this from a very young age and soon after getting married. I vividly remember her working so hard, especially towards winter, to raise money to buy us warm clothes, particularly tennis shoes, because winters in Zimbabwe can be viciously cold. My dad would spend many years without returning to the village or financially supporting us, but my mother never turned her back on us. She could have gone back to her nearby parents' village, and they were able to take care of her, but she chose to stick up for us. In other words, she sacrificed all she had for us to be what we are today. Without her, my siblings and I would have been the destitute, the abused and the downtrodden in the village. But thanks to my mum who sacrificed so much for us. I personally feel profoundly grateful and grossly indebted to my mother. She is my heroine and hope for a living. She is my survival-rock and reason to live. I strongly believe that her Christian values based on Biblical principles, human rights and social justice carried her through this harsh and unbearable life. I don't think that if I was in her situation, I would have passed the 'test'. I would have given up because there was enough justification and reason to abandon us (her children).

The other surprising thing about *Amai* was her endless generosity despite her conspicuous poverty and lack. She would share the little food we had with strangers, particularly the widows, the orphans and the needy in our villages. Initially, my siblings and I did not understand her 'misplaced generosity'. But now we do. *Amai* staunchly believed in the Biblical principle which says *"Blessed is the hand that giveth than the one that taketh"*. She literally lived this scripture. She was also strongly guided by our

African cultural philosophy of Ubuntu and principles of human rights and social justice (Universal Declaration of Human Rights, 1948; Mandela, 1994; Tuwe 2018). It is important to note that these principles are crucially imperative to the entire human race because they are of fundamental value to both the individual and the collective community. They are part of the constitution of one's identity, and one's social inclusion and empowerment (Tuwe, 2018). I also believe that I inherited some of the characteristics to do with human rights and social justice from my *amai*.

My Baba (Father): Simon Mutsau Tuwe

Simon Mutsau Tuhwe, the son of Esther 'Mugaiwa' Musaka and Timoti Tuhwe is my baba. Baba was an ever-jovial joyful man who naturally attracted both friends and enemies. His adversaries had no choice but to like him. Since his parents were divorced, he struggled to secure tuition fees for his education. He would miss classes while doing piece jobs in order to raise school fees. However, it was an 'open secret' in my village that despite missing classes, at the end of each term, baba would be at the top of his class. Not only was he good academically, but was one of the best runners in the entire province. He was also a renowned soccer player. Due to his outstanding academic and sporting accomplishments and performance, the school authorities were sympathetic to him, such that they did not always send him away due to non-payment of school fees.

Due to lack of financial resources, my baba could not complete his higher primary education, which was then known as standard six. This is the equivalence of year seven. Instead, he secured a job at a very tender age. His first career was with the British South African Police (BSAP) as a Police Officer in Rhodesia (now Zimbabwe). He spent most of his Police-career days in Manicaland Province.

Being a traditional man, my baba married two more wives (after my mother), such that at one time, he had three, all living in the same village-compound. Dad continued working in the cities and there, he enjoyed the city life as if he was a bachelor. During those olden days, this was normal within an African marriage setup. Nowadays, it still happens but at a lower scale.

Officially, I have about 23 siblings from the loins of my baba; from a total of five wives. Rumour has it that he had several girlfriends and possibly 'planted' numerous children in most cities in which he once domiciled and worked. We are also told that there is a possibility that we might be having 'mixed-race' siblings from my dad. In a Zimbabwean context, a 'mixed-race' or 'coloured' person is a product of a white and a black couple. If this is true, it means baba had children with white ladies. In those days, it was not allowed under the apartheid system to go out with a white person so if it's true I wonder how baba did it. As a result of this, some of his grandchildren (our children) call him a legend and celebrity 😊.

Due to his natural intelligence coupled with a jovial and positive attitude toward both his superiors and peers, he was quickly promoted through several ranks within the Police force. My baba always projected a happy, joyful and buoyant attitude. Be it at home, work or within community, he was always a happy man. In my entire life, I have never seen my dad angry.

Despite having so many children, baba rarely visited our village. Many young people in my village did not know him. The sad part is that even my younger brother and some of my younger half-brothers and half-sisters did not know him either until there were about seven years. But surprisingly, those rare times he visited, villagers would congregate in our compound to greet and welcome him. Some, especially the younger ones, who had only heard about him and his hilarious and entertaining stories, wanted to see what type of a man he really was. He had this rare and unique ability to relate and connect so well with every age, generation, ethnicity, race and gender. With the majority he met for the first time, it was as if they had known each other for decades. He had both amazing social and 'soft' skills and abilities to quickly and easily build rapport with strangers.

He was tallish, handsome, intelligent, sociable and always smartly dressed. He always moved around with a hair-comb in his pocket to ensure his hair looked good. There are many fun stories about my baba, especially during his working life. While working with him in the same company (Ziscosteel Ltd), each time there was a small congregation of workers laughing and making noise, one could almost tell that it was my baba cracking jokes. One of the old stories is how he 'fixed', embarrassed and 'put in line' one of his abusive British bosses in the Police force. It is told that one day while driving on a patrol trip, the said boss asked my baba, *"Mutsau; where do you come from? I mean your African native village?"* Baba seized this as a golden opportunity to politically and intellectually insult his boss, but in a subtle way. His response was *"I come from England, boss"*. The face of his boss immediately turned red in anger because, in those colonial days, indigenous Black Africans were politically oppressed and economically marginalised. They were basically treated as second-class citizens in their own country of birth. Therefore, telling a white boss that a Black African man was originally from the land of the white men, England, was a serious offence which would cost him his job. But my baba did not care. In anger and denial, the white boss made a U-turn and drove back to the Police Charge Office and reported my baba to the superiors. His aim was to have my dad instantly dismissed from the Police force. At the Charge Office, my dad was given an opportunity to defend himself. That is the grave mistake they made because, remember, my baba was smart and intelligent. He confidently said to the Member-In-Charge and the audience, *"Boss, I did not say I come from England. I said I come from Enkeleee-doorn."* Instead of simply saying 'Enkeldoorn,' he purposely said "Enkeleee-doorn" (pulling the 'eeenkleeedoorn' word) in order to be freed from this case as well as not to lose his job. Enkeldoorn (now Chivhu) is a town, 146 kms south of Harare, Zimbabwe's capital city. Immediately, the Member-In-Charge thundered his 'legal' hammer (thump) and pronounced *"Not guilty. Mutsau, you are free to go"*. Baba was 'discharged' from the allegation. The senior police officer was furious and, at the same time, ashamed and embarrassed. He later sought a transfer and left the police station. Within a short time, baba was promoted.

The other fun story about baba is that each time he was asked to be the acting Police Member-In-Charge, upon return, his bosses could not understand why there was always high staff morale and happiness in the Police camp. They could not comprehend how he was able to motivate staff by boosting and enhancing work-enthusiasm. Staff productivity would go up, and absenteeism drastically dropped. The secret was, unknown to his superiors, baba strategically deployed his work colleagues (Police Officers) to villages and areas where he knew the staff members had girlfriends. In addition, these officers were well financially resourced via 'per diems (bush allowances) and food. Most staff wished that baba could be a permanent Member-In-Charge. They liked him. On the other hand, the superiors valued him. This earned my baba another promotion as he was deemed a good and competent officer with outstanding abilities to motivate and manage staff. Later, he was posted to a different station where he implemented the same strategy, and it worked well for him.

The other reason why baba was liked by his fellow Police Officers and the communities was that he was politically aware of the environment in which he was operating – some of the Police policies and legislations were oppressive for the indigenous people such that he would ignore some of the political 'offences' committed by community members. This made him the darling of the village chiefs and the entire communities in which he operated.

It is with a deep heartache that my father passed on in May 2003, in my 5th month in New Zealand. It was most painful because I could not attend his funeral and burial (in Zimbabwe), mainly because I was new and struggling to settle in a foreign country. Although I had a return air ticket to Zimbabwe, I could not afford to pay for my New Zealand return trip. Besides, New Zealand had just introduced visas in February 2003 for Zimbabweans, and it suddenly became extremely difficult to come to New Zealand. However, sad as it was, the consoling thing was that my wife and I (before I left for New Zealand), had managed to send my dad for a major surgery and special treatment which was expensive. Thanks to my other brothers and their wives who contributed towards the medical bills. Before leaving for New Zealand, I also requested for his parental blessings, which he bestowed upon me. We also prayed together before I left. As we prayed, I knew it was my last time seeing my dear baba.

Although my father was mostly absent in my life and did not contribute in my upbringing as he was supposed to, I respected and honoured him. I harbored no bitterness towards him. May His Soul Rest in Everlasting Peace (MHSREP🙏).

My Ambuya (Maternal Grandmother): Nyanya Lydia Kanda (nee Denya)

Ambuya (Shona) and *gogo* (Ndebele) means grandmother. I will be using these words interchangeably as we do in Zimbabwe. Ambuya Nyanya Lydia Kanda was my maternal grandmother – the mother of my *amai*, Agatha. She was one of the numerous daughters of Chief Chakadonha Denya (Nyika) and Dzanisa Jangara. She was born and raised in Denya village in Mhondoro-Ngezi. The Denyas are very famous in our village. Although my ambuya could not read and write, she was smart and intelligent. It was simply a matter of being deprived of the opportunity to access education. If she had the opportunity to go to school like her youngest brother Titus Matiyenga Denya, she could have accomplished much in the academic world. It's unfortunate that during those days, it was seen as wasting resources to educate the girl-child. Her brother Titus was considered one of the most educated indigenous Black Zimbabwean in the whole Mashonaland West Province in the 1960s. *Sekuru* Titus became a successful Principal in many schools in a number of provinces in Zimbabwe. I adored and admired him. He was one of those who motivated and inspired me in the world of education such that when he passed on in 1999, I had to drive a distance of about 225 kms (dust and dilapidated roads) to pick up his sister (my ambuya Nyanya) from her new dwelling place in Sanyati in order to attend his funeral and burial in Mhondoro-Ngezi.

Titus Denya's desire and propensity for education somehow rubbed off on one of his sons, Denys Denya, the accomplished and polished Chartered Accountant, who is currently working at Afreximbank as the Executive Vice President, based in Cairo, Egypt. This is just to show that intelligence was a commodity in abundance in my ambuya's household and lineage. I guess my maternal grandmother's side also contributed to my interest and appetite for education. Denys is also special to me because he was pivotal in supplying important '*Denya ancestry information and data*' as I researched 'My Dzinza/Family-Tree' material for this book.

In my Shona culture, a grandmother, especially from the mother's side (maternal), is mostly a darling and a friend to her grandchildren. The grandchildren would play all over her and perform all kinds of mischief which they would never dare to attempt in front of their parents, especially mothers. However, this was not the case with Ambuya Nyanya. She was feared and dreaded by all of us, her grandchildren, and other small children in the entire village. She was a straight talker, sharp-tongued, no-nonsense old lady, and a tough disciplinarian. She always wanted everything to be orderly and in the right place. Since the distance between my father's homestead and Ambuya's village (in Mhondoro-Ngezi) was about seven kilometres, I was blessed to have stayed with her and Sekuru Kufonya for about two years when I was a small boy, looking after their cattle and goats. This gave me an opportunity to know Gogo Nyanya intimately. On the brighter side, she would tell you the authentic truth in order to make you a better person. She would do it from a pure and clean heart. My best moments with Ambuya Nyanya were when she would sing Christian hymns and songs of praising and worshipping God every evening after dinner. The singing always came after Sekuru Kufonya's interesting, rich and thought-provoking stories, framed and based on African oral tradition of storytelling practices (Tuwe, 2018) and Biblical parables.

In the later years, when I was working, I became very close friends with Ambuya Nyanya, and I was one of her favourite grandchildren. The main reason was that, each time I visited my village from the city, I would spoil her with nice things she loved, such as sweets, biscuits, fizzy drinks, meat and dried tiny fish (*matemba*). She had a sweet tooth. When I jokingly told her that I had not brought her stuff, she would be furious and tell me off.

Due to old age, my *amai* eventually took Ambuya Nyanya into our homestead in order to give her proper care and love. This gave us an opportunity to 'spoil' and do good things for Gogo. Sadly, Gogo Nyanya had her last breath in May 2003 when I had been only five months in New Zealand. She died a few days before my dad passed on at the age of around 95 years. This means I lost two important people in my life in the same week. For the reasons already explained, I could not attend her funeral and burial in Zimbabwe. However, I was blessed to pay my last respects in 2007, when I first visited my beloved country of birth, after a long continuous five-year stay in New Zealand. I was happy and relieved to see where Ambuya Lydia Nyanya Kanda (nee Denya) was laid to rest. I miss her dearly. MHSREP🙏.

My Sekuru (Maternal Grandfather): Paul Kufonya Kanda

Sekuru (grandfather) Paul Kufonya Kanda was my maternal grandfather. This made him my *sekuru*. His father was Bota Kanda, and his mother was Gungudzo. He originally came from Njanja, near a town called Chivhu, before he relocated to Mhondoro-Ngezi, when he was a small boy. We are told that he grew up as an orphan. Sekuru Kufonya was one of the most gracious and yet humblest men I have ever seen in my entire life. He and Ambuya Nyanya were blessed with seven children, one son and six daughters. His best friends were his children, especially the girls.

Each time Sekuru Kufonya's daughters visited him, there was joy, peace and happiness in the entire household, which was also contagious to the village-neighbours. Sekuru Kufonya was mostly known, in the whole village, for his outstanding ability to narrate traditional African stories as well as interpret them. He had another rare competence of telling Biblical stories in such a flamboyant and convincing way. Each time he narrated an ancient traditional story, he would dramatize and vividly describe it as if he was present when the events unfolded. He was highly gifted. It was said that his gift to narrate stories was buttressed and enhanced by his preaching pedagogical skills. He was the para-priest at a local Anglican Church based at Saint Cuthbert Gasanyama School, where he administered Sunday services without fail. His sermons were vibrant, captivating, humorous and soul-searching.

Every night without fail, especially in summer, small children from around the village would congregate in his grass-thatched hut around a fire and attentively listen to his compelling and thought-provoking stories. He also had the talent and flair of knowing where and when to throw a joke and when to be serious when narrating stories. As I stated before, I felt blessed and honoured to have had an opportunity to live with Sekuru

Kufonya and Gogo Nyanya, under their roof, for two years in their village. Everyone in the village, called Sekuru Kufonya 'Fata' (a Saint) because of his good deeds and genuine love for the people. All the village children loved him dearly. As evidence that Sekuru Kufonya was a God-fearing man, he died peacefully on his knees during a family evening prayer session in 1995. MHSREP 🙏.

I was honoured when they asked me (and my dear wife) to buy his coffin, which is a blessing in my culture. I also played a leading role at his funeral and burial. I guess my passion for human rights and social justice, based on Biblical principles, was influenced by my maternal grandfather.

My Gogo (Paternal Grandmother): Esther 'Mugaiwa' Tuwe (nee Musaka)

Gogo Esther 'Mugaiwa' Musaka was my paternal grandmother, and she was the firstborn with three siblings (two brothers and a sister). Her father was Muzavazi Musaka and her mother was Chimhimbi Madzivanyika. The name of her husband, my Sekuru (grandfather) was Timoti Tuhwe. She was nick-named *'Mugaiwa'* because of her light complexion. She was also known in the entire village for her astonishing beauty. When Ambuya Mugaiwa was pregnant with my father, she was divorced by my grandfather. In my Zimbabwean Shona African culture, when you want to divorce your wife, you give her what is known as *'gupuro'*, which is a token of as little as a gold coin, for example ten cents. This is meant to show that you no longer love your wife and you are customarily divorcing her. The *gupuro* is normally given to the divorced wife in the presence of her relatives as witnesses. I am told that when Sekuru Timoti divorced my gogo Mugaiwa, he gave her my unborn father (pregnancy) as a *gupuro*. He paid no money, not even a single cent. In my culture, this is unheard of. This was the highest degree of disrespect. It meant that he was completely disinterested in the relationship with my ambuya. Sounds as if he had lost all love and affection. Sekuru Timoti took off and my father had to be raised by his mother's parents (the Musakas) and partly his paternal grandfather, Chibikamanhanga.

Since my gogo Mugaiwa was exceptionally beautiful and presentable, within no time, she stole the heart of a Police Officer who fell in love with her. This Police Officer was a Mr Ndumera, originally from Mberengwa, in the Midlands Province closer to Matabeleland. She later married Mr Ndumera and had three children. This meant that my father, a Shona, had now half-siblings who were Ndebeles. Maybe this explains why I have a natural love and appreciation for the Ndebele people.

Gogo Mugaiwa came from a family of renowned political activists. Her brothers, Peter Musaka and Stephen Chipfo Musaka were active in politics and vehemently opposed the oppressive Unilateral Declaration of Independence (UDI) declared by Ian Douglas Smith, the last white Prime Minister of Rhodesia (now Zimbabwe) from 1965-1979. (Lancaster House Agreement, 1979; I. D. Smith, 1997).

Their sons played a central role in the Zimbabwe armed struggle; for example, Peter's elder sons, Ephraim Musaka and Nisbet Musaka (Comrade Mabhonzo), later joined the Zimbabwe Second Chimurenga, which was also known as the Zimbabwe Liberation Guerrilla War (1966-1979). This is the war which led the end of white-minority rule in Rhodesia and ushered us into our political independence of the majority Black Zimbabweans in 1980, under the rule of Robert Gabriel Mugabe (1924-2017). I guess my political activism and consciousness is from my paternal grandmother's side.

I vividly remember Ambuya Mugaiwa visiting us in Mhondoro-Ngezi with my cousin Douglas Ndumera, aunt Agnes Ndumera and their children. Each time they visited; it was a time of celebration. The last time I saw my beloved gogo Mugaiwa was in 1997 when she visited us in Gweru. My wife and I (and our two small children) later drove her to her village in Mberengwa. During the long drive, we had a very good fellowship with her and little did we know that it would be our last time to set our eyes on her. Gogo Mugaiwa later passed on in Mberengwa in 2006, when I was already in New Zealand. MHSREP 🙏.

My Sekuru (Paternal Grandfather): Timoti Tuhwe

Sekuru Timoti Tuhwe, my grandfather, was the son of Chibika-manhanga (Chibika) Tuhwe and Gogo Muguhu. This makes Chibika my *zisekuru/teteguru* (great grandfather. I am also told that Chibika had two wives: a gogo Muguhu, the first wife, who was a beautiful Ndebele girl originally from a South African tribe called baSotho and a local one known as Gogo Mazviitireni Jirongo (second wife). Looks like the issue of polygamy and 'an eye for beautiful women' runs in my father's family. Maybe this explains why I have a strong inclination and appreciation of Ndebele people. For example, most of my friends, including my beautiful wife, have Ndebele blood linkages.

Sekuru Timoti was a short and jovial man who loved the pleasures of this world. I am told he adored and passionately loved beautiful women (like-father-like-son 😃). The women loved him too. He also had an unquenchable quest and thirst for 'Tea Parties' or Concerts popularly known in those days as *'Konzati'. Konzati* is the equivalence of today's boozy parties. Stories are told that he was a great, polished and amazing master of ceremonies (MC) at most *Konzati* and traditional weddings. He would be hired as MC, both near and far from his village. Authoritative sources say Tea Parties and *Konzati* would not start before his arrival. He was the soul and life of the party. His 'MC-ing' skills were second to none. When growing up, we were told that he had outstanding abilities and skills to entertain party guests such that some would fall off their chairs laughing at his tantalising jokes. In summary, he was a talented and gifted public speaker and entertainer. He was also a peace-maker. He never fought or caused troubles. Interestingly, he was both a teacher and a preacher within the Methodist Church.

A unique story about Sekuru Timoti is that a 'huge' announcement would be made at a *Konzati*, that a big man, whom the villagers had never seen, would soon be entering the building and guests were asked to be seated quietly as a sign of respect. Once the guests were quiet and highly expectant, my tiny-framed Sekuru Timoti would enter the full room wearing goat-skin clothes, to the hilarious and wild laughter of the guests. To make matters worse, this would sometimes happen in a church full of congregants. The villagers and the people loved my sekuru.

When he divorced my gogo Mugaiwa, Sekuru Timoti left our village and went to teach at a school in another village called Neusu, which was about 30 km away. There he met and 'stole' the heart of a local woman and finally married her. He later had some children, including babamunini Phillip Musokeri and tete (aunty) Neria. Sadly, my sekuru died at a relatively young age. It is said that he had food poisoning. Unfortunately, I never saw him because he passed on before I was born. I don't even know what he looked like as I have not even seen a photo of him. I wish I had one. He was lucky because I had a few questions for him to answer. Some of my questions are: What made him 'tick', and what was the source of his endless energy? What was the basis of his audacity and propensity to mischievous behaviours, especially at Konzatis. Finally, and more importantly, I wanted to understand why he gave my 'baba's pregnancy' as a *gupuro* to my gogo Mugaiwa, instead of paying a few cents/pennies as per our tradition and custom. To this day, it remains a mystery to me.

Coincidentally, I have been invited to many social gatherings such as weddings and graduation parties as an MC, both in Zimbabwe and New

Zealand. I have been told that I am good at it. I therefore guess that I got some of the skills and expertise from my *sekuru* Timoti. MHSREP 🙏.

This is the story of my life:
A village-boy borrowing from the leaf of his legendary forebearers.

Chapter Three:
My Primary Education
in the Village

Gasanyama Primary School

I did my primary education (grade one to three) at St Cuthbert Gasanyama Primary School, in Mhondoro-Ngezi, Mashonaland West Province. This was an Anglican run-institution. We used to walk about seven kilometres (one-way) daily to school, from our village (Madhondo). More than three-quarters of the distance was covered by crop-fields, thus, there were no homesteads. What it therefore meant was that if we left school late, for whatever reason, we would walk the long-distance home in darkness and far away from where people lived. At times this was scary especially as when we were growing up, we were told of specific places and areas which were said to be known for *zvidhoma* and *tokoloshis* (ghosts). *Tokoloshis* are believed to be dwarfed-humans used by witches and magicians for performing evil deeds and intimidatory acts. So, each time we finished school activities late, it was a daunting and challenging task to face the realities of going through some of the 'evil infected' areas under the cover of darkness. My hair would 'stand' due to fear as we passed through these frightening identified and designated areas.

I hated the winter seasons because it was always fiercely cold especially in the mornings. The grass would be 'white' covered in frost. Yes, in my country of birth (Zimbabwe) there is no snow but we have frost and it can be very cold. Due to poverty and lack, at times we went to school barefooted and our feet would 'crack' and start bleeding because of chilly-cold weather. Apart from the frost, we would be completely wet before arriving at school because of the narrow road that meandered through fields where the grass was generally tall. The combination of 'cracked' bleeding feet and wet clothes in a school environment in winter was physically painful, psychologically detrimental, emotionally draining and socially embarrassing. This could adversely affect one's academic performance in class.

I vividly remember most of the names of my teachers (for example Misters Shumba, Chihoro, Able Muzhingi, Mugwangavare, Masarakufa and Kadzimu). They were all great educators and unique in their own individual ways. Mr Mugwangavare later became one of our first Members of Parliament for Mhondoro-Ngezi, after independence in 1980. However, my favourite teacher was the late Mr Muzhingi. He was passionate about his job. He knew his stuff and how to stimulate his learners. He was so engaging and fascinating both in the classroom and sport-fields, as well as on Sundays at Church. I later learnt that I was distantly related to Mr Muzhingi. He was my distant cousin-brother, from my mother's side.

As already stated, my twin and I were sporty, especially in soccer. My twin was also outstanding in athletics. Despite my poor background and some of the challenges I have mentioned above, I was fortunate that I was one of the top students in all my classes. I clearly remember competing for the first position in grade three with two intelligent girls namely Zvichanzi Madhafi (now Mrs Motsi), who is now a successful farmer in Zimbabwe and Victoria Murerekwa, who later became a State Registered Nurse in Zimbabwe.

From Gasanyama Primary School, together with my siblings, I proceeded to attend a closer and bigger school called Muchemwa Primary School. This was a Methodist run-institution, about five kilometres from our village. The roads were wider because cars, buses, cows and people frequented them. Until now, it is not clear to me why my siblings and I were 'punished' by attending a smaller school which was far away and coupled with other aforementioned challenges. It was only my siblings and I from the entire village who attended Gasanyama Primary School, where we were separated from our friends and childhood acquaintances from our village.

Disappearing from School

After about a year, I went to stay with my maternal grandparents (about 5 kms from my village) and as a result, I went back to Gasanyama Primary School, which was nearer. One day the headmaster at Gasanyama sent us home due to non-payment of building-fund fees. Since I was committed to my education and did not want to miss my classes, I hatched a plan to go back to school and lied that I had gone home and informed my grandparents about the required fees. When the headmaster discovered this, he caned me badly. As he continued to beat me nonstop, I took off and headed into a thick forest. He ordered some of the fastest runners in the school to pursue me but they could not catch me. When I realised that I was 'safe' from the chase, I decided to go to my aunt Nelia Maganda (my father's half-sister) in another village called Samambwa which was about 10 kilometres from my school village. When I got there, I never told her what had happened. I was there almost a week while in my school, the headmaster was in trouble with my family. Everyone thought I had died. My mother was the most affected person. She lost a lot of weight and was deeply pained. When I got home, I was given a heroic welcome by the youth in my village because they knew I had put the headmaster in trouble. Due to this event, the following year I was transferred from Gasanyama back to Muchemwa Primary School.

Muchemwa Primary School

At Muchemwa School, I was now reconnected with our childhood village friends and relatives. Life at school was now more vibrant and interesting. As I mentioned before, my twin Anyway, Chikuru, Taurai and I were in the senior soccer team and that further spiced my schooldays. Our clique of four became very popular at school, especially with girls. They loved us. And we responded accordingly. Unfortunately, mainly owing to a young age, the popularity with beautiful girls got into our heads and we became full of ourselves and this in turn adversely affected our academic performances. However, my advantage was that my mother knew and understood the importance of education and she was strict when it came to doing homework and concentrating on our school. Without the guidance of my mother, I would have lost the plot completely.

School and Life in the Village

School-life in the village was difficult, especially during the cropping seasons, from seed-planting (October-November) to weeding and harvesting time (December-April). Before going to school, we would wake up early in the morning around 4am and work in the fields. There was no warm tap water to bath. We used cold water in buckets. We would only bath 'half-body', thus, the head, the hands and the legs, mainly due to time and lack of facilities. Mostly we only had proper bathing during the weekends – and it was normal. On specific days, there was general work at school, mostly between 1pm and 2pm. General work included working in the school garden, cleaning the toilets and classrooms, as well as clearing the entire schoolyard. Soon after school, we would go back home and work in the fields and then at sunset, we attended to our livelihood animals such as cows, goats and sheep. Ideally, during the cropping season, there was barely any time to rest. Village life was hard and at times unbearable. This gave me the push and drive to work harder in my studies as I did not want this kind of hard village-life.

As for lunch, we mostly carried *maputi* (roasted white corn) or *mangayi* (cooked white corn) and if we were lucky *mutakura* (cooked white corn with beans/groundnuts). *Mahewu* and water were the most common drinks for the majority of us. There was no tea and bread. These were luxurious commodities only a few villagers would afford. As for my siblings and I, we had tea and bread mostly at Christmas.

When going to school, we always had to run because we did not have the luxury of time. Lateness was punishable. Latecomers would be publicly announced at assembly in front of the entire school and get punished later. On the other hand, some parents were in the habit of releasing their children from the fields a bit late. Some students found themselves between the devil and a deep sea. Luckily and thankfully, my mother was civilised when it came to releasing us on time to go to school mainly because she had profound respect for education. She did not want to create some stumbling obstacles in our education.

This is the story of my life:
The African village-boy's primary education in the village.

Chapter Four:
Desire to Join the Second Chimurenga
(The Armed Struggle)

Strategising to Join the Zimbabwe Second Chimurenga Armed Struggle

"Iwe shamwari (hey my friend), let us join the armed struggle and liberate our country from the shackles and jaws of the enemy. The colonisers must go. We need our freedom and emancipation, now!!!!. Our dignity, as a people, is vanished and evaporated." That was me pushing the boundaries, and doing all I could to influence, persuade and cajole my childhood friend and close relative, Lloyd Mutizwa (popularly known in our village as Chikuru Musaka), to join the armed struggle, the Zimbabwe Second Chimurenga. Chimurenga means war.

It was on a rainy and humid Sunday afternoon, in early December 1978, at the age of about 13 years, Chikuru and I sat in my father's old and malfunctional Bedford car which he had barter-traded with about 10 fat-healthy cows. We therefore started to strategise our hatched plan to join the armed struggle, Second Chimurenga in neighbouring Mozambique. As I stated before, the Zimbabwe Second Chimurenga was also known as the Zimbabwe Liberation Guerrilla Warfare (1966-1979), which led to our majority rule in 1980.

Due to our geographical location, our village in Mhondoro-Ngezi was one of the few lucky places that only experienced the war for a very short period of time. For the 13-year war period (1966-1979), my village 'suffered' the effects of this deadly war for 10 months only (March - December 1979). However, short as it may have been, the resultant effects were devastating and ruthless. Both the young and the old perished in this war.

Towards the end of 1978, the news and wild-fire rumours of the war were the topical subjects of discussion in my entire village. Daily, we heard of fascinating and captivating stories about the guerrilla fighters or comrades of the war; mostly referred to as *'vana mukoma'*. Some of the stories that profoundly touched and revolutionised the minds and hearts of the youth, in particular, was that *vana mukoma* did not die in a battlefield. We were told they would miraculously disappear from the sight of the enemy and suddenly re-appear from a different angle and decimate the enemy. One of the conspicuous mysterious narratives was that one comrade would come in a homestead and ask for heaps of *sadza* to be prepared. When the food was ready, he would remove his shoe and shake it violently and the hut would be suddenly filled with armed comrades who would straight away 'dive' and 'dig-in' into the supplied food. Such stories and propaganda intrinsically motivated the young people to join the armed struggle against colonialism, imperialism and capitalism. Chikuru and I were such candidates who were ready to go and liberate our country from the jaws of the imperialists.

The biggest challenge was where to get the money for travelling from a remote village in Mhondoro-Ngezi to a beautiful city called Umtali (now Mutare) which borders with Mozambique. We had to go via Salisbury (now Harare, the capital city), which is 132 km from my village. Back then, the bus fare was cheap since we were paying half the price as school-going children. For us, our individual bus fare from Mhondoro-Ngezi to Harare was one dollar ($1.00) and another dollar from Harare to Mutare. The minimum total transport cost we needed was only $4.00, for both of us. By then, although the Smith regime was under United Nations economic sanctions, the economy was performing well hence these low bus fare prices. We did not care about food and our up-keep as we believed and knew that the people, as a community, bound and guided by the African philosophy of Ubuntu, would provide. We also believed that our ancestors would guide us and provide for us. We were therefore prepared to do anything in order to get the travel-money because we had a bigger national agenda of freeing our country from the chains and bondage of colonialism, social subjugation, economic domination, political persecution and racial oppression. Remember this was at a tender age of 13.

Under the shadow of my baba's old Bedford, we hatched a plan to finance the crucial journey before us. I had one hen (live-chicken) which I sold for $0.80, to one of my nephews in the village. When I sold my hen, my mother asked why I had done that and I told her that I wanted to buy some important school books. Although she valued education, she openly told me, in the presence of Chikuru, that she was not convinced and that my behaviour on that particular day was weird and suspicious.

Fortunately, Chikuru's maternal grandfather (uncle to my father), Mr Stephen Chipfo Musaka, whom he lived with was a businessman. He owned a butchery-shop and a grocery shop at Manyewe Township. The grocery shop was popularly known as Musaka Café - Eating & Booking House (The Kefa). So, Chikuru stole an amount in the sum of $10.00. We now had a total amount of $10.80, which was a lot of money. It was more than enough for our planned Mozambique trip to join the armed struggle. As close childhood-friends who now had a commmon national agenda, we both felt that the money belonged to both of us and we shared everything equally. I must say that my babamunini Chikuru was naturally a generous and a good-hearted person.

Since my mother was increasingly becoming suspicious, she asked me to go and fetch some water from a village dug-well and we seized it as an opportunity to disappear. Just before sunset, we walked to Manyewe Township which was about five kilometres from our village. We made sure we were not seen by the villagers. Along the way we could hide if we saw people who knew us, who were coming from Manyewe Township.

Leaving the Village

When it was dark and all shops closed, we sneaked into one of the rooms at Musaka Café. The following day we woke up as early as 4 am and walked about two kilometres away from the township (closer to Benhura School) to avoid being seen by known villagers who would inform the bus crew not to allow us on the bus. Unfortunately, when we waved the bus to stop, it did not. The crew assumed that we were just naughty village-boys who were stopping the bus for fun. We were shocked but not discouraged. We walked all the way to the next township called Mandedza, a further 10 kilometres.

We spent the whole day at Mandedza Township while waiting for the next bus the following day. We befriended a shopkeeper in one of the grocery shops. There was only one bus to Harare every morning. If you missed it, you had to wait for the following day. Such are the challenges of accessing public transport in most villages in Zimbabwe and other African states as well as developing nations of the globe. At night we initially slept in the bush nearby but mosquitoes had a free feast-party on us. When it started raining, we had no choice but to leave and look for shelter. We thought of going to the veranda of the shop of our 'friend' whom we had met in the afternoon. It became very cold and we helped ourselves by sleeping in a parked car at the shop of our newly founded 'friend'. Luckily, it was not locked. Early in the morning, we approached our 'friend' and confessed and told him exactly what we did. He was very appreciative and actually told us we should have told him that we needed accommodation overnight. He was willing to assist, thus, displaying Ubuntu.

Around mid-day we got into a Harare-bound bus. This was the very first time in my entire life to get into a long-distance bus. We arrived at Harare's Mbare-Musika, the most populous Market and Bus Terminus in the country, around 4 pm. This was my very first time to get into Harare, the capital city. I was mesmerized and fascinated to see so many people all over. The streets were densely populated and everyone was doing his/her own business. It was totally different from my small village set-up. Although it was raining and a bit cold, when we 'landed' in Harare, we straight away rushed to buy some ice cream. Again, at the age of 13, it was my very first time to eat ice cream. The experience was exhilarating indeed.

Since we knew there were many thieves and robbers, in particular at Mbare-Musika, we enquired about cheaper accommodation overnight and we were lucky to find one close by. The following morning, we boarded a Musabaike bus, which was going to Mutare (263 kms). We befriended the bus conductor, *mukoma* (brother) George. By mid-day we were in Sakubva, Mutare. The city of Mutare is about eight kilometres from the Mozambique boarder. It is worth noting that the Zimbabwe African National Liberation Army (ZANLA), which was the Mugabe-led, Chimurenga guerrillas (fighters) were trained and based in Mozambique. While the Nkomo-led, Patriotic Front - Zimbabwe African People's Union (PF-ZAPU) were based and trained in Zambia. Before the colonisers partitioned Africa, Mutare (Zimbabwe) and Manica Province (Mozambique) was one village and one community (Faal, 2009; Lancaster House Agreement, 1979; Mubako, 1975). Right now, I know of families where half lives in Zimbabwe and the other in Mozambique. The colonisers never considered family ties and connections, and other factors such as socioeconomic and emotional injury and injustice caused on the indigenous people of both Zimbabwe and Mozambique. They did not care.

When we got to Mutare, the atmosphere and environment was tense and petrifying because the road that linked Sakubva and Mutare CBD was infested with hundreds of all shapes and sizes of army trucks and vehicles. Some were patrolling on foot. I had never seen so many soldiers within such a short space of time. Although we witnessed this terrifying scenario, we were not deterred and discouraged from achieving our agenda. Around 6pm, we bought a few food items and started walking toward Mozambique. We thought as soon as we crossed the main road, we would be at the border, ready to get into Mozambique and thereby accomplishing our objective. We were surprised that beyond the road, there were many residential houses and we could see many army trucks. We decided to go back and find somewhere to sleep and then resume our journey around mid-night under the cover of darkness. We had no identification documentation (IDs) on us. This was a big risk, especially given our proximity with the Mozambique boarder. There were many roadblocks and if we were caught by the soldiers, we would be shot-dead or the least sent to jail without trail. However, we were so lucky that we never encounter a single roadblock throughout the entire journey. Due to ignorance and childishness, we did not know how dangerous it was to be 'ID-less'.

We returned to Sakubva Bus Terminus and asked where we could get cheaper accommodation. We were directed to a very affordable place called Chipo Murape Booking House, close to the Bus Terminus. We were tired and since we wanted to leave by mid-night we decided to retire to bed early. Just before mid-night, I had one of the most vivid dreams I have ever had. It was so clear and intense. I dreamt of my mother calling me. She was bitterly weeping and grieving. Her sadness and sorrow were conspicuous, but above all distressing, tear-jerking, painful and heart-rending. I started crying and calling her, endlessly (in the dream). My heart broke and bled for my mother. When I woke up, I was in the hands of my dear friend Chikuru. He asked me why I was crying and screaming. Before I explained my dream, he told me that I was literally crying, on top of my voice, and calling my mother. I was also sweating and breathless. My heart sunk in profound pain and unexplainable anguish. It was throbbing and aching in agony. I have never missed my mother as I did at that particular moment and time. After explaining my vivid dream to my friend, I categorically told him that I was going back home, the following morning. He looked at me in astonishing disbelief. But he knew straight away that I was over it. I was determined, at any cost, to go home and be with my dear mother. Before Chikuru uttered a word of persuasion, I firmly told him that if he wanted to proceed, he was free to do so, but as for me, I was going back home, without fail, to my mother. After a long-protracted silence, he said, "*It's okay. We go home tomorrow.*" We went back to sleep.

The following morning, we boarded the same Musabaike bus to Harare. It was great to reconnect with *mukoma* George the kind bus conductor. We arrived in Harare at Mbare-Musika around early afternoon. We were now running out of money. To be precise, we only had $2.oo, which was only enough for both our tickets from Harare to our village. Hunger was beginning to bite but this was overshadowed by the fact that we would be home-bound the following day. Due to thieves and thugs at Mbare-Musika, we befriended a homeless old man originally from Malawi, who permanently lived there. He assured us protection from thugs but we later discovered during the night, he wanted to steal our little remaining money as he thought we were loaded. Fortunately, we had hidden the money in our under-wears. We survived the trap.

The following day, around mid-day, we left Harare for our village. Since we left our village on a Sunday evening, we had five nights in total away from home. We had never taken a single shower nor changed our clothes, including under-wears. I had black tennis-shoes known as 'tenderfoot' and my feet were white as snow. They were beginning to peel off and heavily stinking. Chikuru had some open *pata-patas* (jandals). Since his feet were not covered, they were distinctly dirty but luckily not stinking. Our clothes were the dirtiest I had ever seen. We actually smelt but we did not care.

Heroic Village Home-Welcoming

The moment we touched Manyewe Township, we were taken to *The Kefa* and given food. We were dirty, hungry, thirsty and tired. After we had our food, we were escorted home. When I got home, I could not recognise my mother. She had instantly grown so thin and frail. When she saw me, she could not utter a word. She kept on her piercing look at me but maintained her talking-silence. Much later, she opened her arms and I fell into them and we both wept. I could feel her overwhelming love and tender care. This was the second time in my life causing untold pain to my mother by disappearing such that she thought I had died. I purposed and vowed in my heart that I would never ever again cause such grievous pain to my dear mother. I am glad that I managed to keep my promise. I am now mama's boy.

This is the story of my life:
A village-boy desiring to liberate his country from
the shackles of repressive colonisation.

Chapter Five:
From Village to City

The 'Arrival' of War in My Village

Around March 1979, when the war had engulfed my village in Mhondoro-Ngezi, many people, youth in particular, were excited. I was one of them. The most exciting events were *pungwe* – these were night political gatherings where *vana mukoma* (the comrades) would politically indoctrinate the *povo*. In simple terms these were political lectures. In this context, *povo* refers to the local villagers within the surrounding areas. The main agenda was to instil heightened boldness in villagers to oppose and resist the colonial Unilateral Declaration of Independence (UDI) illegitimate government of Ian Douglas Smith (Lancaster House Agreement, 1979; Smith, 1997). In simple terms, the villagers were taught to be defiant and disobedient to this oppressive white minority regime. People in my village had only heard about the war but not experienced it, hence the excitement to contribute in order to liberate our country from colonisation and white-minority rule.

I vividly remember in early March 1979, when the first ever *pungwe* in our village was held at a *n'anga* (traditional healer's) homestead near Gasanyama Primary School- about five kms from my village. Although there was a curfew (6pm to 6am), imposed by the colonial oppressive white minority regime, the villagers attended in massive numbers. Inspired and touched by the captivating and soul-searching Chimurenga songs, the *povo* thundered and joined in the rhythms and lyrics. The accompanying *kongonya* (skilful dance-moves) by the comrades, were fascinating and intriguing. The enchanting and mesmerising guns that dangled on the backs of *vana mukoma*, as they danced, were a conspicuous eye-catching episode to the *povo*. The more the *povo* listened and pondered on the messages of the songs, the louder the singing became. The *povo* would engage and forget that it was in the middle of the night – this was dangerous as it was curfew time. The possibility of soldiers bombarding and ambushing the *pungwe* and massacring the *povo* was high, but the people were not scared. In between songs, *vana mukoma*, in particular the *political commissars* gave charismatic and enticing political lectures. The *povo* was motivated and inspired by the Chimurenga songs and political sermons such that a lot of young people joined the armed struggle on such *pungwe* nights.

Personally, I was blown away and wanted to join *vana mukoma* there and then, but only got restrained by the vow I had purposed in my heart, that of not re-inflicting heart-pain to my mother. The thought bothered me day and night. My mother immediately saw the keen interest I had in the struggle, especially after seeing the 'real' *vana mukoma* 'in action'. Our aborted Mozambique trip and experience were still fresh in her mind. It worried her a lot. She immediately ordered that I leave the village (and school) and join my father who was now working for the biggest Iron and Steel Company, in the then Rhodesia, called Rhodesia Iron and Steel Company (RISCO), now Zimbabwe Iron and Steel Company (Ziscosteel). Ziscosteel was situated in a small (but neat and rich) mining-town called Redcliff, which is about 13 kilometres from the city of KweKwe, in the Midlands Province. Back in those colonial days, before Zimbabwe became politically independent, residential areas were racially segregated, thus,

Whites, Blacks, Asians and Coloureds lived in geographically separated areas. As for Ziscosteel, Whites lived in Redcliff while the indigenous Blacks were domiciled in a famous township called Torwood, popularly and affectionately known as Karaga.

A Village Boy: First Encounter with City-Life

When I moved to Karaga, it was towards the end of the 1979 first-school-term and I could not secure a place to complete my seventh grade, which was the last year at primary before going to secondary/high school. It therefore meant staying at home doing nothing at that tender age. As the saying goes, *'an idle mind is the devil's workshop'*, I suddenly found myself getting involved in naughty things, just like many other young people. To further complicate the situation, initially my dear mother was still in the village and I was now staying with my dad, his fourth wife and a multitude of my siblings. In the absence of my mother, nobody cared about instilling discipline and good morals and behaviour in us, as young children who needed guidance. As for my ever-cheerful dad, he was busy enjoying his life in Karaga. He was well known and loved by many in Karaga.

My dad would visit the beer hall (Torwood Main Bar) every day without fail and come back home drunk, in the middle of the night. We wondered where he was getting the money for beer. His only other source of private income was from his big and well- maintained garden (behind our company-owned house). He was also a trained Rural Farmer and therefore gardening was in his blood and veins. There were about 25 beds of a variety of vegetables. The majority of Karaga residents bought seedlings and vegetables from my dad; this became a source of his beer-money. I was responsible for watering all the 25 beds daily, without fail, using a can/bucket. A hosepipe was a luxury. Interestingly, I never got given a single cent over the years, from the garden proceeds. Not that I cared, but when I think about it now, I feel I was entitled to a small share for my hard labour 😀. I guess I did not complain because of my dad's genuine appreciation and gratitude towards me. He would sincerely tell me (daily) how hard-working and responsible I was for watering his 'cash-cow' – the garden. Around mid-night (daily without fail), from the beer hall, my dad would dip his finger into the garden-beds and then proceed to my room and wake me up, just to thank me for a job well-done. That on its own carried me through and gave me the energy and enthusiasm to do my daily garden-assignment. However, this childhood experience had a negative impact on me such that I now hate gardening and farming with an overwhelming passion.

Basic food in my father's household was a constant and perennial challenge, because there were too many mouths to be fed. My father was the only breadwinner and his job as a Security Officer/Driver (before being promoted to Ambulance Fire Engine Driver) was not paying him enough for the size of his vast family. The scarcity of food, in my father's household, resulted in a policy which stipulated that whoever was not present during meal times, especially dinner, no food would be kept for them. This situation cultivated a natural instinct and sense of inventing survival tactics. I was therefore cajoled to join some 'bad' boys and started getting involved in *chaputa/Kiya*, which is basically a *'head and tail'* money-gambling game. This was simply betting and gambling. It was either winning or losing. Losing would mean hunger. When my friends and I had a lucky day, we would spoil ourselves with yummy food and also go for entertainment, especially weekend music events hosted by prominent artists such as the late Dr Oliver Mtukudzi (and the Black Spirits Band), Dr Thomas 'Mukanya' Mapfumo (and the Black Unlimited Band), and the late legend Safirio Madzikatire (and the Mukadota Family backed by the Ocean City Band). My mother joined us in town much later, due to the intensity of the war in our village, but the behavioural damage (on me) was already done.

The whole of 1979 was not an easy year for me and all my siblings. I loved school but I could not go. I think due to a subconscious frustration of not going to school like other children, I indulged more into *chaputa/Kiya*, attending musical events and chasing after little beautiful girls. I later joined a gym club and trained as a youth-boxer under the supervision of a skilful trainer popularly known as Mr Powerman or *Mr Kedebu*. This training gave me a false sense of confidence and arrogance. I became egotistic and big-headed. I was generally feared by the majority of youth in our locality.

Becoming a Born-Again Christian

One night, towards the end of December 1979, while coming from playing *chaputa*, and committing other mischievous deeds, I vividly remember my friends and I passing through Torwood Baptist Church. We saw people dancing and singing inside the church building. We got fascinated and decided to go inside. The other agenda was to 'hunt' for beautiful girls.

The atmosphere and environment were completely different. The songs were tantalising and sung in melodically traditional tunes. The loud volume capturing the rhythm and lyrics from box-guitars was amplified through electric transformers. The messages in the songs were profoundly clear and heartily touchy. The captivating and enchanting singing was accompanied by thrilling African dances. The raising and lifting-up of hands in worship was an eye-catcher. Everything was just perfect and in order. My eyes, ears, my inner-soul and above all my heart were caught-up and thrilled by this divine environment. I felt a certain indescribable inner-peace and joy unspeakable.

Soon after the 'heart-searching singing', a neatly-dressed gentleman stood up and 'mounted' on the pulpit to preach the Gospel. His sermon was simple but piercing and penetrating to the intense of the heart, soul and mind. He talked about bad habits and deeds, mostly committed by the young people. It was as if he was reading and filming my dirty life. He was not blaming anyone but clearly pointed out that those who do it are normally under the bondage of sin and influence of darkness of this sinful world. He further reiterated that there is a man who can freely give spiritual freedom and total emancipation from the yoke of sin. He further stated that this man can free those chained in the bondage and shackles of the devil. As the preacher thundered, there were punctuated choruses of "Amen and Hallelujah" mostly from the energetic youth. I loved and cherished the agreement, harmony, and connection between the preacher and the youthful congregation. The air of sincerity and authenticity prevailed and engulfed the entire church service.

At this point, I was almost seated at the edge of my chair and all I wanted was to see, meet and have a conversation with this man who would change my life. As I was pondering who this man could be, the preacher thundered that this man was **Jesus Christ, the Son of the Living and Most High God.** I had heard about Jesus Christ before, but not in the manner in which this was presented and narrated. My heart was pricked and I felt the conviction to accept and receive Jesus Christ, as my Lord and personal Saviour. Before he finished making an altar-call, I just found myself standing in front of the congregation, with a gigantic smile on my face. I felt that inner- tranquillity and satisfaction enveloping my life. It was as if a heavy load was lifted off my shoulders. What surprised me the most was that my best friend (in crime), Darlington Rainos Gava was also in front, wanting to receive Jesus Christ as his personal Lord and Saviour. We looked at each other in full surprise and we hugged and congratulated each other. Later I learnt that the young preacher was Brother Alexander Mahlohlomane Kent Sigxoza, affectionately known as mukoma Zandah. He later relocated to Zambia. The good thing is that later, after about 15 years, I was able to locate mukoma Zandah in Zambia (via social media) and we started to communicate. He was excited when I told him that he obeyed to be used by the Lord as a vehicle to communicate the Gospel to me. I called him mukoma (big brother) and he called me mununguna (younger brother). Sadly, mukoma Zandah passed on in 2021 in Zambia. I was given the honour to be one of the guest speakers at his virtual memorial service, held in Zimbabwe.

Two partners in crime had finally seen the light - Darlington and I. We both started attending youth meetings and fellowships at Torwood Baptist Church. Our lives were revolutionised and totally transformed for the better. Later, I went and confessed and apologised to my father for not being a good son. Although he was not a Christian, he was exceedingly excited and told me that he had noticed a big, positive change in my life. He started calling me '*Mufundisi*'. This means Pastor. My relationship with my father took a completely new positive direction and significantly improved. He always talked about my transformed life.

Lessons Learnt from Torwood Baptist Youth (TBY)

From the day that I became a Christian, I never missed any youth meeting and fellowship at Torwood Baptist Youth Fellowship, popularly known as TBYF and to a lesser extend as Bible Believers Fellowship (BBF). What motivated me the most to attend the youth meetings was the love and welcome I received from all members of the Youth Group – from day one. I felt genuinely loved, accepted and embraced- as I was. No one judged me. In my view, the majority of the youth stood out as good community role models. Good and shining examples were two brothers. One was David Barnabas Chizozo Nyoni, a quiet, organised and humble guy. In addition, he was gracious and intelligent. The other one was Juwel Muzenda. There were three outstanding aspects I really admired in these two guys: (i) the undisputed dedication to their academic studies – they were always on top of their classes (ii) the unwavering commitment and faith in God (iii) how they managed not to be entangled and involved with 'girls' throughout their academic studies, until they almost completed their apprenticeship training. This is as far as I knew it- if they were secretly playing games, I did not see it 🙆.

Their ability to conquer the temptation of chasing after beautiful girls was completely beyond me. Initially, I could not believe it. I thought they were faking and doing it secretly. I never believed that such humble and intelligent boys would stay away from chasing after attractive girls. What made it harder for me to believe was that most beautiful and well-behaved girls openly liked them. They have both done very well in their careers. David is now an Electrical Foreman/Engineer in a mining company in South Africa. Juwel is currently working as a Group Safety, Health and Environment Executive, in Harare Zimbabwe.

Why am I labouring this point? As I stated before, beautiful girls were my weakness and temptation. As a result, I did not believe that any normal boy would do without having a girlfriend. I suppose this was hugely influenced by my background and upbringing, in my village and to some extent, the life of my legendary father, Mutsau (Dr Love) 🤦 😊. The glad tidings is that after becoming a Christian and learning from these brethren, I was totally delivered from the lust of loving beautiful girls. My life was completely converted and transformed. I became refocused on loving God and having a renewed quest and desire for education. As proof for my deliverance and redemption, I only had my first-ever girlfriend when I was already working, in my 3rd year as a Bank Officer. The truth is, without an encounter with the Lord Jesus Christ (at a tender age) coupled with fellowshipping with such good examples of the brethren and teachings from TBYF, the probability of me impregnating someone at a very young age was extremely high. And my life would have been ruined and destroyed. In fact, I strongly believe that I could have died a long time ago. I am still alive simply because of the sufficient grace of God.

Apart from David and Juwel, there were other TBYF members who immensely contributed to my life-growth. These, amongst others, include:

- **Noah Fore** - one of the funniest clowns and comedians in Karaga. He was the master of ceremony (MC) at my wedding. He is currently a Safety Officer in Zimbabwe and leading Peniel Baptist Church (born after TBYF).

- **Innocent Ncube** – my former high school classmate whom I regard as my young brother. His mother became my mother too, such that she would prepare dinner for the two of us daily, without fail, for two consecutive years. Without Innocent's mother I would have starved – see more detail about her below. Innocent later trained as a Metallurgical Technician and a Mathematics High School Teacher. He is currently teaching in South Africa.

- **Fanwell Nyoni** - my other former classmate. Without his help, I could have failed my 'O' Level History subject. I always say, the distinction I have in History is not mine; it belongs to Fannie. Fannie is currently working as an Administration Manager in Zimbabwe.

- **Lazurus Staziyo** – he is popularly known as "Blackman", because of his nice-shiny dark complexion. "Blackman" is a Zimbabwe-trained Registered Nurse and currently living and working as a Nurse Manager in the UK. Apart from work, he leads (together with his wife) a successful Gospel Band called Tehillah Praise Band in the UK.

- **Clever Dhliwayo** – of the entire TBYF, he was the most dedicated to his studies. He would study the whole night. I will never forget one incident, when we were in our last year of high school, Clever and I decided to have all-night prayer at Torwood Baptist Church, seeking the Lord's guidance and excellence in our studies. The mistake we committed was to carry blankets. After praying for about two hours, we decided to have a little nap and then later carry on for the rest of the night, praying and seeking God's presence and guidance. Within the twinkling of an eye, we were shocked that it was already in the morning. We looked at each other and had a big laugh. When I look back, I see mountains of zeal and good intentions. Clever later became an Environmental Scientist and is now running his own successful Environmental consulting company in Harare, Zimbabwe.

- **Martin Samangaya** - Martin is special to me mainly because he played a pivotal and strategic role when I was proposing to my beautiful wife, Annette. More details to unfold later. He is currently living and working in the UK as a Senior Lecturer in Nursing Studies at one of the best universities in the UK.

- **Saul (Sauro) Phiri Fore** - Of all the TBYF young people, Sauro (Noah's young brother) is the most humorous and the one with whom I connect at a deeper level. I call him "my trusted young man, without filters and boundaries". He is one of my best bona fide encouragers and cheerers. He is currently living and working in the UK within the Health Sector.

- **Nathan Tinashe Tuwe** - this one is my younger blood-brother as well as a friend. We are close. To show our closeness, he and his wife decided to have a similar wedding anniversary date as us, thus, 18 April. When we were still together back home (Zimbabwe), we used to celebrate our wedding anniversaries together in nice holiday resorts. Nathan is now living and working in South Africa as an Electrical/Control Instrumentation Foreman.

- **Abedinigo Mathe Malinga** - This was my late beloved brother in the Lord who had become also like family. He later became a Member of Parliament in Zimbabwe. Malinga always liked to joke with me. We clicked and used to laugh a lot. During our wedding, my brother Malinga and his wife Agnetha hosted my in-laws (the entire clan) in their house. Before joining politics, he was a Telecommunications Technician at Ziscosteel. When he joined politics, we were all excited because we believe that it is important for Christians to actively participate in this arena as a way of fighting against corruption as well as influencing good governance and accountability. Sadly, my brother was involved in a car accident and passed on in 2008.

- **Agnes Matorino** – She was the first sister I clicked with at TBYF. She was the most beautiful and cheerful of all the sisters at TBYF. I later became closer to most of her family members such that they refer to me as "Mukoma Tuwe" (brother Tuwe). Sadly, she passed on in the mid-2000s when I was already in NZ. I was pained.

- **Dr Rejoice Malisa** (now Mrs van der Walt) - I first met Rejoice when we were both in grade six at George Hill Primary School, in Karaga in 1980. I preached to her and she accepted the Lord Jesus Christ as her personal Lord and Saviour. When she is happy, she calls me '*Mufundisi wami*' (My Pastor). When in the opposite mood, she calls me "Wena Kudakwashe", thus, "You Kudakwashe". She is now officially Dr Rejoice van der Walt - Malisa. She is currently living and working in South Africa. She has done well, especially in her academics. I salute her.

- **Mai Rosemary Malinga (nee Lunga)** - this book project would not be completed without mentioning the late Rosemary Malinga, who played a pivotal role in supporting me, financially, emotionally, socially and spiritually by feeding me and paying for some of my youth conference fees. She was married to Abednego Malinga's brother and we used to go to the same church at Torwood Baptist Church. I am blessed to have planted a tree at her house in Mbizo, KweKwe. Her family calls it *"The Tuwe Tree"*. I am glad that I am in constant touch with Rosemary's children, especially her first-born daughter, Mrs Jaqueline Sithole (nee Malinga). Each time we visit Zimbabwe, we always catch-up with Jackie. She and her husband are running a successful business in Redcliff, Zimbabwe.

- **Mai Agnes Ncube** – Innocent Ncube's mother became my mother too. She was so kind to me. I think she had noticed my struggles of not having a mother-figure closer by and she quietly decided to step in to fill that gap. I must say that she played that role very well. As I stated before, she would prepare dinner for Innocent and myself daily without fail, for two consecutive years when I was in Form 3 and 4. Without Innocent's mother, I would have starved and probably not completed my high school education. Later in years, each time she visited Innocent's family in Gweru, she would ask him to let me know about her presence and I would take my family to see her. She was more than a mother to me. When mama Ncube passed-on in 2002, I drove from Gweru to Gokwe (203kms) to preside over her burial. Innocent is always saying to people *"Tuwe literally buried my mother"*. This is the little I could do in her honour. I wish I could have done more for her. As a result of what mama Ncube did to me, no matter what trouble Innocent gets into, I am one of the first people to jump to rescue him. To me, he is not just a friend, but a younger brother.

- **Mai Ellen Mataka (aka Mai Shaw)** – When I was in Form three, my brother (the boilermaker) whom I was staying with relocated to

Harare and I moved in with his twin brother who was a lovely brother, but financially struggling. Life changed and became difficult for me. Food became scarce, especially for my lunch. Luckly, as I stated before, my dinner was sorted out via mama Ncube. I had to come up with a plan for my lunch-survival. I started buying soup for ten cents from a Zisco-owned restaurant which was popularly known as "*Kwa Mai Shaw*". This place was named after Mrs Ellen Mataka whose son was called Shaw. She was the supervisor. This popular place provided different delicious meals including sadza (our staple food). After a few days of buying soup for ten cents, mama Mai Shaw started to give me some meat instead of soup only. This significantly improved the quality and quantity of my lunch. I was excited and very grateful. I also discovered that even if Mama Mai Shaw she was not around, I would still get my usual fair share of meat just for ten cents. Without me knowing, she had given an instruction that my soup would be upgraded to a pot of meat. I strongly believe that, as a mother, she had noticed that I was struggling. This completely changed my life. I think without her good and Ubuntu gesture, I would have starved and this could have interfered with my education. I am so grateful to the late Mai Shaw (my mama). As a sign of gratitude, I later looked for Mai Shaw's daughter, Danisa and personally expressed my appreciation. I wish this world would be populated with kind people such as Mama Mai Shaw, Mai Ncube and Mai Malinga, it would be a better place to live. In my small corner, I would want to exercise and implement this kindness to others that I have learnt from these lovely people.

My sincere apologies in advance as I can't name all the great TBYF members and many others from Karaga who were instrumental in shaping my life for the better. I really want to sincerely thank them all and appreciate their valuable contributions in making me what I am today. To God be the glory. We were known in the entire Karaga community as a group of disciplined intellects, economically and socially prosperous young people, but above all as dedicated followers of Christ. By God's grace, we positively impacted the lives of many people, especially the youth in Karaga. That testimony is still intact, almost 45 years on. Again, we give all the glory to the Lord.

While the majority of TBYF members were faithful and doing their best to live right, for the sake of the propagation of the Gospel, we had a few "*Demas and Alexanders the coppersmith*" (2 Timothy 4:10) who were damaging the good reputation by living double-crooked lives. Some got swallowed by the pleasures of this world and entangled themselves in unholy behaviours. In short, they were living double-lives. For example, there was one brother, very active in church activities but well known for being both a drunkard and womaniser. One day the Spirit of the Lord moved at a youth meeting I was leading and he confessed his sins. I had the audacity and boldness to command him to kneel down and denounce his sins. I laid hands on him and prayed for him. Now we always talk and laugh about this incident, amongst ourselves.

Due to the current political and economic instability in my beloved country of Zimbabwe, we are now all scattered around the world, like lost sheep. We dearly miss each other. My heart bleeds profusely. I pray for my treasured nation. God bless Zimbabwe. As we were talking and planning for a possible reunion, the global epidemic (COVID-19) descended upon us. Most of us are still in touch - thanks to social media. In early 2019, I was blessed to initiate and inaugurate a WhatsApp-chat group for the majority of the TBYF members called "TBYF Karaga". I declared myself the Life President of this crucial group. Thankfully, there was no resistance and challenges.

In my view, what contributed to the strong and vibrant TBYF group was the unwavering support and motivation we got from our Pastor, a godly man who was grounded in the Word of God. He was knowledgeable in theology. He gave us our space. This was the late Reverend Joster Katiakunyenga Ngozo of Torwood Baptist Church (TBC) and his gracious wife, the late Mai Felecia Ngozo, affectionally known as gogo Ngozo. I am so blessed to be in touch with their children, Mr Amos Ngozo (baba Abbie) and sisi Connie (Mai Ndlovu).

In addition to the great spiritual support we got from TBC, there were many brethren from other churches in Karaga. We used to congregate at special meetings called *Mubatanidzwa*, meaning Interdenominational Gatherings. To name a few, the late baba Mabvosvo, who was my uncle and a great preacher, the late Reverend & Mrs Kundishora who were mightily used in the ministry of marriage relationships. Our high school teachers Mr Salatiel Munedzimwe, Mr Chihanga and Mr Augustine Machina were supportive in our Scripture Union group at Drake Secondary School. As for the youth from other denominations, the late Abbas Phiri, Kawanga Banda popularly known as Kawanga The Banda and many from the St Bartholomew Torwood Anglican Church Youth. Indeed, Karaga was the best environment for me. It modelled and re-shaped my life for the better. It had good people and strong cultural support structures. People genuinely cared and looked after each other. Without the people of Karaga, I wouldn't be what I am today. May the good and faithful Lord bless the people of Karaga.

Attending the First Christian Conferences – Benevolence of Others

In 1980, when I was in grade six, I had the first-ever opportunity to attend a Scripture Union (SU) Christian Regional Conference at Senga

Chief's Hall in Senga Township, Gweru, Zimbabwe. The conference was engaging and informative. At the end of the conference, I was on 'fire' for the Lord such that I went ahead and registered a SU group under George Hill Primary School (GHPS), at this conference, without the knowledge and authority of the headmaster, Mr John Rhodes Sitsha. When I broke the news on the next Monday, in his 'feared' office, Mr Sitsha was exceedingly excited. He later made an official announcement at assembly that our SU group was allowed to operate at GHPS. This was the ever-first time to have SU group at GHPS. To help me facilitate and run the group, I had my friend Darlington Rhino Gava, the one who gave his life to the Lord on the same day with me. A lot of young people came to know the Lord as their personal Saviour and Lord. Many lives were changed and revolutionised, for the glory of the Lord. There was a significant and noticeable improvement in the academic performance of most of the students who were SU members. The SU group project became a well-known and respected feature within the school corridors.

I only managed to attend this historic and eye-opener conference as a result of the love and benevolence of one of my Christian brothers, Kawanga The Banda. I vividly remember him giving me an amount in the sum of six Zimbabwe dollars (ZW$6.00). This was a lot of money by then because my bus fare (Gweru to KweKwe and back), as a student, was $2.00. I had $4.00 extra money to buy whatever I wanted. Brother Kawanga was in his first-year training at Ziscosteel as an apprentice (Fitting and Turning/Mechanical Engineering). He did not have a lot of money but this was sacrificial giving. His generosity has stuck-up with me up to this day. I have never forgotten about this such that I always remind him (even up to this day, almost 45 years down the line) each time we talk on the phone. He is always trying to distract and deviate me, but I can't be silenced because that gesture of compassion and generosity is like "fire shut-up in my bones". Kawanga is still in Zimbabwe and we are still in touch.

In my view, the two years at GHPS were eventful and productive, both academically and spiritually for me. End of the year 1981, I wrote my final grade seven examinations and passed with distinctions. I was now ready to start my high school academic journey the following year.

While awaiting the final results, during the long December 1981 holidays, I had another blessed opportunity to attend another Christian Conference in Harare hosted by a vibrant youth interdenominational organisation called Abundant Life For All (ALFA). This was my first-ever Christian conference in Harare, the capital city of Zimbabwe. The person who paid for my conference fees was my uncle, now turned close friend Timon Simbarashe Nyatsambo. Although Timon was a few years my senior, we had grown up together in the village, herding cattle and goats. Timon's father Mr Sylvester Mazoe Nyatsambo (The Teacher) was a close cousin-brother to my mother. In my tradition, The Teacher and my mother were brother and sister. As shall be uncovered later, Timon played a pivotal role in my entire life. For example, he later became the leader of my family delegation when I got married and also introduced me to a career that completely transformed my life, both financially and inner-gratification.

Although I have not done much for Kawanga and Timon, the lesson I have learnt from them is that I do not have to possess much in order to bless someone, especially those in need. Apart from my *Amai*, I have seen Timon and Kawanga putting into practice the saying *"Blessed is the hand that giveth than the one that taketh"*. Without necessarily bragging and blowing my own horn, my wife and I are currently paying school fees for some orphaned children from my village in Sanyati, Zimbabwe. Thanks for the practical lessons from Kawanga and Timon. May the Lord continue to richly bless them and replenish where it has been taken from.

This is the story of my life:
An African village-boy goes to the city.

Chapter Six:
My Primary and Secondary Education in the City

Completing Primary Education in the City and Impacting the Lives of other Students

There were only two primary schools in Karaga, Torwood Primary School and R.J Davies Primary School. Due to the war situation, a lot of pupils, mostly the children of Ziscosteel workers, had deserted their villages for Karaga and this resulted in these two good schools not having the capacity to accommodate more learners. Many young people, including myself, wasted the year 1979, doing nothing, instead of going to school. Ziscosteel management decided to turn a residential block of flats called "M" Hostel Building into a school which became known as George Hill Primary School (GHPS). In 1980 I joined GHPS, grade six. I was supposed to be in Form One by then. In my class, there were only two young girls who were of the right age. All of us were older to be in grade six. As a result of the impact of war, this was a common feature in Zimbabwe. The government of Zimbabwe built/opened a number of high schools in order to accommodate ex-freedom fighters, for example Nkukuleko High School in the Midlands Province and Magamba Secondary High School in Mashonaland East Province (Zimbabwe Ministry of Primary and

Secondary Education, 2018). Many ex-freedom fighters who had their education disrupted after joining the armed struggle were given special opportunities to complete their education (including tertiary education). Some of the individuals I know are now human resources management practitioners, lawyers, accountants, medical doctors, engineers etc. This was easily and speedily implemented because the then President Robert Gabriel Mugabe, although a dictator, he was a distinguished and polished academia himself (Nhemachena & Warikandwa, 2019).

As a result of the good influence I got from TBYF, I focussed on my studies and I was always on top of my classes for the two years at GHPS. I passed my grade seven with flying colours. We were fortunate to have a great teacher, the late Mr Jorum Vuma who later visited my house when I was already working. He proudly told my children and wife how smart and hard-working I was at school. I was chuffed and excited for my respected ex-teacher to give such a powerful testimony in the presence of my children and wife. His testimony empowered me to later challenge my children about their academic performance.

While at GHPS, I met one of my best friends in my entire life. I had never seen such a fun character. The guy had the thickest voice and he could laugh the loudest. Each time he laughed, people would in turn laugh at how he laughed. I had never seen such. Both teachers and students loved him for his conspicuous humour. His name was Gift Chakafa. Gift was very good in English Language and was known for laughing at teachers who made grammatical mistakes. He thoroughly enjoyed it and he became well known for it. His nickname became brother 'Bwaaa'. In this context 'bwaaa' means 'breaking' the English language. Though being fun and humorous, Gift was a committed and principled Christian. He also took his studies seriously. I guess this combination is what attracted us to be close friends. Due to my good grade seven results, I proceeded to the next level- secondary School.

Entering Drake Secondary School

In 1982, armed with my impressive Grade Seven results, I secured a Form One place at Drake Secondary School, in Torwood, KweKwe. This meant I would complete my Form four in 1985. Drake was wholly owned and operated by Ziscosteel. More than 90% of the students were children/relatives of Ziscosteel workers. I had wanted to go to St Ignatius College in Chishawasha (near Harare), a prestigious Roman Catholic Advance Level Institute. St Ignatius College was one of the best high schools in Zimbabwe in terms of producing the most outstanding academic results. It was in the same league, academically, with such schools as Gokomere High, Goromonzi High, Fletcher High and St Augustine High (*kwaTsambe*). Unfortunately, I failed their Form One entrance examinations. I later tried Fletcher High School, in Gweru, but I could not secure a place. When I now look back, in retrospect, I thank the Lord because if I had gone to any of these posh and expensive schools, I probably could not have completed my education due to financial constraints and hardships that unfolded later.

Selected for the Best Class

At Drake Secondary School, they would screen students, for Form One, based on their grade seven results. I was placed in the first class, out of seven. Ours was Form One "H" popularly known as 'class *yemashasha*' (class for the intelligent ones). Since I knew that they would screen us again into our third form, I worked harder. Fortunately, I made it into the first class *yemashasha* (3H). Accounts was my best subject. I was greatly influenced by my Form One teacher, Mr Peniel Mhetu. He knew his stuff and he inspired us, his students. He always told us that accountants were the most highly paid professionals in the country, by then. I have always loved office work, especially where I would look dapper in my nice suits. This fuelled my interest in Accounts, as a subject. Most of the time, I would get 100% in

Accounts examinations. As a result of my keen interest in Accounts and desire to work in an office, I developed a negative attitude to practical subjects such as Building and Metalwork (now known mostly as Technical Drawing or Technology). I hated them with passion. I vividly remember in our Form One final examinations getting an above of 95% in all subjects save for the aforementioned two practical subjects, where I scored around 60%. Despite scoring lowly in Building and Metalwork, I came 4th in all combined seven Form One classes (about 300 students) in the final examinations. Had I maintained the average 95%, I was going to secure the 2nd position. It was almost impossible to secure the first position because in all the four years, there was only one student who always occupied number one. His name was Boniface (Bonnie) Mukwenga. The guy was smart, hard-working and humble. Boniface is currently working as one of the directors in a government auditing department in Zimbabwe.

Convincing the Headmaster to Take Accounting at 'O' Level

On the opening day, in our third form, I almost got depressed when I learnt that we were no longer doing Accounts at 'O' Level, but instead Building and Metalwork. Our Accounts teacher, Mr Mhetu had transferred to another school in rural Mrewa- which was about 300 kms from KweKwe. I approached Boniface and told him that it was critical and crucial for the two of us to go and see the headmaster, Mr Joseph Manokore and kindly persuade him to reconsider giving us back our Accounts subject in exchange for the aforementioned practical subjects. I suggested to Boniface that it was prudent not to include other students nor let them know about our agenda otherwise it was going to be sabotaged. I volunteered to be the speaker. He agreed. I made sure that Boniface was included in this fundamental assignment because of his outstanding and unquestionable academic performance. I was academically gifted but not as brilliant as him.

My only advantage over Boniface was that the headmaster knew very well of both my academic record and unwavering commitment to our Scripture Union (SU) group. He liked our SU group because it had huge positive influence on a number of naughty and 'wild' students. We preached the Word of God to them. Every morning, we (SU Group) led prayers and songs at school assembly.

I led a delegation of the two of us to the high office (headmaster). It was rare for students to go to the headmaster's office, unless they were in trouble. When we got there, without an appointment, he quickly demanded to know why we were in his office, instead of studying in our classroom. I boldly said to him, *"Sir, you have destroyed our lives"*. Taking off his glasses, he said, *"What? Explain!!!"*. I continued, *"Sir, the two of us and many others in our stream, not here present, wanted to become accountants but by taking away the Accounts subject from us, it will be a mission impossible. Can you please, Sir, reconsider reinstating the subject and possibly replacing it with the practical subjects. We thank you, Sir, for seriously considering our urgent matter."* I had never seen my headmaster in such deep and profound thoughts. He took a deep breath and a prolonged pause. He gazed on the ceiling and finally said, *"I have heard you, loud and clear. Leave this matter with me and I will come back to you, soon."* We thanked him and left his office. Boniface looked at me in a state of shock and later congratulated me for my boldness and assertiveness. Until this day, I do not know where exactly I got the boldness, courage and wisdom to say what I said and do what I did. However, as a Christian, I believe the Lord was in it.

The following morning, the headmaster walked into our classroom, without talking to anyone, and went straight to the chalk-board and rewrote a revised timetable. He removed Building and Metalwork and replaced it with Accounts. His final words were, *"Ms Mahlazi will be your new Accounts teacher as from today. You no longer do Building and*

Metalwork." Without entertaining any questions, he left. Boniface looked at me in overwhelming disbelief. I was overjoyed within me. I had prayed and staunchly believed that God was going to make a way for us, where there seemed to be no way. At this point none of the other students knew what had transpired behind the scenes. Even up to this day, only a few are now aware. We later went back to the headmaster's office to sincerely thank him for his understanding. The good thing is that a sizeable number of students in our stream, later successfully pursued accounting/auditing as a career. I am personally forever grateful to Mr Manokore, our hero and community champion in Karaga, especially when it came to education empowerment. God willing, I would like to personally present a copy of this book to Mr Manokore, as a simple way of thanking him for all the good work he did for our Karaga community. May the good and faithful Lord bless him and his family.

Becoming School Accounts Club President and Visiting Companies

Miss Mahlazi (later Mrs Jambwa), was given our class. Our bold request changed the entire school timetable. I stepped up my commitment to my studies, especially in Accounts as I did not want to disappoint my understanding headmaster. I made sure that I behaved well especially in the presence of Ms Mahlazi. I approached Ms Mahlazi and suggested to establish an Accounts Club at school. She was happy about the idea and suggested that I see the headmaster for endorsement. I did and the headmaster gave us a green light. The first-ever Drake Secondary School Accounts Club was established and I was voted as its President.

The Accounts Club became vibrant and active. We were able to plan business trips to a number of companies around the City of KweKwe, such as BP, the Post Office Savings Bank (POSB), Ziscosteel and etc. The fulcrum and epitome of all trips was the ones at Ziscosteel. In all these trips, Ziscosteel provided us with free transport in the form of a posh bus. They also spoiled us with yummy eats including cakes on each visit. The Accounts Club was so vibrant and effective such that it became the subject-talk of the entire school, by both staff and students.

Becoming Scripture Union Chair

Apart from being the President of the Accounts Club, I was also voted as the chair of the Scripture Union (SU) group when I was in Form three. Normally, a Form four student (seniors) would always be the chair. This meant I was the chair for two years. We used to evangelise and share the love of the Lord with other students, especially those who had needs. This is the beauty of being in Zimbabwe where there is liberty to freely share one's faith without worrying about unforeseen consequences. At one time our SU group was the best in the National Bible Quiz. Most SU members were top performers in their classes. For example, at one of the end-of-year prize-giving ceremonies, the majority of the best top students were from our SU group. We were very serious about our studies as we did not want to put the name of the Lord in disrepute. I am glad that we left a good legacy at Drake Secondary School. During my time, our SU Staff Advisor Mr Augustine Machina played a pivotal role in supporting and giving us guidance.

When the "O" Level results came out, I had passed and qualified to go for "A" Level. I had a distinction in Accounts. Apart from Mrs Jambwa, I would like to sincerely thank one of the Accounts teachers, Mr Barnabas Sibanda. Although he was not teaching our class, he used to help me each time I had some Accounts questions. Because he was a Christian, he later became my close friend and brother in the Lord. We call each other 'wamai', meaning "my brother from another esteemed mother". When he later had his wedding, I was one of the 'bridegroom-boys'. Mr Sibanda is always telling me that, the first time he met me, he sensed great leadership qualities and huge Christian faith within me. He is always quoting an incident when he loudly overheard me challenging another student who was a non-believer at a public bus stop. He claims I said to the student *"Isu tiri venyasha"*. This means "We are what we are because of God's grace." Mr Sibanda is now in South Africa and we are in constant touch.

I will not have done any justice to conclude this chapter without mentioning my late best friend since my primary school days at George Hill Primary School, Gift Chakafa. Our friendship grew from strength to strength. I have never had a close friend whom I would laugh with, at anything and anytime, like Gift. When it came to 'manufacturing' jokes, he was talented and gifted as his name. We clicked. We parted our ways soon after our final 'O' Level examinations. The parting was emotionally painful. I remained in the city of KweKwe and he went to the rural area in Gokwe and later joined the Ministry of Education as a temporary teacher. There was no social media those days. We only met once, years later, at my flat, when he was passing through on his way to a teacher training college. We had the 'biggest' laugh and reunion. Little did I know that this would be the last time to see my dearest friend. I would have done something significant for him. Sadly, Gift later passed-on while training as a schoolteacher at one of the colleges in Masvingo, Zimbabwe. I miss him dearly. Almost 40 years on, I sometimes vividly dream about him, laughing together. May his soul rest in everlasting peace.

This is the story of my life:
An African village-boy's secondary education in Karaga.

Chapter Seven:
The Genesis of My Career Path
– Part One

Accounting Internship

When I finished writing my 'O' Level examination on Monday the 2nd December 1985, I started my first ever job, the following day. This was an internship position at Ziscosteel Ltd in their Accounts Department, which was supposed to last at the end of March 1986. Ziscosteel used to recruit Accountancy, Business Studies and Economics final year students from the University of Zimbabwe (UZ), which was (by then) the only university in the country. But due to my unwavering commitment to our high school Accounts Club, I was the only non-university student to be offered an internship role to the amazement of my fellow high school colleagues, teachers and the community. I was the least qualified and the youngest of all internships. This had never happened before. To God be the glory!!!!

During my last two years at Drake Secondary school, as the President of the Accounts Club (and my executive), we took the club to another higher level and transformed it into a vibrant entity. We were able to demonstrate how an effective school club would be administered. The contacts we had established with Ziscosteel Ltd and other organisations were very strong and genuine. At Ziscosteel in particular, I had professional interactions with the Chief Accountant and the Financial Accountant, who later offered me the internship job. I have always believed in hardworking, focus and determination.

Since I knew most of the workers at Ziscosteel, because I had grown up in Torwood (Karaga) township, my integration, fit and 'chemistry' into the organisation was easy. Besides that, my father and my four elder brothers were already working for the same company. As already stated, my father was well known by all employees as the most smartly dressed and cheerful Ambulance and Fire Engine Driver.

I was well received and inducted by all the workers in the Accounts Department. It was my first time to see the relationship and interface between accounting theory and practice. It was fascinating. I was really enjoying both the job and the work environment.

In the middle of this enjoyment, I was offered a 4-year apprenticeship training position as a Fitter and Turner (Mechanical Engineering) with Ziscosteel Training Department, starting on 20 January 1986. I had applied for apprenticeship training around August 1985, as 'Plan B' just in case my 'O' Level results were not good enough for Advanced Level. I did not want to be a Fitter and Turner in my life. I knew very well that I was not technically gifted and I was destined for failure if I had taken that route. I had made my mind when I was in Form One that I wanted to be an accountant. That is all I wanted.

As I sought for help, advice and counsel from trusted friends, family, relatives, community and church colleagues, almost everyone told me that I was foolish if I were to decline this rare training opportunity. Apprenticeship training was the 'in-thing' those days. Remember in 1986, Zimbabwe was only into its 6th year of independence and as a result very few indigenous (Black) Zimbabweans were into apprenticeship training.

Because of racial segregation, apprenticeship was mainly reserved for white people. I was openly criticised and labelled unreasonable, useless, opportunity-waster and many other negative names you can think of, for considering not to go for apprenticeship training. What complicated my situation is that my two elder brothers were already qualified artisans (fitter & turner and a boilermaker) and were earning good moneys. In addition, most of my close church-friends were training as apprentices. They all criticised and castigated my dreams, with passion.

Short-Stint Apprenticeship Training

As the 20th January 1986 approached, for me to start my scary apprenticeship training, I was already in total dilemma and near-depression. Since I had not received my 'O' Level results, I had no choice but to leave my exciting internship accounts job to join the boring and miserable apprenticeship training. That was one of the saddest days of my life. Ironically, all the almost 120 trainees, save for me, were visibly excited to start a career with such a massive organisation such as Ziscosteel. After two months of this torturous training, my 'O' Level results came. I had passed and qualified for Advanced Level (5th and 6th Forms). What I knew was that I could not go for 'A' Levels due to financial constraints. My father had many children and could not afford to pay fees for a battalion of his offspring. My elder brother who had a good job (boilermaker) was not working. His twin brother had a low-income job and could not afford to help me. My only available options were to keep on training as an apprentice or resign and look for another job of my interest. I tried to go back to Ziscosteel Accounts department, but they did not have permanent positions. But I clearly knew what I wanted in my life, career-wise. To be an accountant, without fail. I was determined to face any obstacle and hindrance on my path. I had made up my mind when I was in Form One and it was a deal done, within me. I quickly looked for a job at commercial banks, and luckily secured one at the

Zimbabwe Banking Corporation (Zimbank), now known as Zimbabwe Bank (ZB Bank). Barclays Bank, an international bank was about to offer another job.

I tendered my resignation from apprenticeship training end of March 1986. I am thankful to Ziscosteel Training Centre management for being thoughtful and considerate by giving me ample time to make a decision and not cajoling me into signing a government training-bond contract. Had I signed the contract, it was going to be difficult for me to get out of it. I started my banking career with Zimbank in early April 1986.

Banking Career and Private Studies

April 1986 was a great and exciting month for me. As I walked into the Zimbank banking-hall and offices at KweKwe Branch, I was stoked. I could feel that I was now ensconced in a career path that resonated with my soul and spirit. I was employed as a bank clerk. I loved my job. The working environment was great. Both management and staff were kind and supportive. Above all, I was fortunate and blessed to work under a professional and supportive management team under the leadership of Mr Gordon G Savanhu the Branch Manager and Mr Kanengoni, the Branch Accountant.

Firstly, I pay great tribute to Mr Savanhu who was my first ever manager. He was professional and understanding, but firm and fair. I liked his leadership style. He was balanced and strategic. He was kind and warm, especially to me. I particularly liked and learnt a lot from the way he carried himself at work. He bullied no one. Not even a single day did I have a problem with him. The other person who was helpful in my banking career was Mr Kanengoni, the Branch Accountant. He was professional, gentle and always jovial. I never saw him angry. He made everyone 'feel at home'.

I seriously believe that if I had continued with my apprenticeship training, I was destined for a depression and disastrous life, ahead. The fact that I had turned down advice and counsel from close friends and relatives and resigned from a lucrative and financially rewarding trade career path (apprenticeship job), I had constant pressure to prove that my instinct and decision was right. I unceasingly reminded myself of the only option, thus studying (privately) very hard in order to make it in my new profession. I had to. I had no choice. This was not just studying, but working full-time and studying part-time. I knew it was not easy. To make it to the top in a bank industry, one had to acquire a relevant degree or study for a specific professional qualification with such boards as Institute of Bankers of Zimbabwe (IOBZ) and Chartered Institute of Secretaries (CIS). I had none of the above.

I wasted no time. Within a month of joining the banking sector, I enrolled with the IOBZ. After six months, I sat an examination for two subjects (Economics and Money & Banking). My Branch Manager, Mr Savanhu was our invigilator. Our local Banking Hall was the examination venue – my work familiar territory. There were only two candidates, with another guy from the nearby Standard Chartered Bank. When the results came out, I had failed both subjects. I think I had not prepared adequately. This did not discourage me. When I informed Mr Savanhu that I had failed both subjects, he encouraged me to re-register and try again. He never discouraged me nor perceived me as someone who was dull.

In July 2021, after 36 years, while already in New Zealand, I searched for Mr Savanhu and was able to locate him, in Zimbabwe. I then thanked him for all the unwavering support he had given me. After a few but long WhatsApp text messages, I called him and our first-ever call in 36 years lasted for more than one-long hour. Most of the time I was reminding him of all the good deeds and the unwavering support he gave me when I was a mere bank clerk. He had totally forgotten about all his multitude of sincere kindness and genuine help he had given me. In my view, he immensely contributed to where I am today. Apart from reminding him of all the said good deeds and Ubuntu he displayed to me, we shared about our career paths, what became of each one of us since we parted ways 36 years ago. We also updated each other about our families. He kept on saying he is now a proud grandfather. We also laughed about how 'young' we currently felt. We laughed a lot. I was also thrilled to talk to his wife, Mai Savanhu, who was also friendly, respectful and humane to me. We again laughed a lot with Mai Savanhu.

My relationship with Mr Savanhu was professional and genuine. We both had professional boundaries. Why am I mentioning all this? Is it important? Does it add any value in anything? Yes, indeed. Let me explain. During those days, the majority of managers/supervisors were disrespectful to their direct-reports or subordinates – especially if one was a mere clerk, as I was. Maybe this was caused by the fact that we had just attained our political independence (six years old) and most of them (managers) were implementing autocratic type of leadership as they had experienced from their colonial masters/managers. I also believe that one's upbringing and background play a significant role in leadership styles. For example, I later worked under a new accountant who was rough and disrespectful, totally different from the said kind and professional Mr Kanengoni. The other reason why I am labouring on this notion, is a kind reminder that it is good and important to respect every human being, regardless. In my African tradition, this is called Ubuntu (Tuwe, 2018). I thank the Lord because in September 2022, while we were on holiday in Zimbabwe, my wife and I managed to pay a courtesy visit to Mr and Mrs Savanhu at their home in Harare – more details to follow.

Private Studies -Advanced Accounting

As I had dreams to become an accountant, I decided to drop banking studies and pursued Accounting at advanced 'A' Level. I enrolled with the KweKwe-based Zimbabwe Distance Education College (ZEDCO). I would attend face-to-face lessons about three times a week after work. There were only two students in my class. Without notice, our course was discontinued because our part-time teacher, who was an internal auditor at Ziscosteel, was no longer available. My colleague and I had to engage another private part-time teacher who was employed as an accountant at a nearby fertilizer-making company called Sable Chemicals. The same accountant was also teaching 'A' Level Accounting at KweKwe High School, which was in town. Most of his students were my former Drake Secondary School class-mates. I worked hard. I had uncountable sleepless nights. Most of the weekends I used to go and spend the whole day studying at Globe and Phoenix Primary School (GPPS) which was near KweKwe CBD, where I had secured a classroom via my friend Mr Chris Govati Mutopa who was a senior teacher there. I vividly remember one day the headmaster of GPPS, a lovely and respectable old man, saying to me, *"Young man, tell me, what are you studying? What really motivates you to work so hard because I see you spending uncountable weekends reading? I know you are a banker in town and some of your age-mates are drinking and enjoying life..."* Before I responded he said, *"Whatever you are desiring and dreaming for, it shall come to pass...I wish you well."* With these inspiring words, he left. He never gave me an opportunity to respond. I never saw him again. I wish I did. I would have loved to simply thank him for his kind words and encouragement. These words birthed untold intrinsic motivation within me. Up to this day, I vividly recall this inspiring conversation.

Exactly after a year, in June 1987, I sat for my 'A' Level Accounting Cambridge Examinations. When the results came, I got an 'O', which was not a pass at 'A' Level, but the equivalence of ordinary 'O' Level standard. At 'O' Level, I got a distinction (A) in Accounts. This was my first ever 'A' Level certificate, obtained in one year instead of two. Again, I was not disappointed. I was excited and motivated to do more.

When I joined the bank, we were around six new young people comprising of one 'girl' and five 'boys'. By the time I left the bank in October 1988, only the young woman and I managed to remain unscathed by fraud activities that resulted in others losing their jobs – they all got fired. In October 1988, I resigned from Zimbank and re-joined Ziscosteel's Accounts Department.

Accounting Career and Private Studies

Senior Financial Accounts Clerk

My new position at Ziscosteel was that of Senior Financial Accounts Clerk within the Financial Accounts department. The Finance Division comprised of a number of departments such as Cost and Management Accounts, Financial Accounts, Stores, Purchasing and Information Technology. I was responsible for all company debtors. The job was enriching and exciting. The most part I enjoyed were *Debtors' Aging Analysis and Reconciliations*. Not only did these two activities give me a big picture of what was happening within the company debtors' section, but also, that Ziscosteel was the main back-bone and life-line of the Zimbabwean economy. A lot of big, small and medium companies entirely depended on it.

Salary-wise, it almost doubled compared to my former bank position. As for career-path direction, my new job was a huge scaffolding-step in my accounting profession. The work environment was great and friendly. Since I had grown up in Karaga I knew most employees and I had also previously worked with most staff on my internship. This made my integration and settling process very smooth and ease. I blended well. The chemistry was fabulous and natural.

Surrounded by Dedicated Professionals

My biggest benefit for joining Ziscosteel Accounts department was that there were a number of professional and dedicated staff who had done well in their accounting careers, mostly through private studies. The majority had made it from very humble beginnings. Some had done formal education only up to seventh grade - and completed their high school qualifications via private studies while working full time. A shining and vivid example is Mr Edward Madyavanhu. He became my best mentor and source of inspiration, in my private studies. He was a Christian, humble, smart, hard-working and ready to assist other staff. When I joined the Financial Accounts department, Mr Madyavanhu was almost finishing his Accounting Professional studies with the UK-based Chartered Institute of Management Accountants (CIMA). I emulated him and respected him, immensely. I used to go to his house to study with him, as way of learning and appreciating how he was doing it. I learnt a lot.

Budget Officer

After exactly one year of joining Ziscosteel Accounts Department, I was promoted to the position of Budget Officer within the Cost and Management Accounts section. My main role was to look after the budgets for the entire organisation, under the supervision of the Management Accountant. This involved attending all departmental Cost and Management meetings, analysing cost variances, seeking explanations and justification for over/under expenditure from departmental managers and finally documenting the proceedings of the meetings in form of minutes. I gained and learnt a lot of good analytical skills in this exciting role.

My new boss, the Management Accountant was Mrs Annah-Mercy Mashingaidze who was one of the highest qualified people within Ziscosteel's Finance Division as well as nationally. This inspired me to concentrate on my work and even work harder in my private studies. Some of the great and amazing people I worked with in the Cost and Management Accounts department were Innocent Mhazo, Richard Mangi, Elisha Chivero, Peter Banda, Godfrey Chadi, Godwin Sibanda, Philip Hushani, and Raphael Nyoni.

Zimbabwe Association of Accounting Technicians (ZAAT) and Institute of Certified Bookkeepers of South Africa {ICB(SA)} Studies

Before I got my 'A' Level results, I had registered with the then Zimbabwe Association of Accounting Technicians (ZAAT) which is now called Southern Africa Association of Accountants (SAAA). I had thought of pursuing a professional accounting course. I wrote my first two subjects and passed both. I was excited and encouraged to put more effort. I kept pushing my private studies. As a result of the motivation, I got from some of my above-mentioned colleagues, I increased my dedication and commitment to my ZAAT private studies. Within no time, I completed my Part One of the ZAAT qualification and straight away enrolled for the Part Two, which was the final stage. While doing ZAAT Part Two, I enrolled for another qualification offered by the South African-based Institute of Certified Bookkeepers of South Africa {ICB(SA)}. I worked so hard and completed the Associate Level (Part One) and embarked on the final advanced stage (Fellowship Level) of ICB. After passing the advanced stage I became a Fellow member of ICB, thus, using the credentials {FICB(SA)} behind my name. At this stage, I was now a qualified international bookkeeper.

This is the story of my life:
The genesis of an African village-boy's career path.

Chapter Eight:
Meeting the Love of My Life

First Meeting the Woman I Love

Saturday, the 7th of December 1991 was a special day for my friend David Barnabas Chizozo Nyoni and his soon-wife-to-be, Tambu. It was their wedding day in Karaga Township, in the town of Redcliff, KweKwe, Zimbabwe. I was appointed the Chair of the Wedding Committee as well as the Master of Ceremony (MC) for the great day. Two weeks before the big day, as the MC, I decided to go to Harare, the capital city, to buy a special suit for the occasion. I got one, which was later code-named 'Butcher-boy' by my friend, Noah Fore because of its stripes and unique design.

I vividly remember on an early-evening Sunday (around 6pm), I arrived in Redcliff (from Harare) and decided to pass through Jane and Juwel's house. Jane and Juwel were a newly married couple. They were both my friends, well before they got married. In fact, it was me who introduced Juwel to Jane. I was the connector. As I stated before, Juwel was my mentor and youth leader and Jane was my best friend and high school classmate. My friendship and connection (at high school) with Jane was deep and profound – we clicked very well such that some of the students and teachers thought we were going out. The main reason for passing through Jane and Juwel's place was to have a free dinner and then proceed to my flat/apartment to sleep. I was a bachelor. I did not want to cook. I am not even sure if I had food at my flat on that particular night. However, as a connector, this was somehow a way for them to pay me for my free services. 

When I got to Jane and Juwel's house, as a close *sahwira* (friend), I didn't knock. I simply opened the kitchen door, moved in and demanded food. Suddenly, my eyes and attention were caught and arrested by a beautiful young lady. She was seated on a couch (sofa). I had not seen her before. Immediately and suddenly, I 'heard' a convincing and pricking inner-voice saying to me, **"*This is your wife.*"** I straight away told myself that I was going to marry this lady, even if she was already married. That is how strong the conviction was. Honestly, I didn't care. All I wanted was her. I quickly ignored all other factual questions and my own principles when it came to choosing a life-partner such as, *"What if she is committed to someone? What about her background? Was she a born-again Christian? Her values? Her interests and etc...?"*

When I gave her a second glance through the corner of my eyes, my heart jumped into my mouth such that I thought everyone in the house heard it. I nearly fainted. A third glance opened a pandora's box of 'confusion' within me. It was all because of her outstanding and exquisite beauty, her natural curly-hair and her African-light-chocolate complexion. When she stood up to go to the kitchen, what I saw caused and generated massive confusion in my little brain. I had never seen such precision and proportionality. I felt 'explosives' in my heart. Her natural beauty was astonishing and untold. She was not wearing any make-up. All was natural. Yes! It was completely outside this world. I had seen beautiful girls before, but not at this level and natural standard. She was a full-package. She represented everything I had dreamt and desired of a woman. In my heart of hearts, I said, *"Eureka. I have found it."* From no way, I was prepared for anything in order to have her for the rest of my life. All this happened in a split second and within a twinkling of an eye. All along, I had not even greeted her. All this drama was happening in my mind and heart. I was also surprised by myself. The turn of events was unbelievable.

I walked-up straight to her and boldly introduced myself to this "beauty at its best" young woman, who had completely stolen my heart. I looked straight into her gorgeous (but innocent) eyes and her radiating beauty caught my eyes (again) and recaptured my heart. With her hand in mine, I said to her, "*I greet you, my sister. My name is Tuwe. I am the boss of this house. I do what I want here.*" She did not say anything but simply smiled. Then my dear *sahwira* Jane said, "*That one is a crazy guy. Don't listen to him.*" She smiled again. I wish she knew what her smiles were doing to me. They "melted and dissolved" me. The more she smiled, the further her tantalising beauty was unpacked and revealed. She was a complete and flawless package. I loved her straight away. She later said, "*I am Annette. Nice to meet you, my brother.*" In my heart, without uttering any word, I quickly said, "*I am not your brother. Soon, I will be your husband.*" I smiled and said, "*Thank you, sisi.*" I sat down.

Tambu had previously told me that her friend whom she had known for the past three years at a Teachers' Training College was going to be her best-girl (maid of honour) at her wedding. In our brief introductions, it turned out that Annette was the best-girl in question. Annette was staying at Jane and Juwel's place because Tambu and David's place was far from Karaga where the wedding 'Dancing Practice' (*The Steps*) were happening daily after working hours. David and Juwel were close childhood friends. So, it made both social and economic sense for Annette to stay at Jane and Juwel's place.

I was thrilled when I discovered that Juwel was not at his place when I got there. If he was there, it probably could have 'forced' Annette to join Jane in the kitchen leaving me with my friend Juwel, whom I had no business nor interest in, on this opportune day. In other words, he was going to *'pour sand into my cup of tea,'* thus, spoiling my rare life-opportunity.

My heart was already stolen by Annette. All I was seeing, sensing, hearing, breathing, feeling and smelling was Annette's beauty. All I wanted was Annette. If this is what is defined as 'love at first sight', this was it. As Jane was preparing our supper, I had an opportunity to have a casual chat with Annette. It gave me a rare opportunity to talk to her without any 'competition' and divided attention.

In my brief discussion with her, I learnt that her full names were Annette Mutema. She had just successfully completed her three-year Primary School Teachers Training Programme. She was ready to start her first year as a qualified teacher in the following year, in January 1992.

As we were chatting while awaiting dinner, I was busy thinking and conjuring in my mind ways of coming up with a quick strategic plan of *'ring-fencing'* Annette from the other 'hungry vultures' (single boys). *'Ring-fencing'* is a term we used when a boy makes a non-verbal declaration (via actions), that he was in love or keenly interested in a particular girl. The *'Ring-fencing'* concept also sent a clear message to other boys that they should not dare try their luck nor come closer to the girl in question. The message was simply *'Touch Not'.*

Hatching a Plan to Charm and Lure Annette

I quickly came up with a plan. I kindly requested Annette if I could take her to our city of KweKwe, the following day (Monday) and show her around, since it was her first time to be in our beautiful city. KweKwe was popularly known as *'The Now City in Touch with Tomorrow'.* To my surprise and excitement, she agreed. I was electrified with unspeakable joy. My energy levels just shot-up. My confidence was enhanced and invigorated. I could not hide my excitement. As a strategy, I knew that the first most challenging obstacle was now eliminated. I strongly believe that this idea and strategy was divinely supplied. It did not just come from the ivory tower of my distilled human wisdom. No. I believe it was 'heaven-baked' and 'heaven-cooked'.

The second challenge was about reporting for work the following day (Monday). I had taken two days off-work (Thursday and Friday) the previous week, for my Harare-suit trip. Due to the demands of my job, as a Budget/Accounting Officer, I had to report for duty, without fail. I now had a dilemma, to choose between Annette and my job. To make matters worse, I had already promised her to take her to the city of KweKwe the following day. I could not change it. Otherwise, I was not going to get (again) this rare life-opportunity to 'shine' and firmly establish myself and 'my territory'. Within the twinkling of an eye, I came up with a plan. I would ring off-sick the following day. I felt very bad because I knew it was unethical and unprofessional. I had never done this before. But in this case, I had no any other viable option. It was a do or die game.

After supper, I went into the kitchen and had a private chat with Jane. I told her about my profound interest and intense love for Annette and that I really needed her unwavering support in this crucial journey. I also informed her about the planned trip to the city, the following day. As my best friend, she had known me from our glorious high school days and in any case, she had already told me that I was going to be a good and responsible husband. She trusted me and wanted the best for me. She agreed to play her strategic role and 'cards' well for my benefit. I was intensely excited. I left Jane's place for my flat, a happy and relieved person.

As I walked to my flat (about 15-minutes), I am not sure if I was audibly talking to myself as a mad person or not. I don't even know how I got to my place. Whether I met some people or not, I don't know. If I did, I am not sure if I greeted them. Remember, Redcliff was a place where everyone knew everybody. We all worked for the same company (Ziscosteel) which at one time employed around 7000 staff. I was well known in town. When I got home, I mentally re-played all that had happened, from the moment I set my eyes on beautiful Annette.

I had just seen her, for less than four hours and for the very first time in my life, yet I felt this way. A million questions started to bombard my head. Is this normal? Is this what is called genuine love? Isn't this infatuation? Isn't this of the flesh? Is God in it? Did I know her background? Did I know whether she was already committed to someone or not? As a committed and principled Christian, did I know her level of faith and commitment to the things of God? The answer to most of the aforementioned questions was a big NO. To be brutally honest, I did not care. I missed her the more. The more I thought about her, the more I loved her. I simply just wanted to be with her. Without her, I felt empty and incomplete. I had never experienced such a powerful and dominant emotional feeling towards anybody of the opposite sex. Not in my life-time. I was actually surprised by what I was feeling and going through. It was inherently over-powering and conspicuously convincing. Based on how I felt, what I had seen with my naked two-eyes, and the inner conviction within me, I knew straight away, she was the right person for me. Even before I had proposed and got a 'yes', I made a decision to marry her.

I had been praying for a good wife for many years and I knew exactly what I wanted, both spiritually and the physical beauty. As I was growing up, I was very particular and choosy about physical beauty and outward appearance. To be truthful, while I desired a God-fearing woman, I had a high propensity and gravitation toward physical beauty. This is why when the Biblical Adam saw Eve he said *"Wow!!! This is beautiful. Bone of my bone and flesh of my flesh"*. To prove this point, most of my primary and high school friends were beautiful and attractive girls. After high school, I met many beautiful girls at numerous prominent social and spiritual events, regionally and nationally, where I was the Master of Ceremony (MC), but none of them 'moved' me as Annette did. Some made advances but I did not fall-in. I thank God for that because otherwise there wouldn't be any Annette to talk about in my life.

As a result of my public stance and overt preference for physical beauty, most of my close Christian friends nick-named me '*Nyama*' which meant '*A fleshly Man*'. I was open about it because I had witnessed unhappy Christian marriages where most husbands' love and commitment later grew wax-cold towards their wives because they were simply no longer attractive to them. The initial fire and affection would have evaporated. I hated it with passion and I vowed (to myself) to marry someone whom when I look at, in her deep-sleep (without a bath and make-up), my heart would jump into my mouth and feel 'blinded' by her beauty. Did this happen with Annette? Please keep on reading for your own discovery 😃.

Before I retired for the night, I prayed as usual. I started thanking the Lord for my future wife called Annette. I claimed her in prayer. And I staunchly believed it. For me, it was a deal done.

The following day on Monday, I rang my boss and took sick leave. It was granted because it was my first time to take sick leave, in that particular year. Since there were no mobile phones in Zimbabwe (by then in December 1991), I woke up early in the morning and called my friend Jane (on her landline) to let Annette know that I was on my way to pick her up. When I got to Jane's place, I found Annette ready waiting for me. I was thrilled and encouraged by her preparedness. For me, it was a positive sign and good omen that things were flowing in the right trajectory and direction.

I did not have a car, so we walked to the bus stop to catch *Makombi* (private vans used as public transport) to KweKwe. We met my former schoolmate, Shelter Bvochora, who had become a successful professional photographer - and he demanded to take a picture for the two of us. He was both interested and surprised to see me walking with such a beautiful girl. They used to call me 'brother' at high school; signifying that I was not involved in girls. He was both excited and happy for me. He started teasing us and instructing us to get closer to each other as we posed for the photo. I liked it. It was all working in my favour.

KweKwe City Visit

When we got to the City of KweKwe, I suggested going for our breakfast at Wimpy Restaurant, which was (by then) well known as 'the restaurant' in town. Its popularity was centred on its great taste for good food, especially T-bone steak. After ordering our yummy food, I did not waste time. I asked Annette if it was okay for both of us to share our backgrounds so that we know each other in a little bit more detail. She concurred. I was excited. I offered to start. The reason for offering to share first about my life, was to set the pace and tone for the narrative and depth of the content. I really wanted to know her background, especially her upbringing and social values that underpinned her life. To me, that mattered a lot. In addition to my personal life (as outlined in the proceeding chapters), I passionately shared and highlighted on spirituality and social values, especially Ubuntu. To me that balance was pivotal and crucial. While sharing the story of my life, I constantly watched Annette's body language to gauge her interest and concentration, in the discussion. In my humble view, she looked keenly interested in what I was saying. However, she refutes this assertion even to this very day. She maintains she was not at all interested. I haven't believed her. I was both thrilled and encouraged. When I finished, I asked if she had any questions. She didn't have any. Whether she was telling the truth or not, I felt that I had done a good job.

When it was her turn, I made sure that I gave her maximum and undivided attention. In summary, Annette told me that she was the third child in a family of nine (five girls and four boys). Her father Kimeon (KC) Mutema - was originally from Mutema, Gutu in Masvingo Province. Her mother Agnes Cheda's roots were based in Gwaranyemba, Gwanda in Matebeleland South Province. Her father was a teacher in one of the oldest towns in Zimbabwe called Masvingo. Her mother was a full-time housewife.

Although she didn't mention it, I later learnt that Annette was a straight 'A' student – through-out her school days. She is academically gifted. During her narration, I kept on asking her a number of questions as a way of encouraging her to speak and provide more details and context but she didn't say much. I later discovered that she was generally a quiet and reserved person, but smart, calculative and intelligent. She was also firm. I must say that the catch-up with Annette was the genesis of better things to come. We both clicked and enjoyed each other's company. My fears and concerns were alleviated when Annette shared with me that she was a born-again Christian. I felt relieved.

After exchanging our life-notes, which took the greater part of the day, we had a tour of the City of KweKwe. I later sincerely thanked Annette for her precious time and we left for Karaga where the Dance Practice (*Masteps*) was taking place, daily after 5pm.

"Ring-fencing" Strategy

When we got to Karaga for the '*Masteps*', I made sure that the '*Ring-fencing*' strategy was effectively implemented immediately but in a nice and 'professional' manner. As I stated before, we were all well known in this township of Karaga as disciplined young men who were committed to the things of God and with a keen interest in the development of our community at large. Many people, both young and old looked up to us. We knew it. So, I had to exercise extreme care and caution. What made my job easy was my close and trusted young man, Martin Samangaya, who was chosen as the 'Best-man' for this wedding and was automatically paired to dance with Annette (the best-girl). In other words, they were dancing-partners. During the wedding preparations, especially at *Masteps* and on the wedding-day, Martin effectively and efficiently played his '*Ring-fencing*' strategy by behaving and telling all the '*hungry and dangerous vultures*' (boys) that Annette was 'mine'. The message was simply 'Touch Not'. He also behaved and said positive things about me to Annette. It worked perfectly well. To this day (almost 33 years ago), Martin is always reminding me and boasting that were it not for him, I wouldn't be having my sweetheart and beautiful Annette as a wife. He is always threatening to send me an 'invoice'. 😃

As the Chair and MC for the wedding, for the next week, I would go to Karaga every day after work to supervise progress as well as giving moral support to the dancing-bridal party. However, most importantly, I wanted to see Annette and make sure that I 'registered', established and reaffirmed my '*ring-fencing*' strategy. Fortunately, I had unwavering support from everyone. I would also chair wedding meetings in which Annette was a participant. At times, in these meetings, I would go an extra mile to impress her. 😊 Apart from attending the *Masteps* daily, I would buy Annette special and expensive chocolates daily. After the *Masteps*, I would take Annette to Jane's place. During this time, our friendship grew steeply. I could not wait for 4pm, to knock off from work and leave for Karaga to meet my beauty Queen, Annette. My love for her was like '*fire shut-up in my bones*'. I loved her more. She was almost becoming a distraction to my work.

On David's Wedding Day

On the wedding day, I was the MC and Annette was the Best-girl. In my language we say '*Mutambo waiva mumaoko angu*'. This is translated as '*the wedding was in my hands*'. Due to such an important and crucial assignment, I had to make sure I was up for the game. As the MC, who also had a hidden agenda, I was smartly dressed to impress Annette in particular. Although the ceremony was mostly about the official church proceedings, led by the Pastor, I however played a significant role of directing the entire programme. At the reception, I was the main man – in total control.

The reception at Torwood Hotel was where the bridal party showed their African dancing skills. The boys and girls were doing what they knew best. Hundreds of people graced the event. Within our African culture, even if you send invitation cards, you cannot turn away uninvited community members who will have come to celebrate with you. A wedding is a community event. It is their wedding. So, you can't chase people away especially if the venue is public. After the bridal party displayed some of their dancing skills, Juwel who knew about my agenda, paid some money (as part of a wedding gift) so that Annette and I could dance before the crowd together with my friend Noah Fore and his fiancée Rebecca. I was thrilled and visibly excited. Annette was a bit shy but she couldn't refuse. If one didn't want to dance, he/she was required to pay an amount which was over and above the initial baited-figure. In my culture, this is also a way of raising money for the newlyweds. We danced to the ululation and excitement of the crowd. People were genuinely happy for us. I liked it because it was all working in my favour. After the wedding the feedback on my MC skills was positive. I was dying to know what Annette was thinking about my MCing. Unfortunately, I never got the feedback from her, up to this day- 33 years later. If I ask, she tells me off. 🤷

The Golden Mile Motel 'Summit'- Proposing

After laying a solid foundation and building trust in our friendship, I felt that Annette had now developed some confidence and trust in me. I therefore sensed that it was the right time to put forward my proposal and tell her officially that I loved her to the point of marriage. I never wasted time because I knew she was supposed to go back to Masvingo soon after the wedding. I asked to take her for lunch, on a Sunday afternoon, at one of the best motels in KweKwe called the Golden Mile Motel (GMM). The GMM is located along the Harare-Bulawayo highway and only a mile from the city of KweKwe, hence its name. I chose the GMM for two main reasons: (i) it was the best motel in the entire city of KweKwe and its standards, including food, was top notch, and (ii) sentimental reasons: I knew most of the staff, because during my days (working for the bank) we used to have a number of work-related functions and parties there. I knew I was going to have a personalised service that would also impress Annette and that would be in my favour. I was right. She got impressed by the professional personal service and she also enjoyed the food. These days, Annette and I now refer to the GMM episode as the 'Golden Mile Motel Summit'.

After placing our food orders, I wasted no time. I told her plainly that I loved her to the point of marriage and that she had managed to completely steal and capture my heart. I went further and said, "*I have no heart. My heart is entirely in your hands. Please, break it not*". She smiled. She was calm and easy in conduct. She did not beat about the bush. She told me that she needed a bit of time to think seriously more about it and then come back to me. When I got this response, my guts and inner-feelings told me that all was well. I marvelled inside me. What I was not prepared for was a straight 'No' for an answer. To be honest, I don't know how I was going to handle it if I had been given a 'No'.

Accompanying Annette to Gweru

A day after our Golden Mile Motel 'Summit', it was now time for Annette to 'kiss' KweKwe good-bye and leave for her home-town of Masvingo. She had planned to go to Masvingo via her elder sister's place, in the city of Gweru. I decided to accompany her up to Gweru, which is only 60 kms from KweKwe. Since I did not have a car, we used public transport. The trip to Gweru gave us another opportunity to be together. Even in deep silence, it was evident that we were enjoying each other's company. However, it was as if it was a 10-minute journey. I still wanted more time to be with her.

When we got at her sister's place, I was well received. The welcome from both the sister (Winnette) and her husband (Simba) was just but encouraging. As a way of both asserting myself and 'testing the waters' (for my acceptance), I greeted Winnette as *'maiguru'* and Simba as *'babamukuru'*. In my Zimbabwean culture and in particular in this context *maiguru* meant 'big sister-in-law and *babamukuru* meant 'big brother-in-law'. I did this on purpose, from a customary and traditional perspective. When I was leaving their house, I repeated my greeting-salutations. Later on, Annette told me that her sister commented about my greeting-salutations positively. In summary, they both liked me, the moment they saw me. In my African culture, it is crucially important and significant to secure the endorsement of an elder sister or brother-in-law for your boyfriend, especially if you are meeting them for the very first time.

The time to say goodbye was a painful moment for both of us. I could see and feel it because I tested her by continuously talking to her and delaying our parting. She seemed to like it. For me it was a positive tick. We painfully separated our ways. Annette went back to her sister's place in preparation to leave for Masvingo the following day. I caught a bus back to

KweKwe. I don't know how I arrived in KweKwe because my mind, soul and spirit were still in Gweru with Annette.

Daily Communication with Annette

Luckily, Annette's parents had a landline phone at their house in Masvingo. Many households did not have landlines. They were considered a luxury. This was indeed a blessing, especially for me, because I could call and speak to Annette which would have been very difficult, as there were no mobile phones in those days. At times I could call her more than once per day. However, what would surprise me, at times, was the lack of coherent and effective communication from Annette on the other end of the line. It would be a straight 'yes' or 'no'. She later told me that during such times her father would be seated next to the landline phone such that he could almost hear the entire conversation. To make it a bit complicated (and awkward), her father would not leave the room to give her the privacy she needed. Nowadays, Annette and I laugh about it. I am told at one time he complained and said, *"Who is this guy calling you every time?"* Our telephone conversations strengthened and buttressed our relationship.

Besides calling Annette every day, I would write letters and send beautiful cards via the postal system. Luckily, those days in Zimbabwe, it only took a day or two for a letter to be delivered from one town to the other. This meant, Annette would receive a letter from me every day. In addition to the letters, I would post her favourite chocolates, at least twice per week. This became a tradition and habit without fail. I was consistent, through and through. I really wanted to show her, beyond any reasonable shadow of doubt that I genuinely loved her, with all my heart, with all my lungs and with all my pancreas, with all my intestines and with all that was within me. Just before Christmas, I sent her a huge expensive and beautiful Christmas card which worked well in my favour.

The Masvingo First Visit (in the Park) – *'Ndizvozvo!!'* (It's a Yes!!!)

During one of our conversations on the phone, we finally agreed that I would visit Annette in Masvingo on the 30th of December 1991 so that we would celebrate the New Year together. When I arrived in Masvingo, I vividly remember Annette, in her simple plain white dress, coming to pick me up from Mucheke Bus Terminus. What surprised me was that in her simplicity of dressing, she looked even more beautiful and extremely attractive. At a glance, my heart started to 'bleed' for her, this time around, profusely. Maybe I had spent a few weeks without setting my eyes on her. She was accompanied by Irene, who was her three-in-one, thus, her friend, her relative and a neighbour to pick me up from the bus terminus to her place. Bringing a close friend along was a signal that she was serious about the whole thing. Culturally, this also heralded a clear message to the outside-world that she was 'playing her cards' and doing her 'things' openly and transparently, in a dignified manner. She even went a step further and told her two brothers that she was going to take me to her house. If she was not serious, she should have come alone and not informed her brothers. In our culture, you only bring a boyfriend home when you are serious about the relationship.

From the bus terminus, we walked straight to her house, which was about two kilometres. Her two brothers (Nelson and Goodwill) were there. It was the very first time to meet them. They received me well. I felt at home. Both Annette's parents and all her little siblings were in their village in Gutu, 33 kms north of Masvingo.

After dinner, I left Annette's place and walked to my beloved *gogo* (granny) Mabasa's house which was going to be my 'base' each time I visited Annette in Masvingo. In order to provide context, *gogo* Mabasa was a mother to Peter Mabasa who had married my close childhood niece, Beauty

Runyararo Nyatsambo. Gogo Mabasa was so kind, encouraging, caring and above all very humorous. She knew Annette's family very well and as a result, she quickly endorsed her as a 'marrying-type' girl for me. They went to the same church in Mucheke Township, Masvingo. All she said about Annette was positive.

The following day was the 31st of December 1991, the last day of the year. This day is very symbolic and historic to both Annette and I. I left *gogo* Mabasa's place early in the morning and picked up Annette. We went to town in Masvingo and chose to sit in the middle of the ever-green Council Park called Benjamin Burombo. We had bought our yummy picnic food. I did not waste any time. I kindly requested her to give me a comprehensive response to my life-assignment - my 'Golden Mile Motel Summit' proposal. Although she was kind, she was playing delaying tactics. I applied a bit of strategic pressure to get my answer quickly. She later picked up a small stick and wrote on the ground '*Ndizvozvo*'. In my rich Shona language, it means, '*It's a Yes. I agree*'. I passionately thanked her and looked straight into her bright and glorious eyes. I was blinded by the visible and tangible power of love in her splendid eyes. Her face was glowing and brimming with outstanding beauty. I was exceedingly excited. There was pressure within me to kiss her, for the very first time, but another stronger feeling and force warned me not to. Inside me, I was saying "*Yes!!! Eureka. I have found it*". When I looked at my watch, it was exactly 12 noon. I always teasingly tell her that I was 'loved' at midday, it therefore means that '*I am a son of the light, hence, I have no fellowship with the darkness of this evil world*'.

I then insisted on her verbalising the most important and appropriate three little words, "*I Love You*". I waited in vain and she flatly refused to utter those words. She maintained that she had already given me her most suitable response, unless I wanted to hear the contrary. Although she said it in a joking way, I did not want to jeopardise the positive response I had been awaiting. Due to fear of her reversing her reply, I quickly gave in. The truth of the matter is that I am still awaiting the verbalisation of *"I Love You"*. I always jokingly tell her that she never told me that she loved me, up to this day (now almost 33 years on 😊).

As soon as she wrote the *'ndizvozvo'* message on the ground, my mind was taken back to a Biblical incident when the Lord Jesus prudently resolved and saved a certain woman from been stoned to death (by an angry mob) - by simply writing on the sand. In my view, the *'ndizvozvo'* episode, depicts Annette's pool of distilled wisdom, in handling many issues of life. Yes, she is a smart and wise woman who fears God and genuinely loves me, her husband. I always feel her unconditional love.

After receiving my exciting *'ndizvozvo'* response, I immediately requested my 'now official' dear and beautiful girlfriend to go for a photograph as tangible evidence to record and mark this romantic event. She agreed. We went to a near-by photography studio and had two lovely pictures taken (see below). I vividly remember her wearing a red top and a black skirt. Coincidently, we were matching – what a divine and prophetic omen it was 😀. Red is my favourite colour. We both believed it signified a good omen and blessed future. I loved her more than before.

Around 4 pm, we left town for Annette's house. We decided to go via Irene's place since I had not met her (Irene's) mother. When we got to Irene's place her mother told us that Annette's brothers were complaining that I had disrespected them by (i) coming to their house without customary introductions and (ii) taking their sister away for the whole day. They demanded a payment of twenty dollars popularly known as *'nyanga ye nzou'* (elephant's horn) or else they were going to teach me a lesson. It was called *'nyanga ye nzou'* because the note had a picture of an elephant. I chose the former and the matter was settled. The twenty dollars had a lot of economic value, by then. Soon after giving them the money the boys disappeared. They went straight for 'joy'. When Annette's dad came back from the village, the boys did not mention anything about the *nyanga ye nzou* 'fiasco'. This was the beginning of our courtship. When schools opened in January 1992, Annette travelled to Mafuba Primary School, the new school where she was deployed to teach. Mafuba was only 33 kms South of Masvingo town. I continued writing letters, sending cards and chocolates. Every now and then we would meet up in Masvingo on weekends.

Visiting Annette's Tete (Aunt) in Chiredzi Town

In my traditional culture, if a boy and girl are serious in their relationship, she must introduce her boyfriend to her tete (aunt). This tete is normally a sister to the girl's father. After the formal customary introductions, it now becomes the duty and responsibility of the tete to officially inform the parents of the girl of the relationship. At this stage, there is no mucking around. It's a serious signal to the girl's parents that the guy wants to marry their daughter as soon as possible.

In our case, Annette's tete (mai Zirebwa) was living in a town called Chiredzi, in the South-Eastern part of Zimbabwe. Chiredzi is about 193kms from Masvingo and is popularly-known for its massive sugar-cane production and hot temperatures. One weekend, we paid a visit to Annette's tete. The moment I was introduced to my new tete, we just connected. There was a lot of laughing and eating. She received me well. She could not hide her appreciation and excitement. I felt it within my spirit. Tete Zirebwa was a business woman. She later asked me about my totem (*mutupo*) in passing. When I told her that my totem is *Soko-Mukanya*, she simply laughed and later said that I was going to marry my 'sister'.

In my Zimbabwe African culture, a totem is a traditional concept and belief that once upon a time, people of the same totem originated from the same ancestor, hence they are an extended family. Totem is usually based on names of animals which the individual is likened to in terms of character and personality. A totem can cover different surnames, languages and places of dwellings, yet you are still regarded as one large extended family. Therefore, this is the reason why in my culture it was a taboo to marry from the same totem. It is considered as good as marrying your own blood-sister. If you decide to rebel against this traditional belief and practice, and go ahead and marry someone with the same totem as you, it is believed that misfortunes such as bearing children with disability would be your portion in your marriage. If one insists to marry from the same totem, he would be fined a cow which we call in my culture '*mombe ye chekaukama*', thus, 'a symbol of alienating the relationship'. This act is believed to pacify and eliminate the anger of the ancestors in such a taboo-relationship and marriage. As a result, the first question that is normally asked when people get involved in a relationship and most importantly on the day of paying lobola (dowry) is "what is your totem"?

Annette and I had previously discussed this matter and decided to tell nothing but the truth. In fact, we did not believe in the issue of totems and we did not care about it. We knew nothing would separate us from the bond of love we had for each other. Our relationship was founded on God and in Him, we trusted.

Both my beautiful wife and I belong to the '*Soko – Mukanya*' totem. *Soko* is a monkey. The *Soko* Totem's *detembo* (poem) is as follows in my mother tongue (Shona) with some English translation (in *italics* below):

Detembo (Poem) of the Soko – Vhudzijena (Mukanya) Totem

Ewoi Soko, *(Thank you Soko)*

Vhudzijena, Mukanya *(White-hair, The Pompous one)*

Hekanhi Mbereka *(Thank you Bearer of Children)*

Makwiramiti, mahomu-homu *(The Tree-climber, one-who-always-*

barks)
Vanopona nekuba *(Those who survive by stealing)*
Vanamushamba negore *(Those who bath only once in a year)*
Makumbo mana muswe weshanu *(Those who have four legs, the tail being the fifth)*
Hekani Soko yangu yiyi *(Thank you very much my dear Soko)*
Vakaera mutupo umwe nashe *(Those who have the same totem as the chief)*
Vana VaPfumojena *(The descendants of Pfumojena)*
Vakabva Guruuswa *(Those who came from Guruuswa)*
Soko Mbire yaSvosve *(Soko Mbire of Svosve)*
Vanobva Hwedza *(Those who come from Hwedza)*
Vapfuri vemhangura *(The iron-smelters)*
VekuMatonjeni vanaisi vemvura *(The rain-makers of Matonjeni)*
Zvaitwa matarira vari mumabwe *(A good service has been done the alert one, those in the rocks)*
Mhanimani tinodya, svosve tichobovera *(We eat centipedes, we throw ants into our mouths)*
Maita zvenyu rudzi rukuru *(Thank you for the good service, great lineage)*
Matangakugara *(The original inhabitants)*
Vakawana ushe neuchenjeri *(Those who obtained chieftainship through shrewdness and diplomacy)*
Vakufamba hujeukidza kwandabva *(The one who constantly looks back when moving)*
Pagerwe rinongova jemedzanwa *(Wherever they settle there is quarrelling and crying)*
Kugara hukwenya-kwenya *(When seated you are constantly scratching your body)*
Vari mawere maramba kurima *(Those always on the cliffs, who refused to till the land)*
Vamazvikongonyadza kufamba hukanyaira *(The pompous one who walks proudly)*
Zvibwezvitedza, zvinotedzera vari kure *(The Slippery-rocks that are*

slippery to those who come from afar)
Asi vari padyo vachitamba nazvo *(But is friendly to those in the vicinity)*
Zvaitwa mukanya rudzi rusina chiramwa *(It has been done, a lineage that does not refuse to perform a task no matter how it is treated)*
Maita vari Makoromokwa, Mugarandaguta *(Those on the steep rocks and cliffs, one-who-rests-only-when-he-is-full)*
Aiwa zvaonekwa Vhudzijena *(Indeed your kindness has been seen, White-hair).*

(Source:
https://www.poetryinternational.org/pi/poem/5803/auto/0/0/Shona-Praise-Poetry/Soko-Vhudzijena/en/tile)

Later in the day, I was introduced to tete Zirebwa's husband, *babamukuru* (big brother-in-law) Obert Zirebwa. *Babamukuru* Zirebwa is one of the kindest and humorous man I have ever met. The man is always laughing and joking. At the time of our historic visit in Chiredzi, *babamukuru* Zirebwa was a successful businessman in that region. We clicked at once. Our relationship has grown over the years such that in the early-2000s, he looked after us so well in his house in Botswana (where he was working). I had visited Botswana on business with my uncle Timon Nyatsambo. He is now back in Chegutu, Zimbabwe. Each time I have visited Zimbabwe, I have made it a point to see my *babamukuru* Zirebwa.

In summary, I was well received and endorsed by Annette's tete and *babamukuru* and their entire clan. In my culture, these people are crucial in the success of a relationship. If they disapprove the relationship and inform the girl's parents, the affair may fall on hard-rocks. It could be a difficult terrain.

Introductions to Annette's Parents and Family

After the traditional introductions to Annette's tete, I was formally introduced to her parents. Again, I would like to thank the Lord because both parents endorsed me and blessed our relationship, at once. Annette's baba was very impressed by me such that he told his daughter (Annette) that "*That fellow is a squared young man*". At times I tease Annette that I am so special that her father endorsed me at first-sight. From day one, I became very close to both Annette's parents. Surprisingly, Annette's parents did not ask about my totem because most people would ask if they are meeting for the very first time, especially on such a special occasion.

Near-Cancellation of the Affair

I was fortunate that most people who mattered from Annette's clan embraced and accepted me as her boyfriend, especially her parents, her siblings, her tete and immediate family members and her friends. From both traditional and cultural perspectives, this was a clear signal that if we wanted to get married, we could do so, anytime. All those who mattered had blessed our relationship.

During my many visits to Masvingo it happened that one day while at Annette's house, chatting and laughing with her father, an elderly man who was their good neighbour came to see Annette's dad. After I was introduced to him as Annette's boyfriend, the elderly gentleman was excited and straight away asked me "*What is your totem?*" I immediately knew that there was trouble in the making. In Nigeria they call this "*There is fire on the mountain*" I told him "*Soko-Mukanya*". Before I finished, Annette's father asked me to repeat. Which I did. He never uttered a word and stood up and unlocked his landline phone and called his sister, tete Zirebwa. He was fuming on the phone, telling her off. He insisted why she had not investigated and asked about my totem.

From the phone-conversation he called Annette into the lounge. He simply made a declaration that our relationship was over because we were related via our same totem. He further said that he was happy because our relationship was still in its infancy stage therefore it would be easy to terminate it. Inside me, I was loving it because I took it as a test for Annette's commitment and love for me.

Annette was really upset. She later told me that if they were thinking that she would leave me, they were wasting their time. I reaffirmed my bona fide love and unwavering commitment to her. Her father later called Irene's mother, mai Bobo, to come and witness our breakaway. Mai Bobo liked me and was impressed by my relationship with Annette. So, she supported us and gave many examples where people of the same totem had married and nothing happened. Finally, Annette's dad insisted that we terminate the relationship. We did not. We said, as committed Christians, nothing would separate our love for each other, even this traditional belief (totem).

Visiting My Home-Village with Annette

After some introductions to Annette's key and important contacts, I took her to my village in Mhondoro-Ngezi (before we relocated to Sanyati) to meet my mother and my people. From Annette's side, she was accompanied by her aunt Shuvai, a very lovely and humble young woman. My mother and my people were glad to see Annette for the first time. She liked her. She was well received into the family. Annette had already met most of my relatives who lived in KweKwe. They all loved her.

The Engagement

In May 1992, exactly five months after Annette said '*yes - ndizvozvo*', to my proposal, we got engaged. The venue was Annette's elder sister's house, in Gweru. It was on a shiny blessed Saturday. Although we had planned it to be a small event, it turned out to be like a mini-wedding. People came, in big numbers, from all over the country, as far as Mutare, Chiredzi, Harare and other far places. Everyone was supportive and helpful. For example, those were the early days of the huge video recording cameras, which were very expensive to hire for events. But in our case, we had two of these, both for free – donated by well-wishers.

The engagement was akin to family and community reunion. People, friends and family who had not met for years, were able to congregate and reunite under one room, and laugh again. A good example was the presence of a great number of my former schoolmates and youth group members from Karaga Baptist Church - people who immensely contributed to my Christian faith and social well-being. My former Scripture Union Regional Director, Mr Ralton Jenami led the ceremony, shared the Word of God and blessed our engagement. The other highlight was the reunion of my huge extended family – my father's many children from different mothers. From Annette's side, there was high-powered delegation from her tete in Chiredzi, her childhood friends from Masvingo and her colleagues from her former Teachers College. People danced, laughed and above all worshipped and thanked the Lord.

One close friend of mine came and said to me, "*Tuwe, you know what? Kandiro kanoenda kunobva kamwe*". This simply means "*what goes around comes around*" or "*a good return deserves another*". This simply means that if you are good to people, they see it, they hear it and they perceive it. Then on "your day" they will 'return the favour'. This was indeed humbling for both Annette and I. From then on, it taught both of us to keep on doing good and especially helping and ploughing back in our communities which made us what we are today.

Engagement Ring Thrown into The Mud-water

Before our engagement, we set down and planned how and what we wanted in order to fulfil the necessary requirements before being granted the right to wed, by my in-laws. From a cultural perspective, one of the most important requirements is to pay '*roora*' which is the dowry or bride-price to my in-laws. As per my tradition, one cannot have a wedding before paying at least half the dowry price, especially what is called '*rutsambo*'. *Rutsambo* is the core-dowry or bride-price. If the guy is poor and can't raise the required amount, he can pay a deposit and then kindly request to have a wedding and pay the rest later. Some in-laws would only accept such a request, if they trust the poor son-in-law and are satisfied that the young man genuinely loves their daughter.

In our case, we had agreed that I would pay the *roora* around October 1992, which was five months after our vibrant and successful engagement. Due to the success of our engagement, most people, including Annette's family, relatives and friends were using our relationship and how we had done our things as the bench-mark. This was great and encouraging to set such a good example, especially for other young people in our families, Church and communities. However, this had its own associated challenges, pressures and trials. It exerted some kind of financial, social, spiritual and psychological pressures on us. Within five months, I was supposed to go and pay a large sum of *roora* so that we could get the green light to wed. Although we had not specifically discussed it, all along Annette had the impression that I had already saved the money, yet I hadn't. I am not sure maybe I gave that impression. So, one day, while in Gweru, she asked me how much I had saved for the *roora*. I have always told her the truth. So, I informed her that I was about to start saving. She looked at me in great disbelief and asked me to repeat myself. I did. I smelt danger and thunder. I wasn't sure what was to come my way. The next thing, I saw the expensive engagement ring 'flying' and suddenly landing in mud-dirty waters in the middle of the road. I was shocked and speechless. She told me to get my ring and leave her because I was not serious about marrying her. I picked up the ring from the filthy mud-waters and cleaned it. After a brief silence, holding the ring, I profusely apologised and reassured her that I was 'double' serious and more than prepared to save the *roora* money. I also reminded her that I would never ever break my promise of marrying her. I cried, for the first time. Luckily, my apologies were accepted maybe because we had never had any problem or misunderstanding in our relationship. We trusted each other. That saved me. Otherwise, that was going to be the end of the relationship. Though I was shaken by this experience, it showed me that Annette was serious about our relationship and she really wanted to get married and be with me permanently. That was my consolation and solace.

This is the story of my life:
The African village-boy meeting the love of his life.

Chapter Nine:
Traditional and Customary Marriage

Paying Lobola (Bride-Price/Dowry)

One sunny Saturday in October 1992, all roads led to Annette's rural village in Mutema, Gutu. My uncle Timon Nyatsambo who drove all the way from our second biggest city of Bulawayo, led a powerful delegation of the four of us - Timon, Nisbet Tuwe (my late brother) and Juwel Muzenda (my *sahwira*/friend). On our way to Annette's village, we passed through my maternal aunt's place (my mother's younger sister) mai Mutero whose residence was about five kilometres from Annette's village. In my African culture mai Mutero is my mother. I don't call her aunt, it's disrespectful. When we told them about our mission, mai Mutero's husband who is my *babamunini* ('small'-father) decided to accompany us, as our baba and elder of the delegation. We were excited. In my culture, babamunini Mutero is my baba. From a cultural perspective, baba Mutero accompanying us was a big thing and it showed that the elders were blessing our union and marriage. Later, we discovered that baba Mutero was related to Annette's clan. He was a *muzukuru* (nephew). In my African culture, a *muzukuru* can say whatever he/she likes and nobody should be offended. This worked in my delegation's favour.

When we arrived at Annette's village, we parked our car outside her homestead. Annette's uncle, *sekuru* Munhande who was an appointed *Munyai/sadombo* (go-between), from Annette's family had already gone to the village in advance to start the traditional marriage proceedings. From our delegation, baba Mutero is the only one who went inside the homestead because he was a *muzukuru*. In my culture, if you go straight into the homestead before traditional protocols are done, you can get heavily fined.

Annette came to greet us. She was in her simple traditional attire yet she looked astoundingly beautiful. The moment I set my eyes on her, my heart thundered and bled for her. I became speechless. My mouth dried-up. I nearly fainted. She looked transformed. Her beauty had been multiplied and magnified. She was just astonishing and immaculate. All I wanted was for her to be in my arms, there and then, and to gaze straight into her stunning and piercing eyes. I could not do that because her clan would see me doing that and it would attract a fine. In my culture, showing intimate love publicly and especially in the eyes of the in-laws is inappropriate. Tradition restrained me. I could feel the fire burning inside me. I simply greeted her and smiled at her. I melted. And she melted too. I felt it. Love was in the air. My delegation saw it and they started teasing me.

After the initial traditional procedures, we were called into the homestead and allocated a separate hut (house) as our base. Traditionally, all the proceedings are done via a *munyai* who will be conveying messages and physically moving between the two parties (the in-laws). You are not allowed to be in the same room with the in-laws, during proceedings and negotiations. Even if you want to negotiate the *roora*, you do it via *munyai*. You can only congregate in the same room after all proceedings have been concluded.

The issue of *mombe ye chekaukama* was resuscitated, thus, a fine in the form of a cow for marrying someone with the same totem. Baba Mutero was now handy. He jumped in and told my in-laws that he once worked in my village in Mhondoro-Ngezi as a teacher and he knew that my totem was not exactly the same as that of Annette's clan. In addition, Annette's close aunt (mai Sylvester) reiterated that she was once married in my village in Mhondoro-Ngezi and agreed with baba Mutero. They did not entirely believe these two witnesses but agreed that once it has been established that we are of the same totem, I would be required to pay a fine in the form of a live-cow. The proceedings were allowed to go ahead. The good thing is that, this issue was never ever mentioned again. Up to this day, 33 years later, nobody has made a follow-up. I don't know what would have happened without the presence and wisdom of my babamunini baba Mutero and tete mai Sylvester. However, the truth is that Annette and I share the same totem and nothing sinister nor calamity has befallen us, in our marriage. We are happy and blessed.

In my language the main component of *roora* is called *rutsambo*. To make it easier, we requested a list with all the 'charges' and requirements. When I saw the figure for *rutsambo*, I nearly fainted because it was beyond my reach. To make matters worse, I had borrowed some of the *roora* money. I had not saved enough due to massive extended-family commitments. There was also an element of procrastination on my part. That was foolish of me. I had not told Annette – I kept it a secret until after our wedding. After seeing the *rutsambo* figure, I stood up and threatened to leave. Before I knew it, I was told to shut-up and sit down by my *sahwira*, Juwel. I tried to voice my concerns but he rebuked and asked me not to open my mouth until all proceedings were completed. In my culture, no matter how angry one becomes, you still have to respect your *sahwira* and take their advice (orders) seriously. I just did that and all the proceedings went well. Fortunately, we negotiated and managed to have the *rutsambo* figure slightly reduced. I now understand why Annette was pricy. She is so good and priceless. I am now more than willing to pay more.

As per our tradition, after the roora proceedings, our delegation was asked to join Annette's clan, (in the main room) for formal introductions. The introductions went very well. Everyone was happy. I was well received and embraced by Annette's great clan and family. Traditionally, the son-in-law brings heaps of groceries and food for the event. We brought a lot. People ate, drank and celebrated the traditional marriage of Annette. There was joy, jubilation and celebration in the Mutema village. Traditionally, Annette was transformed from being my girlfriend to my wife, at that particular point in time. She became Mai Tuwe. This is the most important part in our marriage because the parents and family of the girl will have blessed and endorsed the marriage. After all was done, we drove to the city of KweKwe in the middle of the night, with hearts full of joy, peace and happiness.

Our wedding

Exactly six months after traditionally getting married, we had a Church wedding on Saturday 18th April 1993 in Torwood (Karaga), where I grew up. We chose 18th April because it's an important national day. This is when Zimbabwe got her political independence in 1980. We had wanted to be patriotic by having our "marriage independence" to coincide with our national Independence Day. However, this patriotic decision nearly cost us dearly. We had initially booked Torwood Hall as the wedding venue. A few days before the wedding I got a call from the Council informing me that the hall was no longer available. ZANU(PF), the ruling party wanted to use the hall to celebrate the Independence Day. We had to change the venue to Torwood Hotel, which was luckily nearby. Rumour had it that some of the youth from the ruling party wanted to disrupt our wedding as they thought we were disrespecting the national Independence Day. Luckily, we were saved by the attendance of our two important guests namely Rev Tuwe (my dad's young brother) who was an Army Chaplain. He was driving an Army truck. The other saviour was Annette's uncle who was a Supreme Court Judge and former Secretary of Justice and Parliamentary Affairs. By virtue of his role, he was a well-known public figure, nationally. Annette was chauffeur-driven in his uncle's government Mecedes Benz. When the party youth saw these two distinctive government vehicles, they retreated and this became our salvation.

I vividly remember all that transpired on our wedding. Both Annette and I were humbled to see so many people from all the four corners of our country congregating to celebrate with us at our wedding. Both our families were fully represented.

Our Marriage Officer was Pastor Patrick Dube. Pastor Dube was my friend from our church-youth days in KweKwe. Coincidentally, we later discovered that he was a *sekuru* (uncle) to Annette. We discovered this when we accidentally met at the funeral of Pastor Dube's father in Mbizo township, KweKwe. In summary, when I called Annette while she was in Masvingo, she told me that she was coming to Kwekwe with her mother for a funeral. I told her that I was also going for a funeral in Mbizo Township. We did not discuss details, as she was in a hurry to catch a bus to KweKwe. We agreed to catch up later when she arrived in KweKwe. Lo and behold, when I got to Pastor Dube's house in Mbizo, a beautiful lady in the form of Annette was there. Again, she caught my eye. Both of us could not believe it. Her mother initially thought I had come to see Annette. But when Pastor Dube explained that I was his close friend from our church-youth days, and that I was an up-right young man, she was impressed. I later heard that she privately asked more about me from her uncle Pastor Dube since she wanted to make sure that her daughter was in good hands. Fortunately, Pastor Dube gave a good testimony about me.

After we were joined together, in a holy matrimony, as husband and wife, Pastor Dube preached a vibrant sermon. In the sermon, he kept on referring to how he knew me as a youth who was fervent and 'on fire' for the Lord. I was both humbled and excited at the same time because it was more meaningful for Annette's extended family to hear from a man of the cloth about my Christian stand and values. Not just a man of the cloth, but a close relation of theirs. Soon after the sermon, family representatives were asked to give their benediction speeches. From my side, Reverend Ishmael Nicolas Tuwe (my father's younger brother) stood up and thundered a chorus called '*Kudza Ishe Hareruya*' which means '*Praise The Lord Hallelujah*'. At the end of the song, he gave a moving and motivational speech, which was mainly centred on how good their village boy (me) was. Generally, Rev Tuwe was fond of me. From Annette's side, Baba Charisi (Charles) Mutema, a cousin brother to Annette's father, spoke on behalf of their clan. He showered praises and honour on Annette. They were proud of their daughter who had done a good thing.

After the special family representatives, the floor was opened up to other speakers from specific constituencies such as close friends and our respective churches. Speaker after speaker said nice things about both the newlyweds save for one of my best friends, Noah Fore who sent the congregants into laughing-stiches. He told all present that from the time I met Annette, my attendance at church significantly dwindled since I was now frequently commuting to Masvingo every weekend. He said it seemed as if I loved Annette more than the Creator. In summary, he concluded that I had backslidden and became a man of the flesh as opposed to one who lives by faith. He actually suggested for an altar-call for me to repent from my 'sins'. The congregants laughed their lungs out. Finally, he invited my new wedded wife to talk to him nicely if she wanted to know my 'deep secrets'. He made a declaration that he had all my '*Mafaera*' which means 'life-files'. The moment he mentioned '*Mafaera*' all my naughty friends stood-up and cheered Noah to go deeper and reveal all my hidden secrets. The congregants laughed the more. Until today, his 'naughty' speech took the thunder of the day – it became the most remembered, more than the sermon. In my Zimbabwean African culture, *madzisahwira* (close friends) are allowed to say anything they want especially at events such as weddings and funerals. The 'victim(s)' are not supposed to take any offence.

The Wedding Reception

Soon after the ceremony, the bridal party left Karaga for Redcliff, for the photo-shoots. Before we finished the photo-shoot, it suddenly started raining. We were all disappointed, because the rains would interfere with the proceedings of the day as the reception venue was an open space (hotel arena). However, we were grateful that it did not rain during the reception. In my culture, if it rains during such an event, it symbolises divine and heavenly blessings. The elders from my clan were excited by the blessings of the rains. They said my marriage was blessed and highly favoured. I now believe them because, almost 31 years now in marriage, we have never had any serious arguments or misunderstanding. I mean it. Not that we do not see things from different perspectives, but we have always come up with amicable solutions to all our life-challenges. Our bona fide love and genuine respect for each other has been growing each day.

Back to Torwood Hotel Arena, where the reception was held, the bridal party did what they knew best – great dancing. Most weekends before the weeding, my boys from my side would travel to Masvingo (140 kms away) to practice the dance (*masteps*). I am told some relationships nearly got established in the process. The entire arena was filled to capacity. People from the community came in big numbers to support. As their Welfare Officer (HR Advisor) who was in charge of looking after the welfare of their families (employees), the community decided to support me by gracing our wedding. For that, I am forever grateful and humbled. The crowd in attendance was one of the biggest in the history of Karaga weddings. Since I was also closely working with all community cultural performance groups, a number of them volunteered to perform at our wedding. Two particular groups captured the attention of the majority, these were *Bheni/Chihodha* and the *Ingquzu* Dancers. The later actually composed a song in honour of both Annette and I titled '*Tinotenda vaAnnette na vaKudakwashe ne Muchato Wavo*' thus, '*We Thank Annette and Kudakwashe for their wedding*'. Most of my work colleagues, former and current bosses attended our wedding. It was indeed an honour to see such support from people of all walks of life and the community at large.

Coming to the bridal dancing party, the guys put in their best performance. The guests were fully entertained. They danced their 'hearts out'. For days, weeks and months that followed, our wedding was the talk of Karaga and Masvingo. We say "*To God be the glory.*"

This is the story of my life:
The Traditional/Customary Marriage and the white wedding of an
African village-boy.

Chapter Ten:
My Career Path – Part Two

Human Resources Officer/Welfare Officer

Nine months into my hot-relationship with Annette, I was promoted to the position of Human Resources Officer/Advisor, from the role of Budget Officer. This new position was popularly known at Ziscosteel as that of Welfare Officer. This was my baptism into Human Resources Management (HRM) profession. This role required someone who had a strong financial background, which I had. Among others, my main duty and responsibility was to manage salary advances and commutation of leave days for all employees. In this context, 'commutation', is all about selling or converting staff leave days into cash. Salary advances and commutation of leave days were mostly given as a way of cushioning financial hardships for employees especially in the event of a death or illness within the nuclear family. I had to adhere and operate within the confinements of a very strict company policy. This made my job difficult and it easily put me in a collision-path with many employees, especially those who had a propensity to live outside their financial means and budgets. As a professional and Christian, I did all in my means to be fair and firm. As a result, I discovered that I gained a lot of respect and fame with both senior management and staff. I therefore strongly believe that it pays to be honest even in small things.

This role taught me how to professionally relate with staff in difficult circumstances as well as being empathetic. Not sympathetic. I learnt a few nuggets on 'counselling'. In addition to welfare duties, I also learnt other HRM functions and responsibilities such as recruitment & selection, employee industrial/relations, records management, job evaluation, organisational development, training and development. On two occasions I was given opportunities to act in a senior role of HR Officer- Manning, which is the equivalence of a Senior Human Resources Advisor.

In my Welfare Officer role one of my very first 'clients' made a terrible mistake. He wanted to bribe me by giving me a few dollars (later) upon the success of his advance application. I seized this as a golden opportunity to show employees that I was not corrupt - but I was there to help them. I had heard some allegations that such practices were happening and I was therefore fully determined to totally eliminate it.

I took my time to comprehensively explain to this staff member, in question, that it was the right and privilege of employees when it came to staff salary advances – it was their money. Not mine. My argument was that a salary advance was a payment in which the concerned employee had to reimburse the company at the end of the month. I therefore saw no reason for them paying me as if I was doing them a favour. I made it clear that I was not doing them a favour but it was an integral part of my job which I was being remunerated for. I also put it plain to him that what he had just done was 'corruption' and therefore a dismissible offense. At hearing this he almost collapsed. I really wanted to drive the message 'home', which I did. I also told him that if I accepted any type and form of bribe, I would lose my job. Lastly, I reiterated that I was a well-known committed and practicing Christian by the majority of employees and the general community within the surrounding Karaga Township and the town of

Redcliff. I put the message across in a compassionate but very strong way as I knew he was going to tell most of his friends and that it would become viral and a public 'gospel', within no time. Indeed, lo and behold, within a few days it was public news across thousands of employees. It worked in my favour. Just imagine if I had accepted the bribe.

I am glad that this strategy worked well for me. This intensified my resolve to remain untarnished in my job. In my three years in this challenging but exciting role, I never encountered such a temptation and problem again. It actually boosted and increased the level of confidence and faith of both staff and management in me. At my work-farewell party, when I resigned to join a different organisation, speaker after speaker reiterated the fact that I left a good legacy at Ziscosteel's Human Resources Management Division, popularly known as Personnel Department.

Acquiring Human Resources Management (HRM) Profession Qualifications

Since I had no formal qualification in Human Resources Management (HRM), I started feeling professionally 'empty'. Hence, I registered with the well-known and respected HRM professional institution called Institute of Personnel Management of Zimbabwe (IPMZ) now known as Institute of People Management of Zimbabwe (IPMZ). I enrolled for a long-distance study programme for a Certificate in Management of Training where I had to attend face-to-face tuitions on weekends and then submit assignments later. This was followed by a final examination. These face-to-face meetings were held at Midlands Hotel, in the Midlands capital city of Gweru, which was 60 kilometres from my city of KweKwe. After passing my Management of Training, I enrolled for another Certificate in Labour Relations which I successfully completed. I was fortunate that I teamed up with other like-minded staff members, mostly Training Officers from our Training Department who were doing the same course. Mr Stephania Samambwa was my closest compatriot in this unforgettable journey. We formed a small but vibrant study group where we encouraged each other to do our best. We used to meet in my office for studies after working hours.

Armed with my two professional IPMZ certificates, I embarked on an IPMZ Diploma in HRM, which I completed within two years via private studies. When I finished my Diploma, I straight away enrolled for my IPMZ Higher Diploma in HRM. While doing the Higher Diploma, I joined the IPMZ Midlands Branch Executive which was entrusted to run and administer certificate courses. Based on my accounting qualifications and financial experience, I was later appointed to the position of Branch Treasurer. By virtue of being the Treasurer, I became the Branch Administrator responsible for managing all the finances, certificate training courses, including final examinations. Due to my connections in KweKwe, I was able to establish another training centre at Golden Mile Motel in KweKwe. This is the same place I proposed to Annette. Our first training group in KweKwe was one of the highest in attendance in the country. This meant more financial resources for both the National Office (Institute) and our local branch. While working with the IPMZ Midlands Branch Executive, I learnt a lot of HRM skills and expertise from the professional gurus in the field.

Personnel Superintendent/Human Resources Officer

When I left Ziscosteel, I joined another organisation called Zimbabwe Glass Company Limited (Zimglass Ltd), in the city of Gweru, in early February 1996 as the Personnel Superintendent (HR Advisor). I was the second-in-charge within the HR department. I learnt a lot of HRM stuff. While in this role at Zimglass, I continued with my private IPMZ Higher

Diploma studies. After three years, I resigned from Zimglass and joined First Mutual Life (FML), the second largest insurance company in Zimbabwe.

Working for an Insurance Company - Executive Sales Agent

I joined FML, Gweru Branch, on 1 December 1999 as a Sales Agent. The insurance industry is predominately known for its high competitiveness such that we had weekly, monthly and yearly competitions and awards. The sales results on individual performance were publicly displayed on notice boards at all local branches and the national office. Such was the competitive nature of the job and industry. By God's grace, from the first day I joined FML (Dec 1999) until I left in December 2002, I was always 1st, at both branch and regional level. Nationally, I was always in the top 25 out of more than 200 agents. As a result of such outstanding performance and dedication, I was promoted to the prestigious position of an Executive Sales Agent, within a year. I was the first ever Executive Agent at Gweru Branch and the second one in the entire Midlands province. Every year, in addition to executive trips for all Executive Agents, I won family regional trips fully funded by my employer. The best family trip was in Masvingo where we stayed at a hotel called *'The Ancient City Lodge'*. It is located just three kilometres from the historic and internationally known Great Zimbabwe Ruins. To cap it all, at the end of 2001, I won the international award called the Million Dollar Round Table (MDRT) and I qualified to attend the MDRT in the United States of America. The MDRT is the most prestigious international award for outstanding insurance sales agents, globally. At the end of my three years in this insurance job, my commissions had increased by about thirteen times compared to my most recent HR role basic salary.

I guess I did well mainly due to my focus, drive and work-ethics. Why did I work so hard? What really pushed me? There were basically two reasons:

(i)   I had left a good-paying salaried job and promising HR career. I was only a grade away from qualifying for executive perks such as a company car, company house and many others. I vividly remember my former Zimglass boss, the HR Executive Manager, questioning me why I had decided to leave the HR profession after having worked so hard and done so well. He told me that I was excelling in the profession and saw no reason why I should quit. The insurance job had no fixed salary. It had no salary-cap. It was commission-based, thus, it purely depended on one's production and the quality of work. Simply put, I wanted to make as much money as I could. I got into it knowing all this stuff and it was not easy. So, I knew that if I did not work hard, it was going to back-fire financially thereby adversely impacting my young family. Our two little children were at one of the most expensive private schools in Zimbabwe, the Midlands Christian School. This decision reminded me of my previous one - when I resigned from the lucrative apprenticeship training career to join the less-paying banking sector. When I look back, I sometimes get petrified, especially if it had not worked for me. However, what I have now learnt is that when God speaks, it is crucially important to listen and seek His grace, favour and faith to follow His will. However, I must admit that this is not easy. Nevertheless, this could be very risky and devastating.

(ii)   I wanted to excel and explore the sales and marketing areas as I had a calculated desire to later become a grounded and well-informed general manager/CEO. My motivation for wanting to become a senior executive was that I had worked and done well in the following professions: banking, accounting, HR resources management and now insurance & marketing.

Initially, I did not believe in insurance rhetoric and later-on, the insurance sales people. I perceived them as crooks and the uneducated who had failed to make it in life. However, there is one person who kept nagging and cajoling me for years to join the insurance industry. He kept on saying that he could see a massive potential in me in the industry such that I would earn three to four times my current salary. I completely ignored his counsel for years and at one time I told him that I was happy to give him free accommodation in my house and business referrals while he was on business in my city, but not me joining the industry. But he persisted. Since my wife and I had huge respect for this fellow, we later seriously discussed it with my dear wife and we agreed to give it a try and that is how I finally joined the insurance industry. It took him a number of years to coax me into becoming an Insurance Sales Agent. This persuasive kind gentleman is none other than my uncle-turned-close friend Timon Simbarashe Nyatsambo. As I mentioned in prior chapters, Timon's father is my mother's brother. Apart from being my uncle (sekuru) Timon has been one of my best close friends, for more than four decades. He is one person to whom I feel safe to 'empty my heart' without any reservations or hesitation. I can trust him with my own life. I mean it. He was my go-between, leading our delegation when I got married. Our relationship is authentic and profound.

Becoming IPMZ National Executive Council (NEC) Member

I was later elected to be the Midlands Branch Chair of the Institute of People Management of Zimbabwe (IPMZ). This automatically made me to become a National Executive Council (NEC) member of IPMZ. As a member of the NEC, I became part of a Board that appointed the National Executive Director/Chief Executive Officer (CEO) of the Institute and directed its affairs (through the CEO). Thus, I was involved and privileged to learn about governance and management. We used to meet monthly for the NEC meetings in our capital city of Harare. Apart from learning governance and management at this high level within a well-respected professional institute, I had an opportunity to mix and mingle with the HRM gurus, at national level such as Professor TC Gwarinda, Mr Ronnie Zinyuke, Ms Dorren Mazingi, Mr Eric Mahamba-Sithole, Major Josephat Zvaipa, Mr Remigio Imbayarwo Mtomba, Mr Peter Mtombeni, Mr Peter Mucherawehondo, the late Ms Judith Chokowore and Dr Mike Bimha. Dr Bimha later became the Minister of Industry and Commence of the government of Zimbabwe.

This is the story of my life:
An African village-boy's career path continues.

Chapter Eleven: Starting My Family

Kuperekwa Ceremony

In my culture, soon after the wedding, the bride is traditionally handed over to the family of the bridegroom. This is called '*Kuperekwa*'. This is a very crucial and significant traditional ceremony in the entire marriage/wedding process. In addition to marriage advice and distilled counselling, the bride is given some key and symbolic traditional kitchen utensils such as *mutvsairo* (traditional broom), *rusero* (winnowing basket), *badza* (hoe), pots and plates. In our case, the entire event was held at my eldest brother Peter's house, in Karaga. Although it was time consuming and tiring, everything went well.

When the *Kuperekwa* ceremony was over, Annette's aunt accompanied us to my flat, (Palm Court) which was to become our new home in Redcliff. Although we were tired and exhausted, we were exceedingly excited to be in our new home to start our new life-journey.

Honeymoon

After resting for a few days, we left our new home in Redcliff for our glorious honeymoon at one of the seven wonders of the world, the Victoria

Falls. Victoria Falls' local traditional name is *Mosi-oa-Tunya*, which means *'The Smoke That Thunders'*. Mosi-oa-Tunya is the original name of this majestic falls. David Livingstone was the first European to see this natural wonder; and then he had the audacity to rename it Victoria Falls in honour of Queen Victoria – who was thousands of kilometres away in England. Although the name Victoria Falls is more popular worldwide, we the locals, still use Mosi-oa-Tunya. While at the mighty Mosi-oa-Tunya, we were staying at one of the best hotels called Makasa Sun Hotel, which was later demolished, rebuilt and renamed/rebranded 'The Kingdom Hotel'. We had a great time of our life. Most importantly, it was exciting to know that finally, Annette, the woman I loved so much was now part of my life, until death do-us part. I loved her more than before.

We engaged in a number of different social and fun activities. Our advantage is that we had a friend, a manager within the hospitality industry based in Victoria Falls who gave us good information and suggested where we could have fun. She also gave us free and discounted entertainment services. For example, we had a sunset dinner in a Boat Cruise on the vast Zambezi River, very close to the Mighty Mosi-oa-Tunya. The views were spectacular. We saw giant hippopotamus at close range. At times we would race with them. It could be dangerous but all Boat drivers were trained and experienced and they knew the behaviours of these animals. The Crocodile Farm was the other interesting place we visited. It was amazing seeing the development and growth of crocodiles from an egg stage to an old reptile. The oldest crocodile we saw was almost 70 years. It was a great experience.

Annette's beauty does not cease to amaze me. I am glad that this is what Annette has been (to me) for the past almost 31 years in our marriage. Some of my friends and relatives say *'ndakadyiswa'*, meaning my wife gave me some African concoction or *juju* (charms) so that I would madly love her. I tell them, if there is such a thing, I am glad it happened because we are so happy in our marriage. I need more and more of it.

In my view, based on what has transpired in our marriage of 31 years now, starting from how we miraculously met, how we simply clicked and the chemistry we had for each other from the first day we set eyes on "each-each"- I strongly believe that our relationship and marriage was a result of God's divine favour and sufficient grace.

Our First Born - Makanaka Tuwe

On Tuesday the 13th July 1993, around 6pm, our joy was completed and fulfilled by the arrival of our first-born daughter, Makanaka Tuwe. She was born at Birchenough Maternity Centre in Gweru. In my Shona vernacular language, Makanaka means 'Beautiful'. Indeed, she was our beautiful African princess. For Annette and I, we were basically saying 'God you are sooooo good and beautiful to us'. Makanaka is affectionately known as Maka, (in short) both in our home and by her friends. Although Annette had gone for a scan, we decided not to know the gender of our baby. We wanted a surprise. As for the names, we had already agreed, whether it was a boy or girl. We made it clear that we wanted our meaningful Zimbabwe African traditional names for our children.

In my culture, if it is the first time for a woman to give birth, normally her mother or a close and trusted female relative would come and live with the pregnant woman a few days before the Estimated Delivery Date (EDD). They would also stay for at least a week after the delivery. This was done in order to give both the moral and psychological support to the 'new' mother. In addition, it was also meant to teach the new mother how to look after the newly-born baby, especially how to bath and feed the baby. In our case, Annette's mother (mbuya Mutema) was on stand-by for us. Since we were living on the sixth floor at my flat, one day the elevator was not working and Annette struggled to walk the stairs. Our medical doctor advised that we stay somewhere where there were no stairs. There were risks to both the mother and the unborn baby. As a result, we decided for Annette to go and stay with her elder sister Winette in the city of Gweru. Maybe because of the effects of walking up to the sixth floor, Annette experienced false birth contractions, and mbuya Mutema had to come, quickly, all the way from Masvingo to Gweru. She stayed for almost four weeks and there was no baby in sight. When she was about to go back to Masvingo, that is when Annette gave birth.

I vividly remember the day Maka was born. I was there throughout the entire birth-process. I gave Annette all the moral, psychological, physical and spiritual support. I remember telling my dear wife, *"Push, push babe; push please. We are almost there"*.

After seeing the pain my wife went through, I vowed to love and respect her more than before. I am glad that by the grace of God, I have managed to do that. Not only did I vow to respect Annette, but my baby-girl princess daughter and all the women-species of this brutal world. I guess this is why I have a special relationship with my daughter.

Our Second Born- Munashe Tuwe

Almost three years later, and to be exact, on Thursday the 13th June 1996, around 10 am, we were blessed, once again, with a handsome son whom we named Munashe Tuwe. He was born at the same place where his sister Maka was birthed. Munashe is a Shona name which means *'In The Lord'*. So, if the two names of our children are combined, thus, *Makanaka Munashe*, it means *'It is beautiful to be in the Lord'*. We really meant it. Looking back in our lives, Annette and I have seen the beauty, providence and sufficient grace of God. We will forever be grateful.

In summary, we had relocated to Gweru, from KweKwe when I got a new job at Zimglass. Then one day, after dinner, Annette asked me to take her on a long walk, as a form of physical exercise. She was heavily pregnant and overdue. Instead of walking she was literally running and I warned her of the likely consequences. That midnight she started experiencing some labour pains and contractions. Early morning of Thursday the 13th June, she requested me to drive her to Birchenough Maternity Centre immediately. Based on what had happened during Makanaka's pregnancy, I dismissed her request. She insisted and threatened to walk. I gave in and I drove her to the Maternity Centre and then proceeded to work. Around 1pm when I was about to go for my lunch break, I called the Maternity Centre and the nurse said that there was a baby. I could not believe it. I asked her (nurse) the gender of the baby and she told me off and said if I was serious and the father of the baby, I would have known and probably already at the Maternity Centre immediately. I did and when I got there, I was surprised to see a baby next to my dear wife. I asked Annette the baby's gender and she refused to tell me. I straight away moved closer and opened the legs of the baby to ascertain it for myself. It was a boy. I was so excited because we now had a fully-balanced equation, a girl and a boy. To God be the glory!!!!!

Our Children Attending Midland Christian School (MCS).

By God's grace we were able to send our children to a very expensive, but well-resourced and equipped private multiracial school in Gweru called Midlands Christian School (MCS). The official language at this school was English. It was a school whose philosophy was purely based on Christian values. Due to my poor background and how I had suffered during my childhood and my entire school-going age, I vowed that I would make sure that my own children would not experience the same 'hell' I went through. As a policy, we drove and picked-up our children from school daily. This was a good idea to send our children to MCS because when we later migrated to New Zealand (NZ), it was easy for them to integrate in New Zealand school system.

Our Grandson Tedros Simbarashe Tuwe

Fast-forward, in February 2022, our grandson Tedros Simbarashe Tuwe was born. This is Munashe's son. Annette and I cannot explain how it feels like to be called grandma and grandpa. We give glory to God for such a wonderful blessing.

This is the story of my life:
An African village-boy starting his own family.

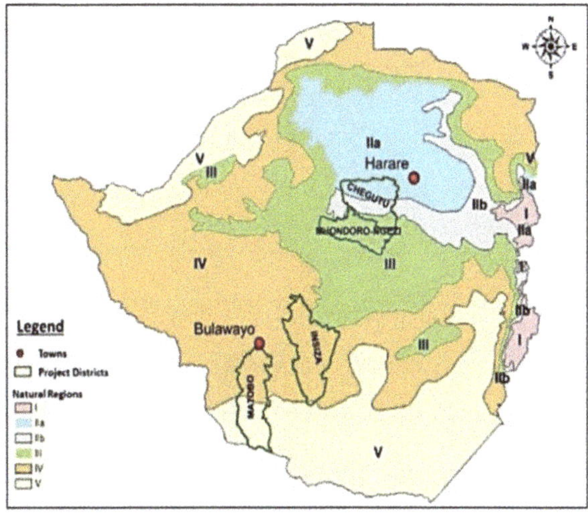

*Zimbabwean Map –
Showing Mhondoro-Ngezi*

*Map of the African continent which spans from the northern
hemisphere to the southern hemisphere. Zimbabwe is in the southern
part of Africa, surrounded by Zambia in the north, Mozambique
on the east, South Africa to the south, and Botswana on the west.*

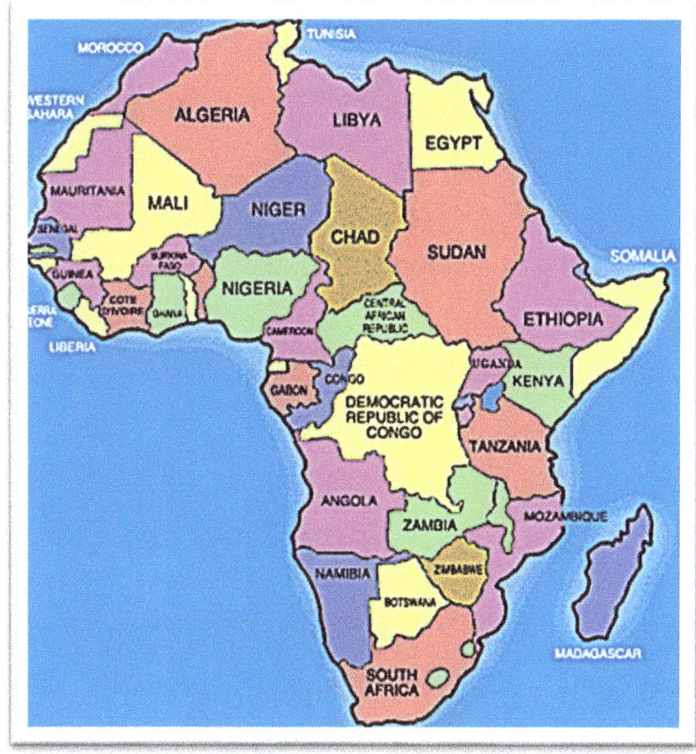

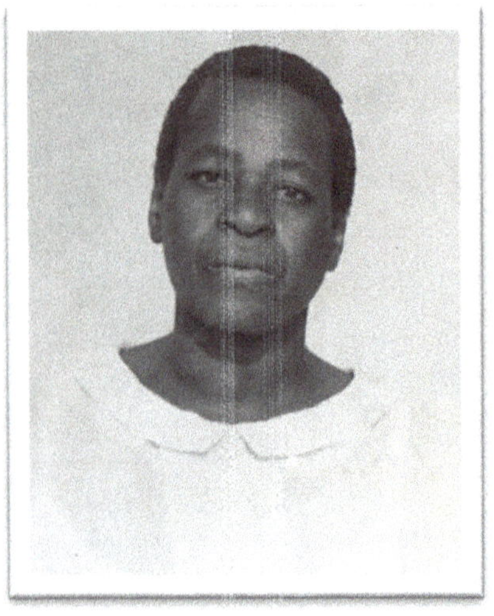

Amai Agatha Tuhwe (nee Kanda)

Baba Simon Mutsau Tuhwe

Amai Agatha Tuhwe with the twins
(L to R: Anyway Tendai & Kudakwashe
Nomore Tuwe)

*Mbuya Nyanya Lydia Kanda
(nee Denya)*

Sekuru Paul Kufonya Kanda

*Annette's Parents with their 1st Born baby boy,
Nelson - 1966*

The following is my *dzinza,* my genealogy or *my* Family-Tree. I felt duty-bound to be the first one in my wider extended family to write about my *Dzinza (Family-Tree)* – otherwise we will be a people without a history. Thanks to my daughter Makanaka Tuwe who created this 'Family Tree' (below). Just as Dr Martin Luther King Jr said *"Our lives begin to end the day we become silent about things that matter"* (Carson, 1998).

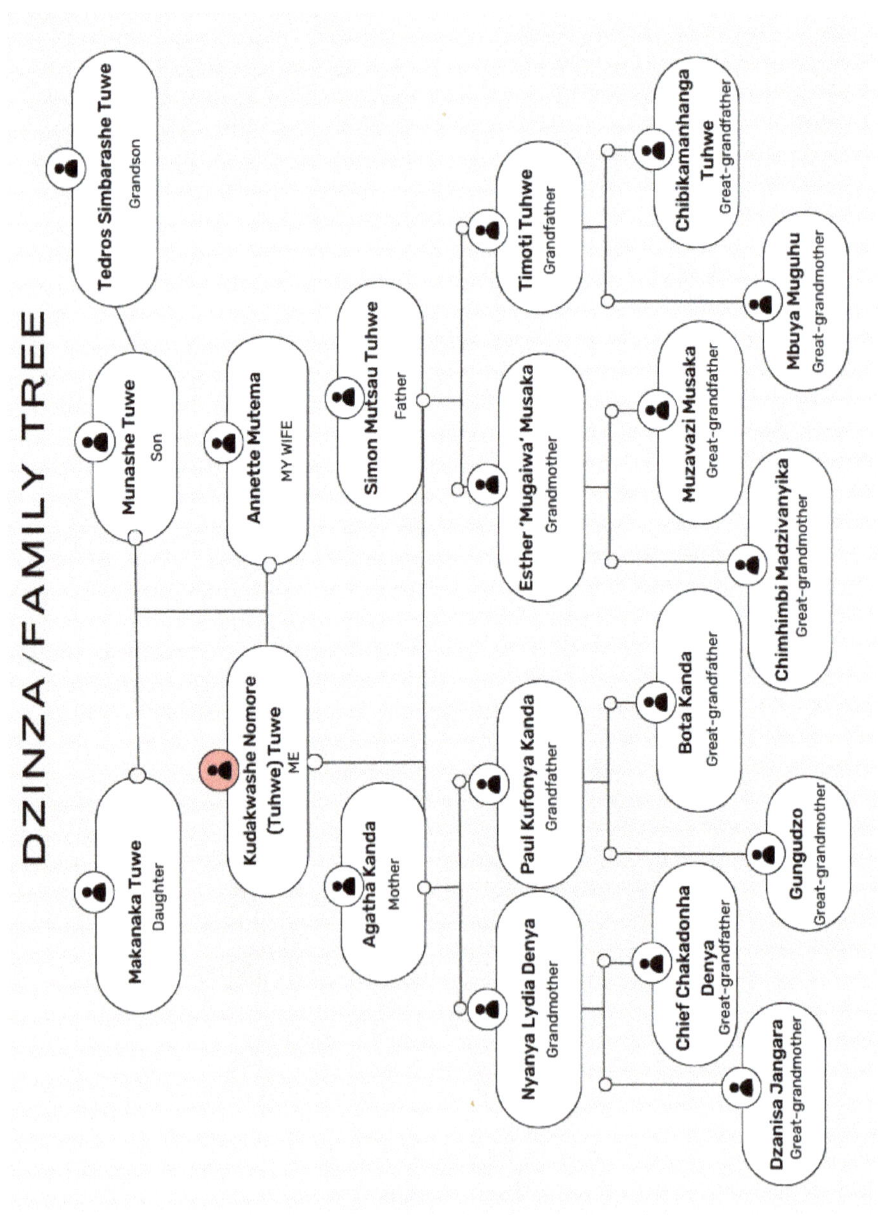

Above Left: 1986   *Right: 1987*

Young Kudakwashe

Annette and Tuwe: The Very First
Photo in Redcliff, Dec 1991.
(Courtesy of my former Schoolmate)

After Annette Said 'Ndizvozvo'- at
Benjamin Burombo Park in
Masvingo, 31 Dec 1991.

Tuwe & Annette's Engagement Party, Officiated by Rev Ralton Jenami (May 1992)

Above and below: Kudakwashe & Annette Tuwe's Wedding, 18 April 1993

Above: Kudakwashe with his in-laws
Below: Kudakwashe with his parents
and best man
at the wedding, 18 April 1993

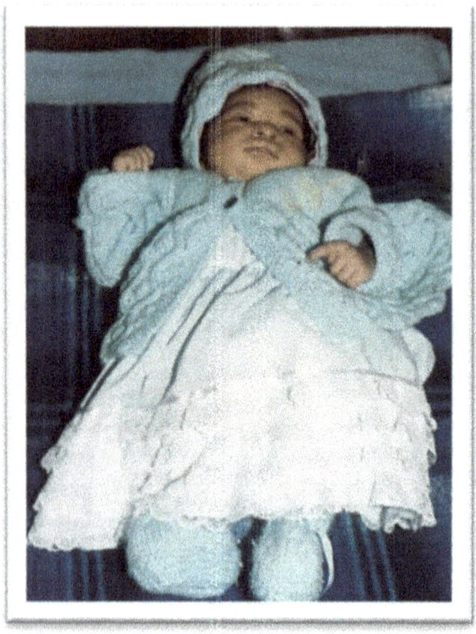

Baby Makanaka
Redcliff, Zimbabwe (1993)

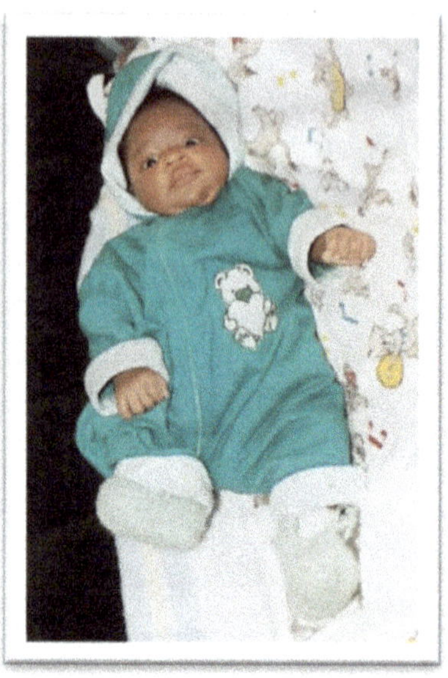

Baby Munashe
Redcliff, Zimbabwe (1996)

Makanaka (2013)

Munashe (2012)

Above (2001)

Tuwe Family

Below (2010)

*Above: Tuwe & Annette
at the FML Awards 2001
Tuwe receiving the National Top-25
Star Performance Award
from Mr Makoni
(Board Chair)*

*Right: Tuwe speaking at the IPMZ
Midlands Branch AGM as
Chairperson (2001)*

*Left: Tuwe & Annette at
the FML Awards 2002.
Tuwe received the
National Top-25
Star Performance Award*

Above: Harare - Capital of Zimbabwe
Below: Auckland, largest city in New Zealand (City of Sails)

An example of a marae - a Māori community centre

Left: Tuwe, with his MBA Degree (2006)

2009
Middle: Annette & Tuwe in Auckland

Bottom: Tuwe with his beloved mother mbuya Tuhwe and mother-in-law gogo Agnes Mutema (nee Cheda) at the Family Party in Gweru

Left: Tuwe at Esibayane Lodge in Manzini Eswatini where he was staying Manzini

Right: Tuwe at the Manzini club

Tuwe dancing with the Traditional Dancing Group at Lobamba Cultural Village, Eswatini

The Village Homestead we built for my mother in Sanyati – 2012

2014
Gogo Agatha Tuhwe's 80th Birthday

Left: Tuwe with Gogo at the party

Below: the 80th Birthday Cake

One Day after the Party
Left: Tuwe with his mother
Below: Mbuya Mutero (mbuya Tuhwe's younger sister) and Tuwe dancing

*Above Left: 2012
Dr Tuwe receiving
First Prize 3-Minute Thesis award –
Master of Philosophy Category*

*Above Right: 2015
3MT First Prize - PhD Category*

*Left: Tuwe Presenting at the AFSAAP
Conference at Deakin University in
Melbourne, Australia (2015)*

*Below: Annette and Tuwe
at 3MT, University of Queensland,
Australia*

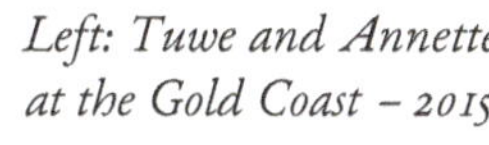

Left: Tuwe and Annette
at the Gold Coast – 2015

2016 - Trip to Zimbabwe
Left: Hugging Amai on
arrival in Zimbabwe
Centre: the welcome cake
we received on arrival.
Below:
with Amai and Annette

Below: Saying farewell to my Amai before returning to NZ.

Above: October 2017 – Fiji

Below: Tuwe submitting his final PhD Thesis to AUT

2017

Right: Tuwe and Annette at Chiguvare Primary School

Below: Tuwe playing African traditional drums at the primary school.

Below Right: With Mr Tembo and donated books for Chiguvare Primary school.

Below Left: Children reading the donated books.

Dr Tuwe's Graduation Day: Friday, the 14th December 2018

Above: Tuwe with his three PhD Supervisors - Prof Camille Nakhid, Prof Ian Shirley and Dr Carol Neill.

Left: Supervisors and their Spouses Dinning (2018)

Tuwe and Noreen Welch, the former renowned Zimbabwe Broadcasting Corporation (ZBCTV) News Reader – now retired in Whakatane, 2019

Above: Dr Tuwe (in red T-shirt) at his first-ever Community Engagement event in Wellington. (Dec 2020)

Below: Dr Tuwe receiving a certificate of appreciation from Rachel Qi, the President of the Wellington Multicultural Council (2021)

Above: A catchup with the Savanhus at their home in Chisipiti, Harare (2022).

Below: Tuwe and his Amai in Redcliff (2022)

*Annette and
Dr Tuwe with
grandson
Simbarashe Tedros
Tuwe (2023)*

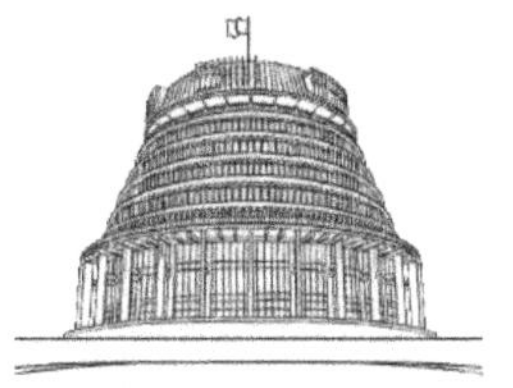

Chapter Twelve:
An African Village-Boy Leaving Zimbabwe for Aotearoa New Zealand

Reason for Leaving Zimbabwe

Once upon a time, Zimbabwe was the bread-basket of Africa and the world. We exported food, minerals and a number of other commodities. At independence in April 1980, our currency was one of the strongest in the world. The citizens earned good wages and salaries. People could afford to send their children to good schools, feed their families, go on holidays, locally and internationally. Life was sweet, meaningful and exciting. But come the late 1990s, tables were suddenly turned against this good life. The once vibrant economy of Zimbabwe started to decline sharply and deteriorate. In my view, the economy was not performing well, as it was supposed to. There was a lack of good governance and accountable leadership.

At this point, a few Zimbabwean professionals started leaving the country, mostly to South Africa followed by the United Kingdom (UK). South Africa had just gained her Black majority independence rule in 1994 and as a result there were many job opportunities created by the massive exodus of whites fleeing the African National Congress (ANC)'s Nelson

Mandela-led government. As for the UK, she is our former colonial master, hence the culture and familiarity attracted our people there. For me and my immediate family, we were still economically and financially sound such that when most of my friends started leaving Zimbabwe, I vowed that I would not leave.

In fact, I vividly remember boasting that I would assist all my close friends who wanted to leave by providing them free transport to the airport. I even told people that I would be the last person to 'lock' Zimbabwe. Based on the stories I had heard such as racial abuses and employment-related discrimination where professionals were made to do minimal and unskilled jobs, I became more convinced that I would not leave the country of my birth and a good-paying job and then become an alien in a foreign land.

Since I was working in the insurance industry, I would easily see that the economy was worsening daily. My commission-based salary was beginning to take a nose-dive decline and yet I had two children at an expensive private school, a house mortgage, a car loan and many other daily expenses. The citizens had no disposable income to buy insurance policies. Those with existing insurance policies, were starting to cancel them, due to financial hardships. The system in an insurance industry is such that if you are paid on commission basis, any policy cancellation would adversely affect one's income. The company would reclaim and deduct all or some of the commission paid before – depending on how long the policy has been in force. This was called 'clawback'. If one had significant cancellations, they would get a minus pay, thus, getting nothing and still owing the company. In 2002, I decided to leave, especially for the benefit of my children. I wanted a better life for them.

Applying for a UK Visa

Due to such an economic decadence and decline, coupled with a volatile political environment, our once little-heaven Zimbabwe became an unbearable place to live. The more I thought and cogitated about the future and welfare of my young family, the more I had a strong inner-push to migrate and leave the country. Since most of my close friends had left for the UK, I started seriously thinking about migrating there. Why the UK? As I stated before, the UK is Zimbabwe's former colonial master and we share a lot in common such things as the English language, the food, work ethics and culture. I also wanted a new country whose official and main language was English. I was not psychologically prepared to learn a new language. By then, Zimbabwe was still a member of the Commonwealth. This meant that as a Zimbabwean citizen, there were no visa requirements to travel to the UK. All I needed was to purchase my ticket and jump into the next plane.

So, I started preparing to leave for the UK. The first thing I did was to sell my car in order to raise the ticket fares. Luckily, we had two cars, my wife's and mine. The other advantage was that, due to a free-falling economy, cars were more expensive than houses. Unfortunately, the week I wanted to book for my ticket, the UK government introduced visa requirements for any Zimbabwean travelling to the UK. I was worried and devastated. The visa requirements were strenuous. I got all the supporting documents I needed from one of my Zimbabwean close friends who was now a citizen of the UK. I also included all the title deeds of our assets as a way to demonstrate that I would come back home at the end of my visit. To ensure that all my papers were in order, I requested my brother who was a Member of Parliament (MP) to run them (papers) through his friend at the British Embassy. The response from the British Embassy was affirmative and encouraging. I was excited and confident that I was now eligible to relocate to the UK.

Due to the introduction of the visa requirements, anyone who wanted to visit the UK was supposed to attend and pass an intense (and scary) interview. I was one of the very first people to be interviewed. I vividly remember it was on a Wednesday the 4th December 2002, I drove 275kms from my city of (Gweru) to Harare to attend the interview. Based on my well-prepared documents and the confidence birthed from the British Embassy's response, I was already seeing myself walking on the streets of London - with my hands in my pockets. I thought the interview was just a formality. When I got to the interview room, it was full of people who wanted visas. The environment and the message in the atmosphere heralded a sad story - that everyone wanted to leave the country, as soon as possible.

I joined a long queue, served by four UK Immigration Officers (two men and two woman), who had just arrived in the country – two weeks prior. I befriended one of the security officers manning the queues who told me that if I got served by any of the three other officers, my chances of being granted a visa were greater. But he strongly warned that if it was the 'big-man' and gigantic male officer on Counter One, I was likely to be declined. He advised me to make a short prayer so as to avoid the big-man. Before the end of our conversation and the beginning of my short prayer, the big-man man shouted 'next'. I started sweating and remained stationary. He pointed at me to come. I nearly fainted. Armed with all my impressive and well-prepared documents, I approached his revered and feared counter. Within a few minutes of perusing my papers, he declined my application. I asked him why and he said he felt that if I was granted entry into the UK, I was likely not to come back to Zimbabwe. I tried to reason with him, but he had no time for me. He shouted again 'next'. Within the twinkle of an eye, my game was over. The UK trip was no more. I was shattered. I could not believe what had just happened.

Annette's Reaction to My Visa Decline

As soon as I left the UK Immigration offices, I called Annette and shared my sad story about my visa application. I expected her to be worried and concerned but she was very casual and unmoved. After calling her I drove to her sister's house (Winnette) who now lived in the suburb of Greendale in Harare – after relocating from Gweru. When I broke the news to her, she behaved in the same manner as her younger sister (Annette) – very unmoved. I smelt a rat, but I could not figure out what was really happening. Since Winnette had recently returned from a 6-month visit to the UK, I asked her about the country and whether I had lost anything. She sounded disinterested in me going to that far land - the UK.

When I went home, Annette showed no concern about my declined application. Later, when I was already in New Zealand, I discovered that she was not keen for me to go to the UK as she had a strong feeling and conviction that if I had gone, she and the children would not be allowed to join me. Because of her convictions, Annette, her sister and other close friends had actually prayed and fasted for my application to be declined. The other contributing factor to Annette's concerns and anxiety was that we intensely loved each other and we both hated to be separated, even for a short period of time. We were only married for nine years and everything was going on well. When I look back, I believe Annette was right. The UK was not meant for us as a family. We know a number of our close friends who took many years for their papers to be in order and their marriages suffered. Some separated and divorced. The majority claimed asylum and they are still waiting for responses, almost 22 years later. Some could not even attend funerals for their spouses, children, parents and siblings since they are asylum seekers. This is sad indeed. I thank God for giving Annette the foresight and insight.

Preparing for Aotearoa New Zealand (NZ)

In principle, Annette and I had agreed that we needed to leave Zimbabwe as soon as possible, but she was not in favour of the UK as a destination. As I stated before, we wanted an English-speaking country and one which took seriously issues of racism and any form of discrimination. So, after my UK application was declined, I started doing my serious research for a destination that suited what we were looking for, as a family, especially for our young children who were only aged nine and six. Luckily my *babamukuru* (brother-in-law), Simba Magadzire, (Winnette's husband) had once visited New Zealand (NZ) on work business and he said that he had interacted with Kiwis (New Zealanders) both at work and at a social level and found them to be good and humane. He even stated that he was well received at their church services. Since I respected Simba so much, I took his word as gospel-truth and I started focusing on migrating to NZ.

It so happened that one of my work colleagues at Ziscosteel Ltd's Human Resources Division, Nobel Admire Pasi, popularly known as NAM, had just migrated to NZ. While we were at Ziscosteel, NAM was working at the Training Centre and I was at HR Offices. We closely worked together. I am glad that our relationship while at Ziscosteel was good and healthy. I thank my mother who taught me to be always at peace with all men because you may never know when you will 'bump' into each other and criss-cross your life-path, tomorrow. I also happen to be related to NAM's wife, (Mabel) and we knew each other. This made my assignment very much lighter and easy. In my culture, I called Mabel '*amai*'. I phoned NAM's place in NZ and Mabel answered my call. She was happy to hear from me especially that I wanted to come to NZ. She was very encouraging and above all very polite and welcoming. Within a few minutes, she had supplied me with all the details I needed. I vividly remember the contents of our brief but important telephone conversation with Mabel. That call changed and revolutionised my life and that of my family. I then made up my mind to go to NZ. I was required to supply a physical address and contacts of someone I knew, who was already in NZ, if I had any. I also needed someone to pick me up from the airport and a place to stay during my first few days, while I settled in a new foreign land. This is where Mabel and NAM became handy and crucial.

By then Zimbabwe was still a member of the Commonwealth, and as a result, Zimbabweans did not require a visa to visit NZ. Since I had already sold my Astra (car), I quickly bought my NZ air ticket. I was very lucky because my ticket was cheap and one of the very last ones to be sold in Zimbabwe dollars due to high inflation. The rest were going to be sold in United States dollars. Since the tickets were cheap and in Zimbabwean dollars, I wanted to purchase for my wife and our two small children and leave the country together, because my concern was that since UK had introduced visas, NZ was likely to do the same. My wife thought it was not a good idea. She suggested that I go first and settle then she would follow with the children. Although it made sense since we needed time to sort out a number of issues such as renting out our properties, Annette arranging leave from her workplace and many other matters, I was deeply worried about the likely possibility of NZ introducing visas, soon after the UK – before they joined me. This would adversely affect us as a family, me in NZ and the rest of my closest people in Zimbabwe. We both did not want such a nasty situation to occur.

Bidding Farewell to My Father, Mother and Mother-in-Law

About two years before I decided to leave Zimbabwe for overseas, my father had some health problems which required a major operation. My wife and I had to send him to see a specialist medical doctor in Harare, which was very expensive. Thanks to my other brothers and their wives who contributed financially to this cause. Special thanks to my younger brother Ophias Tuwe and his wife Lorah who took care of baba before and after the said operation in their house in Mt Pleasant in Harare. After a couple of weeks baba was discharged and briefly stayed with us in Gweru. My wife and I had offered him to stay with us permanently in Gweru but he turned down the offer.

A week before my scheduled flight to New Zealand, I made a special trip to bid farewell to my sick father, who was living in Amaveni Township, KweKwe – with another wife. I had already told him of my plans to leave the country mainly due to the bleeding-economy, triggered by political instability. When I told him that I was leaving Zimbabwe for New Zealand in a week's time, he agreed. I asked him to bless me. He did. I then requested him if we could pray together - and he agreed. As I held his hands in mine, I felt that it was my last time to see my dad. Thankfully, I did not breakdown. Neither did he. After a brief but deep father-son conversation, I left. The parting was painful but I had a profound sense of peace within me because I had played my part by paying his medical bills. Above all, he had blessed my life and journey, to a far-off indigenous land.

I am glad that I had a blessing from my father because as I reiterated, my father passed on in May 2003, exactly five months after me arrival in New Zealand. I was unable to return home for his burial. May His Soul Rest in Everlasting Peace – MHSRIEP🙏.

A few days before I departed Zimbabwe, we went to my village in Sanyati to bid fare well to my mother. Then we had another trip to Masvingo to bid farewell to my dear mother-in-law. These farewells were not easy, there were emotional and painful as I did not know when I would come back home to see my beloved people.

Last Moments in Zimbabwe

About two days before I felt Zimbabwe, we were in Harare to do the final shopping, preparations and bidding farewell to my family members and close friends. On the day of my departure (Sunday the 29 December 2002), my maiguru Winnette prepared a special traditional meal for me, which we call *sadza*. I did not have a good appetite but she insisted that I must eat with her, in her remembrance. I obliged. Little did I know that it was my last 'supper' with her. She later passed on in 2004. MHSRIEP 🙏.

We arrived at the Harare International Airport on time and did all the boarding requirements. There was a large number of my family and close friends who came to bid me farewell. When the time to leave for the Departure Lounge came, it was hard for Annette and our children, especially my daughter Maka. Annette tried to be strong for our children and did not cry. But as for Maka, she literally followed me and was only stopped by the Airport security staff from crossing behind the counters. She burst into tears. It was bad seeing my daughter cry. I am very close with my daughter. As for our son, Munashe, he was too young to comprehend what was going on. He was excited that I was going so that they would follow soon. I turned and waved to my family for the last time and disappeared into the Boarding Lounge. My heart was bleeding, especially for my wife and children. I had no choice but to do it, for their benefit.

My First Ever Flight: Zimbabwe to Aotearoa New Zealand

My flight was scheduled to leave Harare International Airport, Zimbabwe for Wellington, New Zealand, on Sunday the 29 December 2002 at 1.30pm. I had to go via Oliver Tambo (OT) International Airport in Johannesburg, South Africa, and then Sydney International Airport, Australia. It was my very first time to see a real plane within such close proximity and later on to 'jump' into it. It was a dream come true. I was excited. I liked and appreciated the experience. As soon as our plane took off, they began to serve food, starting with children. Guess what? I thought they had left me out and I politely called out to the Flight attendant and said, "*I think you have missed me by mistake*". She smiled and said, "*We are serving children first Sir. Soon, we will be serving the adults, Sir*". She was very polite and professional but I was embarrassed. The gentleman seated next to me smiled and jokingly said in my mother tongue, "*Mwana asinga cheme anofira mumbereko*" meaning "*if you don't ask, you don't get*". All he wanted was to make me feel comfortable.

Within one hour 45 minutes, we safely landed at OT International Airport, in Johannesburg, South Africa. Since this was my first flight in my entire life, I expected the landing to be smooth and nice; similar to that of a car. I was wrong. It was rough and bumpy. I actually panicked and screamed. In my view, it was the roughest landing. Each time I land, that not-so-good experience always flashes back.

I had never seen so many planes and big ones too, at OT International Airport. After about three hours, we checked into a Qantas Airlines, massive plane bound for Sydney, Australia. The experience of flying across some of the largest oceans and seas of this world for 14 hours, non-stop, was amazing and fascinating. It was indeed a life-time memorable experience. The other thing I enjoyed on this long trip was the yummy food and the friendly services of the crew. Now after having travelled many parts of the world, I rate Emirates Airlines the best followed by followed by Air New Zealand and in third place is Qantas Airlines. In my experience, Air Canada has been the worst. There was something I learnt on this long flight, which has stuck with me to this very day. There was a man seated next to me. Around 3am, he stood up and changed into his religious regalia and started doing his rituals (worshipping and praying), right next to me, in the hallway. He was comfortable and confident. He seemed not worried about people around him. My lesson was his commitment to his religion or his God. I was impressed and encouraged. Although I did not know his religion, I admired his audacity and unwavering commitment.

After a long 14-hour flight, we landed in Sydney. While in Sydney, I called NAM Pasi just to remind him the time I was landing in NZ. I'm glad I called because he had thought I was arriving the following day. Within an hour I boarded a Samoa Airways plane which was bound for the New Zealand capital city of Wellington. After about two hours, we landed at Wellington International Airport, at 12 midnight on 31 December 2002. It is important to note that in summer, New Zealand is 11 hours ahead of Zimbabwe, so when coming from Africa, you lose a day.

Although the Immigration and Customers Offers asked me a few questions and opened my big suitcase as well as having their dogs sniff my bag, I was treated with respect and dignity. I was given three months' Visitors Visa – but for some unknown reasons, I thought it was valid for six months. Luckily, I discovered it a few weeks down the line. Otherwise, there are no excuses for overstaying. You simply get deported. When I got to the Arrivals Lounge, I was so excited and relieved to see Mr NAM Pasi waiting for me. I had heard awkward stories, especially at Heathrow Airport (UK) where people make promises to pick you up at the airport and they do not come. A few people have been sent back to Zimbabwe.

NAM drove me to his house in Wainuiomata suburb in Wellington. It was good to see my '*Amai*' Mabel and family. I was well received by the entire family. I spent a week at NAM and Mabel's place and moved into my own Boarding House in the city of Wellington. I will forever be grateful for NAM, Mabel and their family, for looking after me so well. NAM and family later relocated to Australia but we are in constant touch. As a result, from the good lessons I learnt from them, I vowed (to myself) to be kind to all humankind especially those who are new in the country. In the majority of cases, it can be very difficult to settle. As migrants in a new country, we face a lot of challenges in many different forms, such as financial, social, emotional, psychological, cultural and spiritual. However, if you find someone who is kind and already familiar with the place to show you around, such as NAM and Mabel, it makes life easy.

This is the story of my life:
An African village-boy leaving Zimbabwe for overseas,
Aotearoa New Zealand.

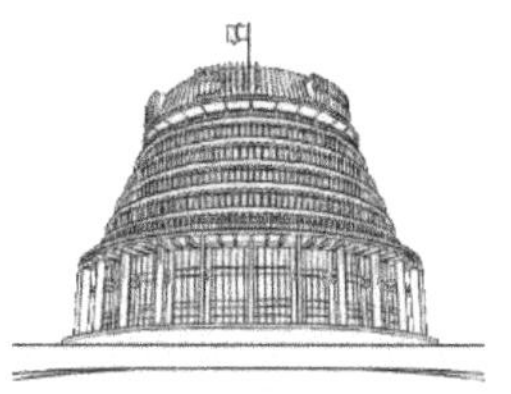

Chapter Thirteen:
My Employment and Career Journey
in New Zealand –
Initial Humbling Jobs

Toilet Cleaner

As I reiterated, my last job in Zimbabwe was that of an Insurance Executive Agent. Prior to that, I had worked in a number of different, exciting and rewarding portfolios such as Senior Human Resources practitioner, Budget/Accounting Officer and a Commercial Banker. Given my humble (poor) background, I think I was doing well in my career. Life was good and comfortable. But as I stated before, the economic situation which was triggered by political instability 'forced' me to leave my beautiful home-country, my familiar territory, my vibrant communities, my close friends, my relatives and my beloved family. When I left Zimbabwe, I had US$850 cash and a suitcase. Nothing more. Now when I look back, retrospectively, it reminds me of the Biblical Jacob who had nothing but a rod/staff in his hands when he crossed the River Jordan, to join his uncle Laban (Genesis 31:10). Initially, I thought this amount was going to take me far but I later discovered that it was not enough because generally accommodation in New Zealand is expensive. I therefore had to get a job fast because I needed money for rent, food, transport as well as supporting my young family and the extended family back home. Pressure began to mount.

Luckily, when I left Zimbabwe, I knew exactly what I was getting into, especially employment-wise. I was prepared, both mentally and physically. I had heard stories from most of my Zimbabwean family members and friends who had migrated overseas, especially the UK, that the majority of professionals were 'converted' (overnight) into rest-home workers, care-workers, cleaners etc. Rest-home work in the diaspora is commonly known in Zimbabwe as '*DotCom*'. Most overseas companies were reluctant to offer jobs on merit, especially to people of colour. This is commonly known as employment-related discrimination and racism (Butcher et al, 2006; Creese 2010, Lauer, Wilkinson et al. 2012, Tuwe,2018).

I did not care what type of job it was. My philosophical approach and attitude were: '*I am not here to impress anyone. I have a simple agenda, thus, getting a job as soon as possible*'. All I wanted was a job, while I settled in a foreign land. I was very intentional, focused and strategic. I was convinced and convicted that with God on my side, if I played my part well, faithfully and professionally, all was going to be fine. He would do the rest, especially that which I could not. I believed God for a good job. When? I didn't know. All I knew was at the appropriate time, it was going to happen. Remember, I am a man of faith.

I was fortunate enough to have found a new friend, originally from my country of birth - who understood our struggles as migrants in a new foreign far-land. The very first time we met, we clicked. She loved jokes. She was jovial and kind-hearted. She had an inclination to narrate stories, mixed with half-baked truths and questionable authenticity ☺. I straightaway viewed her as a clown and embraced her as a *bhururu*. Bhururu is a close friend whom you crack jokes with, normally without filters and boundaries.

Her name is Ruth Pasi. Ruth is NAM Pasi's sister. She was working at a rest home in Newtown, Wellington.

One day, she called me and 'demanded' that we met at a bus stop near her Rest Home. When I got to the bus stop, she looked at me and started laughing. When I asked her why she was laughing, she said, "*Wakapedzesera kudya sadza riinhi?*"- meaning "*When was the last time you ate sadza?*" Sadza is our yummy traditional meal in Zimbabwe. In other African countries they call it *Ugali/Ufufu/Papu*. When I questioned her why she was asking such a question, she bluntly told me, "*Miromo yako yakachena zvenzara chaizvo huye uri kunzwisa tsitsi.*" The English translation is "*Your lips are white as snow. You are hungry and you look pathetic.*" Again, she laughed. As a clown and *bhururu*, I knew that such a laughter and direct talk was engrossed and 'marinated' with some kind of good news. When I asked her to "spit it out", she told me that she had secured a job for me. I looked at her in disbelief. The main reason I was surprised is that it was only my second week in the country and most companies were closed for the long Christmas and New Year's holidays. I therefore did not expect to get a job that early. When I asked her what type of a job it was, she laughed again. When I gave her an 'evil' look, she said, "*Matanyera. What else can you expect?*" '*Matanyera*' means a cleaner. I later discovered that it was not just a cleaner, but a Toilet Cleaner at the nearby said Rest Home, closer to Wellington CBD, the Diplomatic Capital of Aotearoa New Zealand. Although it was the lowest job I had ever done in my entire life, I was grateful and excited for my very first job in a foreign land. I praised the Lord. After I was introduced to the manager, I signed my contract. I shall be forever grateful to Ruth. She later relocated to Sydney, Australia. We are still in contact. For example, one of Ruth's daughters stayed with us in Wellington in 2022 when she was doing her university internship. We laugh a lot on the phone, especially when she starts her gossiping and lies. We also talk heaps about the struggles we faced as we settled in our new found home, Aotearoa New Zealand. We are a family, now.

Influenced by the way I was brought up by my mother, I have always believed in hard-work and professionalism. My policy is *"Work as unto the Lord"*. Within days at my new-found job, there was a talk, in the entire Rest Home, of a well-polished, professional and hard-working new Toilet Cleaner. They even added, *"He speaks fluent English too. He is highly educated and organised"*. I heard it, loud and clear, but remained focused. All I did was to focus on doing my work, diligently. Most workers, especially ladies started to be friendly to me. They became generous by way of giving me food, and extending companionship and fellowship at work. In summary, I was wholly accepted and loved by most staff. I was humbled and excited at the same time. I was also grateful because at times it is daunting and stressful to settle in a new job and to make it worse, in a new country. At times 'old' staff members can 'congregate' and plot to be unfriendly and make one's life hell on-earth for a new staff, especially if you look different and speak with an accent. As someone who had experience in working with people (human resources practitioner), I was aware of such unfortunate and uncalled-for schemes and attitudes. I also knew how to mitigate and navigate.

Home-Alarm Sales Representative

While doing my toilet-cleaning job, I got another one as a Sales Executive, selling Home Alarms. It was commission-based. No basic salary. Since I had successfully worked as an Executive Agent in Zimbabwe, I thought this job was 'a walk in the park'. I was wrong. It was very difficult for me. It involved door-knocking, mostly from 5pm - 7pm, when the majority of residents were back from work. The responses from householders were a mixed-bag. Some were very kind, polite and professional. Most of the nice ones wanted a social conversation with me, mostly triggered by the way I looked and my distinctive accent. They were also keen to know where I was originally from and what made me come to New Zealand. Our agendas were diametrically different. I wanted to "close a sale" and make money and they were after 'playing and socialising' with me. On one hand, others were rude and unwelcoming. They would slam their doors in my face and not talk to me. If they did, it was rough and unkind. The job became increasingly difficult. For the two months, I did not earn a single cent because I never made a single sale. My financial-salvation was through my cleaning job. When the NZ government decided to grant one-year Special Open Work Permits (SOWP), to all Zimbabweans who were already on the soils of New Zealand as at 20 February 2003 (New Zealand Beehive News, 2004), I resigned from the Home-Alarm Sales job as I could clearly see that there was no future for me. The SOWP was the genesis of many Zimbabwean nationals later obtaining their NZ permanent residency and citizenship.

Dish-Washer at the New Zealand Airport

After resigning from the challenging Home-Alarm Sales job, I secured another casual role as a dish washer at the Koru Lounge situated at Wellington Airport. This was around end of February 2003. The Koru Lounge is owned by Air New Zealand and they provide food/meals to both domestic and international passengers who are its members. Both the staff and passengers were great and kind to me. I loved this job because I met and interacted and served people from all walks of life, including the then NZ Prime Minister (PM) Honourable Helen Clark. On one particular day, while the PM was collecting her own food, I came very close to her as I was replenishing the food-trays; she smiled and greeted me. One of the staff members could clearly see that I had not known that I had just talked to the PM - he then asked me if I knew the guest. I told him I didn't. When he mentioned that she was the PM, I did not believe him because where I had just come from (Zimbabwe), the President/PM would have been served food by his own staff. He would be heavily guarded by bodyguards and the entire airport invaded and bombarded by soldiers and plain-cloth military/security personnel. Passengers would be stopped, questioned and at times searched and harassed. But in this case, I did not see anyone with a gun or any identifiable bodyguard. I was also surprised when I later learnt that in NZ, the PM also stops and observes traffic lights (robots in Zimbabwe), just like anybody else. In Zimbabwe, when the President is passing through, all traffic pulls off the road and stops immediately. Any movement may cost your life or invite a savage beating, on the spot. I would wish such practices and simplicity to happen in my beloved country of birth.

My Family Immigration-Salvation as a Dish-Washer

As I mentioned before, my dear wife would not entertain my idea and suggestion of all of us relocating (at once) to NZ as a family. The NZ government introduced Visas on 21 February 2003 for any Zimbabwean visiting NZ. My prophecy that NZ was likely to follow the UK, was suddenly (and sadly) fulfilled. When I heard the news, my heart bled and "jumped into my month" - I was scared that my family would not be able to join me. Just as the Biblical Job said, "*That which I was afraid of had befallen me*". I became extremely worried and deeply concerned because there was no way I would be separated from my beloved young family. I loved them dearly and treasured them as refined gold, especially my beautiful wife. They loved me and missed me too. I straightaway applied for a Visa for my family to join me and this was rejected. The reasons were, my managerial skill-set was not on the NZ Immigration Skills Shortage Category. In short, they did not need my managerial skills. Secondly, my wife was a Zimbabwe-trained primary schoolteacher. New Zealand did not require her skills too. They said maybe if she was a secondary-trained teacher in subjects such as sciences, home-economics and mathematics. I couldn't envisage a life without my beautiful wife and my two little children. This adversely affected me in a deep and profound way, including my work. I was determined to go back to my beloved country of birth, though I would have preferred to have my children grow up in NZ, for a better future.

So, one day as I was doing my normal duties at the Koru Lounge (Airport), one of the elderly ladies named Chris, who worked at the reception, had befriended me, approached me and said, *"Are you okay Tuwe?"* I said 'yes'. Her follow-up question was, *"Are you sure that you are, okay?"* Again, I said 'yep'. She left. After about 10 minutes she came back and asked the same questions. I gave the same responses and she left. She came back the third time and asked the same questions. This time I was actually getting annoyed and agitated such that I nearly told her off. In my heart of hearts, I was wondering why she was bothering me. Though she was my good friend, I started feeling as if she was invading my personal space and I did not appreciate it. She proceeded and asked me how my family was and where they were. I told her they were in Zimbabwe. As if it was not enough, she asked why they were not with me. I then lost it and told her how the NZ Immigration was insensitive and inhumane, especially when dealing with people of colour like myself. I went further and expressed my disappointment regarding the trivial job(s) I was doing yet I was highly qualified and experienced. She smiled, gave me a pat on the back and left. Within no time she came back and said, *"Tuwe I feel you and I now understand why you are sooooo down today. It's not the normal jovial Tuwe I know. Guess what? I know someone who may help you and that person is passing through here tomorrow and if you would like, I can arrange for you to briefly talk and present your case?"* I agreed to the arrangement and she smiled again and left. I did not take her seriously.

True to her word, the following morning while I was washing dishes, she came and pulled me to a private office and there I was genuinely welcomed and greeted by a young lady who introduced herself as a very senior government official (politician). She told me she had been briefed about my story. She asked me about my work-related experience and qualifications. I seized this rare opportunity and bluntly (but politely and respectfully) told her that I did not know that NZ treats its skilled and highly qualified migrants in such a bad way. She blushed. She promised to assist my family to join me and that she would be in touch with me soon. Again, I did not believe her, especially that she was a politician. In my country of birth (and indeed many other countries) politicians lie with a straight face and they don't care about it – they do not feel guilty at all. Indeed, true to her word, within three days, I got a letter from her office; bearing glad tidings that my family would now join me in NZ. The visa application was re-lodged in the normal process and granted. In summary without the professional intervention of this very senior government official, my family would not be here in NZ. I would have returned to Zimbabwe and probably my life and that of my family would have taken a completely different trajectory.

I will forever thank and appreciate the help of this senior government official. It's sad that after a few months of assisting me the senior government official resigned or lost her job. I really felt for her. She was humble, professional and humane. After a few years, I later met her in another city at our big African Community Event where she was the guest of honour. As a National Programme Manager - African Communities, I was also a visiting guest-speaker. I asked her if she remembered me and my story. She didn't. When I stood up to give my speech, before she did, I publicly acknowledged her and what she had done for me and my family. People present and my community really appreciated her Ubuntu and humane way of dealing with people. From this experience, I learnt that it is important for those in high offices to help the vulnerable members of our communities – without demanding bribes.

Without my dear good friend Chris, I wouldn't have met this senior government official. Chris was an elderly white Kiwi lady, married with grown-up children. She made sure that I was happy at work and all was well with me. She even talked about me with her family - her husband and children. Before my wife and two small children arrived in NZ in October 2003, she donated heaps of household stuff, including a double bed, chairs and a table. Her husband dropped them off at my house in Upper Hutt. I don't know why she liked, respected and treated me in such a special way. I now believe that she was God-sent. May the good Lord bless her soul and family 🙏.

Before my family arrived in NZ, I had left my airport job to join a government department. This meant, I could only talk to Chris on the phone. Later, when my family arrived from Zimbabwe, I called her house wanting to make arrangements for my wife and children to meet her and her family. My wife and I wanted to sincerely thank Chris and her family, in person, for standing in the gap for me (and us), in such a great way, that we never ever imagined or dreamt of. In my African culture, it is acceptable to express your gratitude over the phone, but where possible, it is more meaningful and appropriate to do it face-to-face. I have recently learnt that in Māori and Pacific cultures, they also prefer this face-to-face approach which they call '*kanohi - ki te - kanohi' korero* (in Māori) and '*Talanoa*' (in Pacific languages) (Edward Riini, 2020).

When I called, Chris' husband answered my call and I requested to talk to my friend Chris. There was a long-deafening silence on the other end of the line. I asked if he was still there and he said '*yes*'. I asked if everything was, okay. His reply was, "*So, Tuwe you don't know?*" I said, "*What?*" At this moment my heart was pounding and my legs were knocking against each other. I was shivering. I was not at all prepared to hear what I now had anticipated. He finally said, *"I am very sorry Tuwe. Your friend Chris passed on"*. In our discussions, I was later told that she succumbed to cancer. She had not told me and this is why I was so shocked. It took me a long time to believe that my dear friend Chris was no more. I felt the pain. Chris had genuine love and care. As far as I am concerned, she was a human being who regarded people, great and small, all races and genders as equals. Although Chris is gone, I will never forget about her, her good family and what she did for me and my family. I have learnt a great lesson from my dear Kiwi friend Chris; thus, I will do all my best to assist any human being who is in need – regardless of their background, race, creed, gender, political affiliation and etc. As a Christian, I strongly believe that Chris was God-sent to assist me and my family in this daunting immigration process as well as settling in the great nation of Aotearoa New Zealand. An elderly white lady, bonafidely and heartily assisting her friend, a young African village-boy. This is genuine love with no boundaries and strings attached. If this world was populated with such people, it would be a better place to live and domicile.

Car-Yard Sales Representative (by Day) and Cleaner (by Night)

After the airport job, I joined a Car-Yard Company as a Sales Representative, based in the suburb of Porirua in Wellington. This was hugely commission-based with a small basic salary. Again, I thought I would do well based on my previous successful sales career in Zimbabwe. Again, I was wrong. I would serve a lot of customers but when it came to other issues such as credit-rating/checks, my prospective clients would not pass. The majority of residents in this location faced a number of socio-economic challenges hence the poor credit-ratings. Although this was beyond my control, it adversely affected both my earnings and job performance. There was a high staff turn-over as a direct result of these credit-rating issues. My earnings were adversely affected, and yet I wanted to save money for the air tickets for my family. I had no choice but to look for another evening job(s). I finally secured three more additional cleaning jobs to be done after my 6pm-Car Sales job. This meant I had four jobs per day. I vividly remember one day working a total of 20 hours straight (from 10 am to 2am the next day). It was tough, especially considering that in Zimbabwe I was an Executive and had never done a cleaning job in my entire life. My lowest job in Zimbabwe was that of a Bank Officer, which was great, by international standards. Although it was for a short time and unsustainable doing four jobs, I had to scale down. I also considered my health. I resigned from the Car Sales and two more cleaning jobs. I went back to the airport, again as a casual Dish Washer. This was back to my familiar territory - reconnecting with good old friends.

Corrections Officer/Prison Officer

While I was scaling down on the number of jobs, I was also searching for a better permanent job. I now wanted to settle since as I knew my family would be joining me. I had sent out several job applications. Luckily, I got a permanent position with a government department as a Corrections Officer or commonly known in other countries as Prison Officer. My close friends in Zimbabwe used to call me "*Mukoma Mahobho*"- the equivalence of a shop or gate security officer. 🙆 😊 The training was for six weeks. I really enjoyed the training. The free food, during training, was amazing. I lived very close to the Prison Training College and as a result I used to go home (after training/work) and then come back to the College for dinner. I would go early for breakfast. I gained a few kilos.

After graduation we were deployed to different Prison units/departments. This was the first job in New Zealand which I would say was a good one and the pay was equally decent too. There were also heaps of overtime. For me it was okay because I was staying alone, closer to work and I wanted to raise money for my family's air tickets. It worked well for me. Although the job was generally fine, I found some of the culture within of the organisation challenging. Surprisingly, I found most inmates easy to deal with as compared to staff. I found it strange. After almost two years, in 2005, I left and joined another government department as a Youth Worker.

Youth Worker

Because of my experience as a Corrections Officer, I quickly secured a position of Youth Worker. Although this role involved dealing with some of the young people who had challenging behaviours, it was better than the one at Corrections. The culture at the centre where I worked was good, especially the Centre Manager. He was a good fellow. I was also blessed to have lovely staff 'on the floor'. However, like any other organisation, you are bound to find some people who are not-so-easy to deal with.

After about a year, I left my youth worker job and joined a private community organisation, which was wholly funded by the government. My new role was that of National Programme Manager – African Communities – see more detail later.

This is the story of my life:
An African village-boy's Employment and career journey
(initial humbling jobs) in Aotearoa New Zealand.

Chapter Fourteen:
Cultural Intersectionality –
An African Village-Boy
Staying with Pacific Families and
Working for a Māori Iwi Organisation

Staying with a Tongan Family - Parallels Between the Tongan and the African Cultures

When I relocated to live in Wellington City (from Mabel and NAM Pasi's place), I later discovered that some tenants at the Boarding House where I was renting, were of a dubious character. So, I decided to leave. Fortunately, since I had established good working relationships with most staff members at the rest-home, one of the ladies asked me where I was living and if I was happy there. I told her that I was not happy. She told me that she had a nice cottage/sleep out at her house and if I was interested, I could move in (rent). I replied in the affirmative. She would talk to her husband and let me know the following day. Within half an hour she brought the good news – that she had agreed with her husband that I could move in the sleep out, anytime. I was excited for such wonderful and considerate people. After my one-week notice at the Boarding House, I moved to my new dwelling, closer to the Wellington International Airport where I later worked.

Since I did not have a car, my new landlords offered to pick me up from the Boarding House. It was easy because all I had was one big suitcase. Although I was staying at the sleep out, my new landlords always invited me at their main house for meals and socialising. This Tongan young couple and their three young children were God-sent. They loved me and looked after me very well. The mother of my Tongan landlord loved me the most. She called me her '*African son*' and I called her '*My Tongan mama*'. They took me to their relatives' homes, Church, parties, family gatherings, weddings and funerals. Even after leaving their place, I used to visit them and spoil their children. When my wife and two small kids joined me in October 2003, this Tongan family was one of the first people to welcome my family at our home in the suburb of Upper Hutt, in Wellington. They brought food and special gifts- one of them was a warm "two-in-one" blanket.

Later in years, during the last days of 'my Tongan mum', the family called me and informed me that mama was seriously ill in hospital, in Wellington. I was now based in Auckland (638 kilometres away), but I managed to visit her in the hospital and I prayed together with the family. Unfortunately, when she passed-on, about a week later, I missed her funeral, but I sent my condolences.

Staying with a Samoan Family

After about four months of staying with my great and awesome Tongan family, I moved to Lower Hutt and stayed with a Samoan family. The husband was a Pastor and a great musician. The wife and the children were lovely people. I was embraced in the family as their very own. I attended their church services, family gatherings, community events, etc.

Working for an Iwi (Māori) Organisation

Later, I had an opportunity to work for an Iwi or Māori organisation based in a beautiful city called Whakatāne. The city of Whakatāne is the heart of the Eastern Bay of Plenty in New Zealand. From endless coastlines to ancient forests, Whakatāne is blessed with breath-taking landscapes, rich culture and plenty of sunshine. Above all it houses one of the most beautiful beaches in the country, Ohope Beach. I was blessed to have lived in Ohope Beach suburb for the two years (2019 -2020) I was in Whakatane. Working for a Māori organisation gave me an opportunity to experience Maoridom. In this context, Maoridom refers to the world or sphere of the Māori people in Aotearoa New Zealand.

The Māori are **the tangata whenua,** meaning the people of the land, the indigenous people of Aotearoa New Zealand. From a Māori perspective, an Iwi forms the largest social units in Māori culture. The word Iwi means 'peoples' or 'nations'. According to Morrison (2015), within Maoridom, Iwi are made-up of smaller groups called hapū (tribes) and whanau (families). From my African Zimbabwean culture, the Iwi is the equivalent of a tribe. For example, in Zimbabwe we have several tribes such as Shona, Ndebele and many others. In comparison to my Zimbabwe culture, a hapū is similar to a *'dzinza'*. The *'dzinza'* concept is mostly rooted and entrenched on the rich custom of *'mutupo'*. Mutupo in English means totem. It is unfortunate that the English language lacks the rigor to comprehensively explain some of these rich African cultural concepts, notions and philosophies. As explained before, a totem is a traditional concept and belief that once upon a time, people of the same totem originated from the same ancestor, hence they are an extended family. Whanau is equal to *'mhuri'*, which is the family, both immediate and extended.

While in Whakatane, I was blessed to live amongst people from an Iwi called Tūhoe. Tūhoe is one of the Māori Iwi around Whakatane and also bears the sobriquet (name) *Nga Tamariki o te Kohu* which means "*the children of the mist*". In my two years working and living amongst the Māori people, in the paradise of Whakatane, the first thing I experienced was the warm reception I got. I was embraced by all and sundry, the staff (at work) and the community as one of their own. On my first day at work, they arranged a special welcome ceremony for me, known as *mihi whakatau*. A whakatau is a form of welcome ceremony similar to a *pōwhiri*, but less formal and more flexible (Morrison, 2019). It is an official welcome speech for a new member. Depending on the occasion, some organisations hold what is known in Māori as **pōwhiri**. A pōwhiri is a special Māori tradition ceremony to welcome people mostly onto a Marae. A marae is the place where Māori values and philosophies are reaffirmed. The marae is socially integrative in the sense that it fosters identity, self-respect, pride and social control. People from all walks of life are respected and welcome. It is one institution where the visitor can meet the Māori-on-Māori terms and come to a better understanding of what it means to have an inclusive society. Māori oratory, language, value and social etiquette are given their fullest expression on the marae (Morrison, 2015). A marae provides a special opportunity for visitors to experience Māori traditions in action (Morrison, 2019). In terms of comparison, within my Zimbabwean culture, a marae is equivalent to a concept and philosophy of *"Dare"*. Dare is a traditional gathering where cultural values are supreme and everyone's views, regardless of social status, are respected (DARE, 2021; Tuwe, 2018).

At the end of my whakatau ceremony, I was given a few minutes to talk about myself. I straightaway felt the connection with the people and the land. A sense of safety and security enveloped me. I straightaway shared the story of my village-life, as a village-boy in Zimbabwe, e.g., drinking water from dug-wells, no tap water, no electricity, herding cattle, goats and sheep in the bush and walking long distances to school. After the delivery of my brief speech, most staff members and management came to me and said that they were impressed by the story of my village-life. They were able to quickly draw some similarities between my village-upbringing in Zimbabwe and that of the Iwi set-up and environment in their local places such as Ruatoki Valley, the Taneatua Village, the Waimana Village (which I affectionately refer to as 'The Waimana Gorge') and Waikaremoana (The Lakes). Each time I introduced myself, I used to jokingly say, *"My name is Tuwe and I am from The Waimana Gorge."*

However; I need to point out that there are minor differences on the way funerals (tangi in Māori) are done in Zimbabwe compared to other cultures I have described above. For example, in Zimbabwe there is a specific time for body viewing. It is normally short and soon before the burial. While for the Māori, Tongan, Samoan, Niue and most of the Island settings, the body of the deceased is openly displayed during the mourning period. Family members, relatives and friends are welcome to touch and be in close conduct with the body. I have seen some even kissing and talking to the body. In my social and informal discussions with several African colleagues, regarding the notion of not displaying the body of the deceased during the mourning period (as other cultures), it has been mentioned that it looks like there is an element of fear of the dead. Some have vehemently dismissed the fear-factor and argued that it's all to do with the culture of respecting the departed.

Other Islands

At the time of writing this book, I have been living and working in Aotearoa New Zealand for 22 years. As a result of my long stay in this country, I have had opportunities to interact and learn from many people from different Pacific Islands such as The Cook Islands, Solomon Islands, Niue, New Caledonia, Vanuatu and Papua New Guinea and Fiji. They have great cultures. For example, I was privileged to visit Fiji in 2017 where I experienced their great culture.

Cultural Commonalties and Similarities

While I do not claim to be an expert of the abovementioned cultures, during my interactions with them in my stay in New Zealand for the past 22 years, I have come to realise that these cultures have some commonalties and similarities with my Zimbabwean-African culture. They overlap and interconnect in a number of significant ways such as the concept of extended family, the free will to share food as a community, weddings, funerals and religiosity. In all cultures, the concept and notion of nuclear family is non-existent. Everyone is part of the whanau/family. This is the very opposite of the western culture. The other intertwined relationship and interwoven links for these cultures and mine intersect in the 'venn diagram' of humanity and generosity. For example, in Zimbabwe, I have witnessed that it is very common to see someone just turning up at your house in the city (from the village), without any advance appointment. They can stay for days, if not weeks, without telling you the purpose of their visit. And it is generally considered uncultured and rude to ask them the purpose of their visit and ask them when they would be returning to the village. This is not part of our African Ubuntu philosophy (Tuwe, 2018). If you ask them, one should be prepared to 'defend' themselves because before they know it, the news of *'kushaya hunhu'* (unAfrican) will be the talk of the entire village. I have also discovered that the abovementioned cultures and mine have a huge reliance on storytelling as opposed to documentation as a way of passing information from one generation to another (Achebe, 1959; Ngugi wa Thiong'o, 1986, Tuwe, 2018). As a result of some of these similarities and communalities, I fitted in quickly well within these cultures.

Europeans (Pakeha) - Parallels Between them and the African Cultures

Based on my interaction with some of the Europeans (Pakeha), I have seen that the major difference between the Pakeha culture and the African culture is on the concept of extended family. Most Pakeha do not practice this phenomenon but believe in the concept of nuclear family. Most Pakeha who are my friends have openly asked or rather challenged me as to why I bother looking after and supporting some of my extended family members. Some have openly put it out there that sometimes, Africans and those from cultures that believe in extended family, are in the habit of unnecessarily burdening themselves, both financially and psychologically, by helping a clan or battalion of people who are supposed to look after themselves. Some of them think that such practices are as good as promoting laziness and lack of responsibility and accountability.

The other difference between the Pakeha and African cultures is that of making prior appointment when visiting people in their homes. Within an African context (and other stated Island cultures), although appointments are important and crucial, it is also okay and acceptable to visit my family member, relative or friend without a prior appointment. In the majority of cases, they would actually prepare a hot and yummy meal, not just a cup of coffee (without bread 😀), for the unannounced visitor. But when dealing with most Pakeha, they are likely to insist on a prior appointment, unless it's an emergency.

This is the story of my life:
An African village-boy in Aotearoa New Zealand,
exploring Cultural Intersectionality.

Chapter Fifteen:
My Family Joining Me in
Aotearoa New Zealand

The Pain of 'Forced' Family Separation

Before I left Zimbabwe for New Zealand, every Sunday after church service (without fail) I used to take my family for lunch mostly at one of the most beautiful restaurants called Bata Shoe Company Golf Club. I was a Club Member and my subscriptions were paid for by my employer (First Mutual Life Assurance Company). After lunch, we would visit friends and have a good time. My family, especially our small children, loved these Sunday rituals and fellowships with our friends.

When I came to New Zealand, every Sunday afternoon after church (Zimbabwe time), I would phone my family. I thought this would somehow replace our Sunday ritual lunches at Bata Club. I did not want them to feel empty and lonely. For the first few months it was okay because they thought they would join me in NZ. But after their visas were declined, and knowing that they were not coming, the atmosphere changed and took a different detour. Sunday afternoons were like a funeral for my family, especially our son, Munashe. He would wail loudly and tell his mother that he wanted me back. He missed me profoundly. As for my daughter, Maka, she was a bit mature and she tried to be brave for her mother but she would also lose herself. Each time I called home, my children would cry and openly tell me that they wanted me back.

The last stroke was one particular Sunday when I called. Annette received the call and she could not say 'Hello'. She burst into tears. She cried loudly and uncontrollably. My main concern was how the children would take it, seeing her in such a bad state. When I asked the whereabouts of the kids, she had sent them to our friends' house. At least, I was a bit relieved because I did not want the kids to see their mother, whom they loved and respected so much, in such a terrible state. She told me that I had promised her that in three months' time, we would be together in NZ. She reminded me about our wedding vows and how much we loved and respected each other. She also reminded me about how well we were doing as a family. Finally, she said there was no real need for us to leave our country. I went blank. I had no reply. I was moved, troubled and lost in thought. That night I did not sleep. This is when I went to work (at the airport), the following day, stressed and almost depressed and my dear friend Chris noticed it. My humble advice is, where possible, couples must stay together. Don't live separately. It is not worth it. Life is too short.

Family Preparing to Join me in New Zealand - After Ten Months

When the visas for my family were granted, my wife and I started preparing for their coming. They could have come straight away but my wife wanted more time to sort out a few things, including making sure our immovable assets were in good management hands, for example our houses and a plot. We also thought it prudent for her to take an extended leave from work, just in case. I had done the same before I left Zimbabwe and it worked well. When one of my Kiwi Christian friends heard that I was preparing for my family to join me in New Zealand, he asked if I had enough money for the air tickets. He gave me a soft loan with no interest, which I later repaid in full settlement. He gave us a lot of time to repay. Annette and I are forever grateful for these divine helpers in the hour of our need. As a result of such practical benevolence shown to us, we have purposely decided to help others, regardless of their background. We strongly feel that we owe it to serving others, as a form of expressing our gratitude to the Lord and those people who assisted us, especially in the hour of our greatest need. In our view, it is also a way of giving back to our communities which have sacrificed and done so much for us.

Unforgettable Family Reunion

I vividly remember one evening on Monday 6th October 2003, around 11pm, gracing the Wellington International Airport to receive my family from Zimbabwe. I waited for a very long time such that I was beginning to get worried though my wife had called me while at Sydney International Airport, Australia. I later became settled after I had asked another passenger from the same flight if he had seen a lovely beautiful African family. He smiled and his response was affirmative. I was excited. Within no time, I heard a loud voice from afar *"Baba avo. Ndivo"* meaning, *"There is dad. It's him"*. That was my son, Munashe. Before I knew it, the young man was all over me. He ran and left his mother and sister 'suffocating' with heavy luggage. My daughter Makanaka was the second to jump on me. She was overjoyed to see and reconnect.

Last but not the least was my beauty Queen-Annette. She wanted to pretend and portray a dignified image of a married African woman, but I would not have all of that. I lifted her up and kissed her. I had not seen my beautiful wife for nine long-months. That was the longest we had ever been apart in our 10-year marriage. Annette looked more beautiful than ever.

By this time, I was working for the Prisons and living in Upper Hutt which was about 40 kilometres from the airport. We walked to my small 2-door Juno Cynos Toyota car. I opened the boot and it could not accommodate the three large suitcases. I tried to put the bags at the back seat, but the doors were too small. We had to re-arrange the contents of the bags to have them fit in both the boot and the back-seat. Although my wife and children were happy to see me, they were not impressed by the small car I had bought compared to the two we had back home. My car was condemned and castigated there and then.

When we got home, they were not impressed by the 3-bedroomed house I was renting. The walls were 'crying' and watery. No insulation. The house was old and cold. Having stayed in a cottage and at a boarding house, I viewed my rented house as a 'palace'. I tried to explain but they did not give in. I was not disappointed because I knew exactly where they were coming from. I fully understood them, but in my heart of hearts, I was saying, *"Welcome to my world. You will soon see how unfair and uneven the world is"*. In Zimbabwe we were blessed with a brand new massive 4-bedroomed house which had a huge ensuite and a double-lockup garage. Our children had each their own bedroom. Our fence or durawall was made of stones and had a razor-wire on top. Our cottage was modern and beautiful – it actually housed a family. The yard was spacious. We had a big vegetable garden. We had a full-time maid and a part-time gardener. The lady assisted in the main house and a young man worked at our plot/small farm. Life was far better in Zimbabwe than in New Zealand.

Why I am labouring to explain all this? I think it is important because a lot of people, especially some of the Kiwis, think that in Zimbabwe we live in caves and trees. No. We don't. During my first days, some would ask if we had cars and houses. At one time someone said to me, *"Your English is so good. Where and when did you learn it?"* Out of frustration, coupled with sarcasm, my response was: *"Thanks mate. I learnt it at the airport when I arrived in the country – few months ago"*. Strangely, the person was foolish enough to believe it. In my further interaction and inquisitive investigation, I have discovered that some of the Kiwis are not well-travelled, and some are generally not knowledgeable about the geography of the world which has become a global-village. Just like Dr Martin Luther King Jr said, *"This world has become a global-village such that one can have breakfast in Africa, lunch in Dubai and dinner in the USA"* (Carson, 1998). Zimbabwe is one of the most beautiful countries in Africa, if not the world. Its people are friendly, hospitable and hardworking. It's unfortunate that the negative publicity in the media is biased and exaggerated. Due to its global reputation of cleanliness and smartness, Harare the capital city used to be called *"The Sun-Shine City"*. To restore its former glory, most of the once beautiful buildings and infrastructure require minimum face-lifting and renovations.

Enrolling Our Children in School

When our children arrived in New Zealand, we enrolled them at a near-by school, Trentham Primary School, in Upper Hut, Wellington. Makanaka was accepted in year five and Munashe in year two. They both passed their assessments. As I stated before, their integration in the New Zealand school system was easy because in Zimbabwe they attended a multiracial school (Midlands Christian School). While we insisted on the use of our vernacular language (Shona) at home, our children spoke fluent English. Apart from preserving and protecting our language and culture, we knew it was good for our children because no matter how long they live in New Zealand, they will continue to be bombarded with the question: where do you come from? Even their children's children will be asked the same question.

On their first day at the new school, my wife took them. Our children were the only Black African students. Annette said the moment she left the children at school, she felt as if the other half of her being had been cut-off and thrown away. She was heartbroken. She was 'bleeding' inside. She was anxious because although she was a Zimbabwean-trained teacher, she did not know how the New Zealand education system operated and how the children were going to be treated, racially. When she got home, she cried until she went back to collect them. When she asked the teachers how the kids fared, the reports were positive. This was confirmed by the children later when she asked how their first day was. Her unfounded worries subsided. As for me, I was not worried because, since I had been in the country for ten months, I had not experienced any social-racism. But at work, I had, mostly in a subtle and covert way. As I did in Zimbabwe, I would ask our children daily how they were doing at school. I also told and conscientized them not to accept any form of bullying and racial discrimination. I instructed them to report (to the teacher and us at home), anything they felt was a racist behaviour towards them. I had also assured them that if there was any problem, I would handle it myself and visit the school to find out the truth. I seriously meant it and my children had faith in me because they had seen me confronting and challenging racist cases.

Enjoying Our New-Home Country

For the first month after the arrival of my family, I took them places around the capital city of Wellington. Over the years, we have had the privilege to visit a lot of cities and towns, holiday resorts and tourist attraction areas in New Zealand. Luckily, we had a number of our close friends scattered in New Zealand cities such as Hamilton, New Plymouth and Auckland, whom we had worked together with in Zimbabwe. We visited them and had a lot of fun. When we first visited Auckland, the biggest commercial city of New Zealand, the highlight was Auckland Sky

Tower. The Sky Tower is located in the city's central business district. It's a telecommunications and observation point which gives a clear view of the greater part of Auckland city and the surrounding environment. It is 328 metres (1,076 ft) tall, making it the tallest freestanding structure in the Southern Hemisphere and the 27th tallest tower in the world (https://skycityauckland.co.nz/sky-tower/). As a result of its height and unique design, it has become an iconic landmark in Auckland's skyline.

Te Whakarewarewa in Rotorua was my favourite place. I will never forget this place because of its richness and uniqueness in Māori culture and heritage. Te Whakarewarewa Valley provided us with the first exclusive experience and introduction to the unique Māori culture and heritage. According to the electronic information, Te Whakarewarewa is New Zealand's only living Māori Village in Rotorua. This Village is owned and operated by local residents, providing an intimate look and conspicuous experience into day-to-day life in a Living Māori Village. The experience is exceptionally traditional and unique.

For over 200 years the local Iwi has welcomed visitors into their backyard, opened their doors and shared their unique traditional ways of living and distinctive culture. They have also shared their yummy food and gorgeous geothermal treasures. The highlight for me and my family was the Māori traditional songs, dance, and the use of box-guitars. As we entered Te Whakarewarewa Valley, I would easily and quickly see and identify some cultural features and similarities with my Zimbabwean culture. For example, if you visit the Great Zimbabwe Monuments and Victoria Falls, *you* would have the same feeling and sensation. Immediately, I was taken back to my beautiful home-country Zimbabwe.

This is the story of my life:
My family joining me in Aotearoa New Zealand.

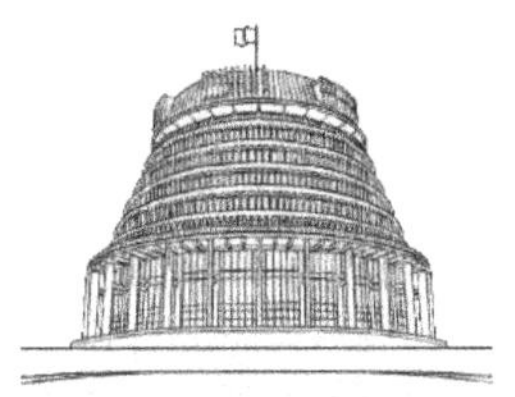

Chapter Sixteen:
Quest for Education in New Zealand – Overcoming Challenges and Obstacles

Qualifications Acquired in Zimbabwe (before relocating to New Zealand)

In addition to my academic credentials, I had acquired, inter alia, the following professional qualifications in Zimbabwe, before leaving for New Zealand:

- Advanced Diploma in Bookkeeping/Accounting, thus becoming a Fellow of the Institute of Bookkeepers of South Africa {FICB(SA)},

- Certificate in Accounting offered by the then Zimbabwe Association of Accounting Technicians (ZAAT), which is now called Southern Africa Association of Accountants (SAAA),

- Certificate in Management of Training offered by Institute of Personnel Management of Zimbabwe now known Institute of People Management of Zimbabwe (IPMZ),

- Certificate in Labour Relations offered by IPMZ,

- Certificate in Insurance – Institute of Assurance of Zimbabwe,

- Certificate in Asset Management – Institute of Assurance of Zimbabwe,

- Diploma in Personnel Management/Human Resources Management, thus becoming an Associate Member of the Institute (AIPMZ) and

- Higher Diploma in Human Resources Management (AIPMZ).

Before I left my beautiful country of Zimbabwe, I was about to embark on a Master of Business Administration (MBA) study programme.

My Master of Business Administration (MBA) Executive Study Programme

As stated before, due to my poor financial background, when I completed my secondary school education ('O' Level), I could not proceed with my higher education ('A' Level). Instead, I got a job as an apprentice - a job I hated with passion, then resigned and joined the banking sector.

Given my upbringing and background, I had worked very hard to acquire some of the above-mentioned qualifications, through private and part-time studies while working full time. Based on my maturity, work-related experience in a number diversified industries and the stated qualifications, I qualified for an MBA programme in Zimbabwe. I was excited to dive into this programme, which was very popular and financially rewarding in Zimbabwe. Career-wise, those who had completed the course, were quickly promoted into senior executive positions in many fields because the programme covered many areas of business. So, when I migrated to New Zealand in December 2002, I never wasted time. I enrolled with Massey University for a 2-year MBA Executive Programme, beginning of February 2004. Massey University is one of the best New Zealand universities, especially in management and business studies. This was a part-time study programme and I was working full-time. We initially used to have face-to-face sessions (2-3 weekends per month; two full days) and later in the last stages, we were meeting three full days (Friday – Sunday). These were full days, starting from 8am to 6pm, with very short breaks in between. This was a demanding programme, both mentally and physically. When we initially started, there were 23 in our class, but only about 13 graduated. A week before we started attending the face-to-face sessions, the university organised a great dinner function for the students and their spouses. The purpose for the event was to psychologically prepare the students for what they were about to get into. On the other hand, it was also meant to solicit the support of the students' spouses, in this tough academic journey. In one of the speeches, it was emphasized that MBA was a tough and demanding course such that it was also referred to as the Marriage Breakdown Association (MBA), because historically, a number of marriages of MBA students had broken down. At this dinner event, our oldest student was 73 years. This was the last time we saw this gentleman. He never came back for lessons. We don't know if he was scared by some of those speeches.

Since I was on a work-visa, I had to pay international fees which was very costly. In addition, I did not qualify for a government study-loan so I had to pay 'cash', upfront. Since my salary from a government department was just slightly above minimum wage, I struggled to pay my tuition fees. I also had a family to feed and look after – including those back home. I will forever feel indebted to my wife (and children) who made huge family financial sacrifices by allowing me to undertake this expensive course. Metaphorically speaking, it was like taking from nothing.

In my class, I was the only student who was not in a managerial position. The rest were senior managers and executives. However, despite all these challenges, I was always above average academically, and at times performing better than some of these executives.

Apart from financial challenges, I initially faced the difficulty of relating and understanding local examples given in class, for instance, when lecturers and students were using local organisations and companies, as business scenarios. I had been in the country for only one year and I did not know the main players or companies in specific industries and sectors. For example, they would talk about Fonterra NZ, as the main player in the dairy industry and I could get lost. However, although I encountered all these obstacles, my academic performance was within the class average.

In addition, I was doing shift work (full-time) such that at times I would knock off on a night shift at 6am and be in class at 8am. Juggling shift-work and studies was tough and challenging. I vividly remember one Saturday morning, straight from a night shift into the classroom, and the lecturer announced that we were writing an Economics test. I had not read anything. I had not even opened the 'fat' pack from the university. I got the shock of my life. I nearly dropped dead. It was our very first day to do Economics and since I had not opened the study-pack, I did not know we were going to start with an examination. As we had done for all other subjects, I thought we will be 'grilled' and 'bombarded' with data first then a written examination at the end. It was my fault. I felt bad. I blamed myself. At the end of the examination, I knew I had failed. When the results came, lo and behold, I had dismally failed. From that day, no matter how busy or tired I was, I vowed to religiously read all the material in advance, before classes. That was the only test I failed. My only salvation was to later work extra hard on the final 'big' assignment in order to compensate for this dismal and embarrassing failure. Indeed, I later scored highly in the final assignment and thereby bettering my overall average grade. I learnt the hard way.

On a lighter note, our Economics lecturer was perceived as fun and a clown by all students due to his popular daily statement. He would say, *"Students don't worry. Economics is a tough subject. Even myself I don't understand it. I have been teaching it for the past 20 years"*. The entire class would burst into laughter and ask: how can someone who is supposed to be a guru on the subject matter and an encourager to his students, talk like that?

Apart from the aforementioned problems, I was subjected to elements of unfair treatment and racial discrimination by one particular senior lecturer, who was later promoted to a very senior position. Unfortunately, instead of supporting and protecting me, he transformed himself as my chief persecutor and oppressor. He really wanted me out of the programme such that I had no choice but to legally threaten the university. I sent the university a strong-worded letter which was drafted by my lawyer. Since I was three quarters to completing my MBA, he (senior university official) even encouraged me to terminate my studies in lieu of a Postgraduate Diploma in Business Studies. I turned down his 'cheap' offer. I told him that I had enough diplomas and all I wanted was an MBA qualification. I stood my ground. When I sensed that he wanted me out of the programme, I stepped up my commitment to my studies and improved my grades, so as to ensure that he had no case against me on my academic performance. He later confessed that my grades had greatly improved. In my view, the guy was cunning, racist and unprofessional. Again, in my view, he did not deserve to be senior member of the university-staff. I really do not understand it when institutions of higher learning such as universities promote such people. Universities should be the conscience of our societies, where prejudices and any form of bias and discrimination should be exposed and shamed. But unfortunately, this is not so with a number of international universities - I have heard similar sad stories, especially from people of colour.

Most of my fellow students were good save for a few who were subtly racists. Fortunately, I would not take any of that nonsense. I stood my ground. The problem is that some of them once they think or perceive that you are weak, they would make you a "racial punching-bag".

On the other hand, fortunately, I had a lot of support from other students in my class, particularly one of my African colleagues who was a qualified Veterinary Surgeon - he knew his stuff, especially in Finance and Accounting. He was very good at figures and sciences. He was also vocal and would not take any racial connotations kindly. He would challenge anyone including lecturers, especially when he felt that there was some injustice being exhibited.

Despite all these challenges, the MBA journey was insightful, inspiring and rewarding. I learnt a lot of stuff which has carried me through to this day. The highlight for me was making a final choice between two options before graduating. Option one was to do 14 core subjects plus a dissertation (project). Option two was doing 14 core subjects plus two extra elective subjects to make them a total of 16. There was a choice from four elective subjects. I chose the second option and took *Change Management* and *Governance* papers as electives. I really enjoyed the two said elective subjects. I learnt a lot. I later graduated on 24 November 2006 at the Palmerston North Campus. It was both a great moment and an emotional one. My wife and two young children were happy to see me walk across the stage to be capped with a "cap of knowledge". Although I had a lot of support from my wife and children, I really wished if my mother was there. It was her day, considering how she suffered and sacrificed to see me through my education. Indeed, it was a real struggle, to say the least. While I was celebrating this special achievement, I was already reflecting and strategizing my next academic step - PhD which I had always wanted to do.

Postgraduate Certificate in Health Research Methodologies

After my MBA, I wanted to embark straight on my Doctor of Philosophy (PhD). I wasted no time and approached one of the most educated and respected members of our African communities who was based in Auckland. His name is Dr Love Chile, originally from Nigeria. He was an Associate Professor within the Faculty of Social Sciences and Public Policy at the Auckland University of Technology (AUT). He gave me all the relevant information and good advice. I enrolled for a PhD with his faculty. My application was turned down on the grounds that I had not done a dissertation/research project as part of my MBA. I had to do a Postgraduate Certificate in Research Methodologies, to qualify to enrol for a PhD.

I chose a Postgraduate Certificate in Health Research, since by then I was working in the health sector. In addition, my employer would assist financially if I was studying a course which was relevant to my job. I successfully completed the Health Research Methodologies Certificate. For unknown reasons, although I had enjoyed and successfully completed a paper on "Research Methods" when I did my Higher Diploma in Human Resources Management (in Zimbabwe), I struggled in the current Research Methodologies course. After being asked to resubmit one of my assignments, I approached my lecturer and argued my case, but it was fruitless. I had no choice but to resubmit, if I wanted to complete the course.

Postgraduate Certificate in Qualitative Research

After completing my Postgrad in Health Research Methodologies, I embarked on a second Postgraduate Certificate in Qualitative Research.

This was out of my own choice since I knew my research was going to be a qualitative one as opposed to quantitative. Again, by the sufficient grace of God, I successfully completed this course.

Postgraduate Certificate in International Refugee Management

When I completed my Qualitative Research, upon advice from Dr Chile, I decided to do a third Postgraduate Certificate in International Refugee Management (Internal Displaced People). The rationale of doing this course was that I knew I wanted to do a PhD which would involve people from refugee and migrant backgrounds, as participants. When I completed this course, my lecturer, Dr Chile told me that I was the only student (since this course was launched at this university) who had attended all classes and completed the course on time, with a distinction. In my view, I attribute this success to Dr Chile for his unwavering support in my studies.

My Master of Philosophy (MPhil)

After successfully completing the abovementioned three Postgraduate Certificates, I enrolled for a PhD programme with AUT. I was excited. I thought I had it all in my kit, but I was totally surprised when I was told that I had to initially start the programme as a Master of Philosophy (MPhil), for the first six months and then transfer to a PhD, based on good progress. Thus, if my performance was below standard, I would not proceed with the PhD programme, but would be awarded an MPhil. I wanted to know why. I was told that "my sins" were that I had not done a dissertation/research project for my MBA. I argued that I was informed that I could go on a PhD programme once I had completed one Postgraduate Certificate but, in my case, I had done three (two extra). My arguments fell on a hard rock - I could not win the case. Again, I had no choice but to start my PhD programme as an MPhil. I was disappointed because all I wanted was to do my PhD, not starting another Masters. I had already earned my MBA. I felt powerless and hopeless.

However, with the help and professional guidance of my supportive and committed supervisor, Dr Chile, I worked very hard and did very well. I was always ahead of the schedule. I would qualify to have my MPhil translated into a PhD, but just before six months, I had a robust discussion with Dr Chile and I decided to continue with my MPhil so that I could, at the end, have two masters (MBA and an MPhil). This would strengthen my CV. In addition, the topic for my MPhil was *"The challenges of health promotion within African communities in New Zealand,"* yet both Dr Chile and I knew that my passion was in Human Resources Management/ Employment Matters not Health Promotion - so he advised me to consider examining *Employment Challenges* as a topic at PhD level. I concurred and took his prudent advice on board.

Winning the 3-Minute Thesis (3MT) Competitions and Graduating - MPhil

I won the first prize for the 3-Minute Thesis (3MT) Competition, for the Masters category in 2012. This is where a student presents his/her thesis in 3 minutes, covering specific required areas such as key research objectives, research methodology, research theory and intend ed outcomes. In August 2012, I graduated with an MPhil. Thanks to Dr Chile for all the support. I must also sincerely thank my dear wife and children for the support in this journey.

Doctor of Philosophy (PhD) in Social Sciences and Public Policy (Majoring in Employment Matters/Human Resources Management)

After my MPhil, I enrolled for my PhD, again with the Auckland University of Technology (AUT), in April 2014. Dr Chile had taken a long sabbatical leave and I was fortunate to be supervised by Dr Camille Nakhid (who later got promoted to professorship within the same Faculty of Social Sciences and Public Policy. Professor (Prof) by Dr Camille Nakhid (popularly known as Dr Camille), a professor within the same Faculty of Social Sciences and Public Policy. Dr Camille is originally from Tebogo Trinidad. Her husband, George Schuster, is a pious man, originally from the Island of Samoa. George is one of those who were praying for me and providing the much-needed moral and spiritual support in my PhD journey, especially after some telling-off from Professor Camille. I was blessed to have known and closely worked with Prof Camille for a long time before she became my supervisor. For example, she was the Chair for our first ever Auckland Council-based Ethnic Peoples Advisory Panel (EPAP) from 2011 to 2014. The role of EPAP was to advise the Mayor of Auckland (Supercity) on Ethnic issues. We had also worked together at the Waitakere Ethnic Board (WEB), where I was the President. WEB is a voluntary community organisation that advocates, promotes and represents the interests of all ethnic communities to both local and central government in Waitakere Area (West Auckland), New Zealand.

My secondary supervisor was Dr Carol Neill who was a Senior Lecturer within the same Faculty. Due to some foreseen political reasons, it was decided that I have a third supervisor. His name was Professor Ian Shirley, again from the same faculty. He was also the Pro Vice-Chancellor and the New Zealand's first professor of Public Policy and an advocate for social justice. He established the Institute of Public Policy at AUT. Professor Ian

Shirley was highly knowledgeable and well respected within the academic fraternity.

The topic of my PhD thesis was: *"African Communities in New Zealand: An Investigation of their Employment Experiences and the Impact on their Well-being using African Oral Tradition of Storytelling as Research Methodology."* The main reasons of choosing this particular topic were:

- During the course of my MPhil, all of the participants expressed their employment experiences as a major challenge and barrier to their progression and social advancement in New Zealand. However, I did not deal with this issue since it was beyond the scope and limitations of that study (MPhil).

- My personal experiences with employment-related challenges, both in Zimbabwe and New Zealand, had a huge influence in the choice of this topic.

- I was keen to determine and understand the main key employment experiences and challenges faced by African communities in New Zealand and the impact of these challenges on their well-being.

- I was also interested in understanding why qualified and experienced Africans encountered difficulties in getting jobs in their professions in New Zealand.

Although I was technically a part-time student, the university policy was to admit only full-time students for a period of four years to complete a PhD programme. As a part-time student and a full-time worker, I was expected to take four years to complete the programme just like any other full-time student. By then, I was employed by the New Zealand AIDS Foundation (NZAF) as a National Programme Manager – African

Communities. To be honest, without the support and great work environment at NZAF, I would not have completed my MPhil and later on embarked on a PhD journey. With the unwavering support of my supervisors, my wife, my children, my family, friends and NZAF, I worked very hard and was able to submit my thesis for examination after a record three-year period. I really enjoyed my PhD journey and I had no major problems, save for external examinations. In my view, my MPhil was more difficult and challenging than the PhD. Maybe I was now used to the world of research and a bit knowledgeable on carrying out academic research investigations at that level.

Winning the 3-Minute Thesis (3MT) Competition for my PhD Thesis

Before graduating, I won the 2015 3-Minute Thesis (3MT) Competition for my PhD thesis. Being the best PhD student for the 3MT, I represented AUT at the international final competitions at the Queensland University in Brisbane, Australia. All my relevant costs were covered by the university. I had the pleasure of taking my dear wife Annette, on this trip – but I paid for all her costs. We visited the famous Gold Coast in Australia. We have since code-named this Gold Coast trip *"Our Second Honey-Moon"*.

Initial Submission of my PhD Thesis

As I stated, after three years of studies, I submitted my PhD thesis for final external examination. The university had just changed their policy, from having three external examiners to two. When the change was introduced, as students, we complained that the policy would disadvantage students especially when one examiner gives a pass and another one a fail. Our argument was that if there are three examiners, the above scenario would not happen. The university refused to consider it. I was very vocal on this issue. Little did I know that I was going to be one of the very first victims of this new 'oppressive' policy.

One morning I got a call from my primary supervisor (Dr Camille) and she told me that I was needed the following day at the university offices. When I asked her the agenda, she said she did not know. I straight away smelt a rat. My intuition started flashing "red lights". I knew something was not right. I attended the meeting the following day. One of the Professors and Dean from another faculty was chairing the meeting. Without wasting time and nor mincing her words, she said, *"Tuwe, we don't have good news for you. We have received your PhD thesis results and they are not pleasing. Unfortunately, you have to resubmit and you have 12 months to do that. As the university, we have put a plan in place to help you. I will be looking after you and your supervisory team. Your supervisors will be there to help and support you. You have to do what needs to be done. Here are the reports from your two external examiners. Do you have any questions"*? There was a deafening silence. Initially, I felt empty, then later angry. I thought I was in a trance. I got confused. I could not believe what I had just heard because I thought my PhD was *"a walk in the park"* compared to my MPhil. It turned out that I was totally wrong.

I was full of anger and irritation. I felt let down by the university external examination system which I perceived as oppressive. The only thing I was able to say (much later) was, *"Is that all? I have no comment. I have to read the reports first"*. I stood up and left the "dark" room. My two supervisors followed me to my primary supervisor's office. I did not know what to do or say. I remember telling my supervisors that I was not going to be bothered. I did not care about a piece of paper because I had all the knowledge and information in my head. I was in total denial. What made it difficult for me to believe all this was that just a few months before the final examination, I had just won one of the most prestigious University Award, the 3-Minute PhD Thesis and represented the university at international finals.

After going through the reports from both external examiners, I noted that one examiner had almost failed me (re-submit) and the other had passed me. There was no consistency between the two examiners. In my view, the one who had 'failed' me had taken the contents of my thesis personally rather than from a professional and academic perspective. Again, in my opinion, what "worked her up" and irritated her was the research methodology I had used coupled with the way I condemned all forms of racism, discrimination and injustice (including white supremacy and white privilege). She was a white woman. The other one who passed me was an Afro-African woman. I saw them later (in the flesh) as they were interrogating me during the "Defence of my Thesis". For my research methodology, I had used the unique and new "***African Oral Tradition of Storytelling***" (AOTS) because of three main reasons:

- As a researcher, I am African,
- My topic was purely based on African phenomena, and
- All my participants were Africans.

I therefore deliberately purposed to refrain from using any of the westernised methodologies. Then for my underpinning research theories, after careful considerations, I decided to utilise Labour Disadvantage Theory (LDT) and Critical Race Theory (CRT) to explore the phenomenon of employment-related experiences faced by New Zealand-based African communities. I had chosen this methodology and these two theories because they were more appropriate to address the issues of labour disadvantage, racism and discrimination in a comprehensive way (Bell, 1985; *Ngugi waThiong 1985;* Li, 1997; Meager, Bates, Dench, Honey, & Williams, 1998; *Young,* 2000; Rigg, 2005).

Defending My PhD Thesis

In her report, the external examiner who had 'failed' me made it clear that she wanted me to change my African methodology in favour of a westernised one and to tone-down my language, thinking, critiquing and findings. I refused to bow down to all these demands as I viewed them to be unjust and unreasonable, especially from an academic perspective. I believe that academia must be objective critical thinkers of our societies. Even though I was supposed to make the required corrections and then resubmit for examination, I was allowed to go ahead and defend my thesis. After about a month, I defended my thesis, via Zoom. I took this chance as an opportunity to show-case to this particular external examiner who had 'failed' me that I knew my stuff. I had no choice but to demonstrate my deep knowledge of the subject-matter, my methodology, my underpinning research theories and my original contribution to the board of knowledge. I was bombarded with heaps of questions, some tricky and tough ones. I did my best to prove my salt and worth. This was my only chance to display my in-depth knowledge on my topic. I vividly remember, at one time during the defence, I literally stood-up and demonstrated some of the following importance and distinctive uniqueness of using African Storytelling as research mythology:

- The African Call and Response Technique
- Pedagogical Skills - The Art and Science of Narrating African Stories
- African Spiritual Connections
- Dialogical and Communal Affair
- Repetition Techniques in African Stories
- The Power of African Stories
- Functions and Roles of African Storytelling

After briefly explaining each of the above unique efficacies, using African pedagogical skills, calculated moves and dramatizing, I sat down. There was dead silence in the room. The convenor (chairperson) asked if there were any further questions from both external examiners. There were none. The convenor informed me and my supervisory team that he was going to compile a report and give it to us later. For unknown reasons to me, I never received that report, up to this very day. I requested it and I was told that it would not be given. They refused to explain the reasons. I told them that this was unfair and unprofessional. Again, I was ignored and I lost the case.

As soon as we left the room, both my supervisors were visibly happy and impressed by the way I defended my thesis. My primary supervisor said that she had never seen me this *'alive and in-action'* especially when I suddenly stood-up to demonstrate and dramatize the aforementioned distinctive uniqueness of using African Oral Storytelling. They were both excited by my outstanding performance and impromptu idea of dramatizing. They said what I did had a huge positive impact on the perspective of the examiners, especially the one who had asked for a 'resubmission'.

Resubmitting My PhD Thesis

Although I was given 12 months to make all the required corrections and resubmit, I only took about four months. In fact, when I went for my defence, I thought I was supposed to have completed all my corrections. So, I worked very hard to implement all the required corrections by the time of my defence. This worked in my favour.

Instead of toning-down my critiquing and analysis, I added more 'hard and sensitive' stuff. This annoyed the examiner who had initially 'failed' me. She later refused to remark my thesis. The university had to engage a new and fresh external examiner. I did not care. All I wanted was fairness and justice. The new external examiner gave me a distinction. Not even a comma or any aorta of correction was done to my thesis. I was given a written glorious report, which clearly started that my thesis was one of the best mainly because I was consistent through and through yet the topic was difficult and sensitive. The report also mentioned that I had enormously contributed to the new body of knowledge especially by appropriately using the concept of 'Communities', and a unique African research methodology of African Oral Tradition of Storytelling. The application of an exclusive African philosophy of Ubuntu was also highlighted as an outstanding contribution. I have kept this report for the record.

It was a blessing in disguise to have Professor Ian Shirley as my third supervisor. When Professor Shirley heard the manner in which I was treated, he resigned as my third supervisor in protest. I later discovered that he had done this as a strategy to have no conflict of interest and fight in my corner. He wrote an email to the University and copied me where he openly told them that he felt that I was mistreated and discriminated, in the process. He gave a comparative example of the other students he was supervising and stated that my work was better and therefore I should not have gone through all these unnecessary challenges. He challenged the university. Based on what I saw and experienced Professor Shirley doing, I straightaway understood the reason why he was New Zealand's first professor of Public Policy and an advocate for social justice. I witnessed him practically performing and playing his role as an advocate for social justice. He was a fair man who did not allow issues of race, colour and creed to interface with his work. I will forever respect my third supervisor, the late Professor Ian Shirley.

My PhD Graduation

I will never forget the historic day on a sunny Friday, the 14th December 2018, when I was capped and received my Doctor of Philosophy (PhD) degree in Social Sciences and Public Policy (Majoring in Employment Matters/Human Resources Management). To make it look, sound and feel really African, my primary supervisor, Professor Camille Nakhid 'demanded' that, on the day, I do something exclusively African, aligned with the contents of my PhD thesis. I therefore requested my fellow African brother and friend originally from Uganda (Dr Alfdaniels Mabingo) who had just graduated with a PhD in *"Dance Education and Pedagogy"* from the University of Auckland to come and perform traditional African drums, just before I got capped. Dr Mabingo was accompanied by another great African drummer on this mission. To make it outstanding and purely African, we decided that when my name was called out, I would not step out to be capped, but to wait for Dr Mabingo to do his thing. We agreed that there was *"no hurry in Africa"*- we would take our time and 'shine' as it was my day. When my name was called, I remained stationary and immovable. The Vice Chancellor who was capping us was confused, so was the entire audience. Then from nowhere Dr Mabingo broke the dead silence. The whole auditorium was filled with tantalising and amusing African drums. The audience stood up and joined in the African way of clapping of the hands, stamping of the feet and ululation of the mouths. The audience went mad. It went on for about two minutes and everyone enjoyed it. The Vice Chancellor spent a reasonable time congratulating me because he knew about all the struggles and challenges, I had gone through. Our plan with my brother Dr Mabingo worked perfectly well.

Last "Supper" with Professor Ian Shirley

Prof Shirley did not attend my graduation ceremony; he was in ill health. I therefore thought of quickly organising a dinner, a few days after my graduation, in honour of him and my two supervisors, who had worked so hard to help me in my PhD journey. My three esteemed supervisors came with their partners and I brought my beautiful wife, Annette. Indeed, it was a great communion. We ate, laughed and fellowshipped. Each of my supervisors gave a brief speech. Prof Camille talked about how I 'conquered' and 'defeated' the external examiner who wanted to pull me down and discourage me. Dr Carol Neill spoke on my resilience and focus. Professor Ian Shirley reiterated how committed I was in the face of what he called unfair treatment of an intelligent African student and a man of colour. The brief speeches from my learned supervisors were indeed motivating and inspiring. My supervisors were teasing me by constantly calling me "*Dr Tuwe*". It sounded strange because I was not used to it. I will forever be grateful to my supervisory team. I have never seen such a committed, principled and professional team such as this. Above all, they were all advocates of fairness and social justice.

After their wonderful and encouraging speeches, it was my turn to say a few words. I heartily and profoundly thanked my learned and committed supervisors. I also asked my beautiful wife to say a few words. She initially turned down the offer but Professor Camille could not have any of that. Annette had no choice but to say a few words, teasing me to the excitement of everyone present. Annette and Professor Camille are now good friends. Each time we meet, they normally 'gang-up' against me especially 'attacking' me for my dislike of cooking at home. I hate cooking with passion, but love doing dishes and vacuuming the house. However, Professor Camille thinks I am a lazy boy. 🤷‍♀️😃

Professor Ian Shirley was accompanied by his wife Mary. After the dinner, as we were walking to the carpark, I went to Professor Ian Shirley to further express my gratitude for all the help he had given me as well as attending the dinner. He was struggling to walk but was in a good and cheerful spirit. I was really touched by his willingness, commitment and love he had for me as his student. We had a brief but deep chat. He encouraged me to keep on focusing on the positives. At the very end of our brief conversation, he said, *"Dr Tuwe, you have a bright future in front of you. Keep going"*. His words had a deep impact on me. Least did I know that these were his last words and this would be the last time to see him.

Sadly, exactly six weeks after my graduation, (on 20 January 2019), I got the devasting news that Professor Ian Shirley had passed on. I was shocked. Unfortunately, I had just started a new job on the 7th January 2019 in Whakatane which is 320 kms away from Auckland (where the professor domiciled) and I could not attend the funeral. My heart bled for my kind and professional Professor. However, I was able to call and talk to his wife Mary, to pass my deepest and heartfelt condolences. May his soul rest in everlasting peace.

While I faced several challenges and obstacles in my academic journey, I am grateful that I managed to complete my intended and dream qualification: thus, a PhD.

End of 2023, I completed Level One and Two Māori Te Reo Course and will; be graduating April 2024.

This is the story of my Life:
The struggles and successes of my academic journey.

Chapter Seventeen:
Managerial Jobs in
Aotearoa New Zealand

When I arrived in New Zealand, I was surprised to see some of the employment ill-practices I had seen in Zimbabwe, during my days as a Human Resources Practitioner. In Zimbabwe, some of these ill-practices were in the form of discrimination based on regionalism, tribalism, favouritism and *chikamarism* (nepotism), especially when it came to staff-hiring. As regards regionalism, during the days of the Federation (before independence), Zimbabwe, Zambia and Malawi were basically regarded as one nation by the colonisers, hence there was free trade and movement of people. Zimbabwe was known as Southern Rhodesia, Zambia as Northern Rhodesia and Malawi as Nyasaland. This resulted in people originally from Zambia and Malawi permanently settling in Zimbabwe. Soon after independence, Zimbabwe was once referred to as the *"Bread Basket of Africa"* such that there was a flood-gate of many professionals especially tradesmen (fitters & turners, motor mechanics, electricians, boilermakers and etc) coming from mostly neighbouring African countries such as Zambia and Malawi into Zimbabwe. So, when it came to recruitment there was generally a tendency of favouring original Zimbabweans at the expense of those with a Zambian and Malawian ancestral background. I stood against any forms of discrimination as I believed in employing people based on merit, competency and job-suitability, not the country of origin. I created a number of enemies in the process.

As regards tribalism, in Zimbabwe we have many tribes and languages. At times hiring managers were employing staff based on tribal lines. As for me, I hate tribalism with passion and therefore it had no room and vocabulary within my sphere. Initially it was not easy. However, I later gained huge respect for fairness from both employees and management in all the organisations I worked for.

When I landed in Aotearoa New Zealand, I could not get a job within my profession -Human Resources Management (HRM) - nor any other fields I had experience in, thus, accounting, sales and banking. I applied for many jobs which I believed I was qualified for, and by mid-2006, I had received more than 150 unfavourable responses (regrets) from prospective employers. I kept a record of my applications. This was despite the fact that I was about to complete my Master of Business Administration from a reputable New Zealand university. As someone who had a keen interest in employment matters, I decided to join the New Zealand Institute of Human Resources Management, but this did not help my employment situation. I still could not get a job within the HRM profession. I was devastated and frustrated. While in Zimbabwe most employment issues were centred on tribalism and regionalism, in New Zealand I felt it was mainly racism. I also felt that the equivalence of the Zimbabwean tribalism and regionalism is called 'networking' in New Zealand. Some hiring managers employ their friends and colleagues in the name of networking. Most of the "networkings' happen in pubs and exclusive social gatherings.

However, my biggest question was: why was I unable to secure employment within my profession or related areas, yet I had both the experience and professional qualifications? This question hugely remains unanswered event to this day. The other concern I had is that most NZ employers demanded Kiwi (New Zealand) work-related experience yet in Zimbabwe we had top executives from places such as Europe, Australia, USA, Asia and even New Zealand who did not have Zimbabwe work experience. In my view, this is unfair and unjustified. As a result, this unexplained and unethical practice ignited a keen interest and unquenchable quest within me to research this phenomenon in my PhD thesis.

National Programme Manager

In chapter 13, I briefly narrated some of the non-managerial jobs I did in NZ. In this chapter, I will focus on some of my managerial jobs in NZ. Just before completing my MBA in May 2006, my major breakthrough came. I really thank the Lord for His faithfulness and provision. I secured my very first managerial job in NZ, after 3.5 years, in the country. What I call "a real job". I was employed by the New Zealand AIDS Foundation (NZAF) now known as Burnette Foundation Aotearoa as National Programme Manager - African Communities. I was responsible for all African Communities in New Zealand. This is one of the roles I really enjoyed in my career life in New Zealand. I felt empowered and respected. It was not a tokenistic role. I had four Regional Community Engagement Advisors reporting to me. These Advisors were based in our four major cities of Auckland, Wellington, Christchurch and Hamilton. I was in-charge of my team and budget. My decisions and contributions, both financially and strategically, were genuinely valued and respected. I was embraced as a member of the management team.

While at NZAF, I managed to complete my MPhil, three Postgraduate Certificates and almost 90% of my PhD. In addition, the organisation partly supported me financially in my studies via a *"Staff Development Assistance Programme"* – a policy the organisation used to help and empower their staff to professionally develop. I later discovered that a number of organisations in NZ, both in private and public sectors, do not have such great staff development programmes. I will forever be grateful to NZAF. The work environment was great and conducive to higher productivity. I was also blessed to have good and supportive direct-managers. As I will report later, I had many great opportunities to travel both nationally and internationally, mostly presenting at conferences. I was with NZAF for 11 years until 2017 when they did a restructure and I was made redundant. This restructure affected a number of staff members across the organisation - due to lack of funding to sustain some of the community development programmes. In my view, the redundancy process was handled in a fair and professional manner. I had no concerns with the entire process.

National Engagement Lead/Manager

Before I finished my redundancy notice with NZAF, I was fortunate enough to secure a one-year fixed contract position (April 2017- April 2018) with Statistics New Zealand (Stats NZ) within their Census Division. My role was that of National Engagement Lead/Manager - Culturally And Linguistically Diverse (CALD) Communities. In New Zealand, CALD communities are commonly known as Ethnic Communities. In this position, my main function was to effectively engage, inspire and encourage all our New Zealand-based Ethnic communities to participate in the March 2018 Census. Same as NZAF, I had a great team of four Regional Community Engagement Advisors reporting to me. The job involved a lot of travelling nationally, visiting communities in all the regions in New Zealand. My Team did a great job. We managed to reach and surpass the threshold and targeted rate of participation. I left my exciting role end of April 2018 when my contract expired. However, I am still in touch with some of the team members at Census. They invited me in February 2022, to share (virtually) a powerful poem on "Empowerment and Emancipation" at one of their Team-building workshops. The feedback was positive. They really enjoyed it.

Human Resources Management with an Iwi (Māori) Organisation

While on my fixed term job with Statistics New Zealand (Stats NZ), I started applying for several jobs in my areas of expertise but nothing came up until my contract expired. I spent seven months out of employment and rigorously looking for a job. However, I took advantage of that time to finalise my PhD thesis. Soon after my graduation, I joined an Iwi (Māori) organisation based in Whakatāne. I was part of their HR Team, which I had an opportunity to lead. I was also blessed and fortunate to be a member of their Management Team for the two years I was there. Although I loved the beautiful Whakatāne, my biggest challenge was that it was too far from my family who were living in Auckland, 320 kms away. I used to drive to Auckland every Friday after work and go back to Whakatāne on Sundays, late afternoons and at times wake up around 4am on Monday mornings. I was now getting tired of driving long distances. In addition, the separation from my wife and children was becoming unsustainable. Although my wife would visit me once in a while during weekends, to give me a bit of rest, it was clearly becoming unmanageable and cost ineffective. Both of us were beginning to feel the fatigue of living apart. Since we came to New Zealand, we had never lived apart. The longest was ten months when I had come to New Zealand while my wife and children remained in Zimbabwe. That was the longest time staying apart and as I mentioned before, I nearly packed my bags to go back home.

Due to the long distances between Auckland and Whakatāne, I started looking for a job, seriously. I would check the NZ Government job website daily. At times there were as many as 3000 different jobs and I would go through all of them, searching for what was suitable for me. There were many HR jobs in Auckland and nearby places, but I could not secure any. Depending on the job requirements, at times I had to understate and downplay my higher qualifications e.g., my PhD. At one time when I applied for a General Manager - HR position in Auckland, after the initial phone interview, I was told that my accent was not that good. Knowing that the reason given was cheap and untrue, I escalated the case and complained to the Chief Executive Officer (CEO) of that organisation. The CEO later apologized and told me that she found that my accent very clear and my English very deep and profound. The apology was too little and too late. All I needed was a job. I later learnt that the person who initially interviewed me on the phone and complained about my African accent was going to be my junior, if I had secured the job. In my view, from a human resources management perspective, involving a junior staff member in the hiring process of his/her potential boss is both unprofessional and unethical. I found it inappropriate. However, I was once involved as a panel member in interviewing my future boss (CEO) in the initial stages of the entire process – it worked well because we did it as a group panel. After two years in Whakatāne, I got a very senior role with a government department.

While living in the paradise of Whakatane, I was blessed and privileged to connect with one of the most famous and popular former Zimbabwe Broadcasting Corporation (ZBC) TV News presenter, Noreen Welch. She relocated from Zimbabwe to New Zealand well before I did. Most Zimbabweans remember her as a result of a fun incident that happened when her and the late Tsitsi Vera were reading the main news, live on TV. When I first met her, that was the very first thing I asked her to explain. We had a big laugh about it. My wife and I have developed a very good and professional relationship with Noreen.

Regional Manager – Community Engagement & Partnerships (Central Region)

After a long search, towards the end of September 2020, I 'bumped' into a role that attracted my heart and captured my eyes. The title was that of *Regional Manager – Community Engagement (Central Region)* with the then Office of Ethnic Communities (OEC), under the Department of Internal Affairs (DIA). I was reluctant to apply because I had applied for many jobs to this organisation without any success. Since I was not going to lose anything, I submitted my application. A day later, I got a call from one of my friends and former colleague (the late Baljit Kaur) at Waitakere Ethnic Board (WEB) – which is a community voluntary organisation. I was the WEB President and Baljit was our Office Coordinator. We had worked very well together and she had high regard and respect for my work ethnics and professionalism. After seeing the advert, she was so excited to tell me about this role at OEC. When I told her that I had already applied, she was so thrilled. She actually said if they don't give me the job, the least they could do was to invite me for an interview. For me this was a confirmation.

After a week, I got a call from OEC congratulating me that I was shortlisted for an interview. I could not believe it as I had received numerous regrets from this organisation. However, I was so excited. I started seriously preparing for the interviews. I told myself that this was my only chance. There were two options for the interview, face-to-face or by zoom. I chose zoom because if I had chosen face-to-face, I was going to pay for the travel and accommodation costs. The interviews were held in the capital city of Wellington – almost 700 kms from Auckland.

The interview was tough and demanding but I was equally prepared for it. I never left anything to chance. I gave it my all. Above all, I really enjoyed it. I went through the entire process including psychometric tests, both written and verbal. In summary, I got the job and would start on the 1st

December 2020. The following day I submitted my resignation for my HR job at TUT.

About two months in the job, the government announced that the Office of Ethnic Communities would be upgraded to a fully-fledged ministry called Ministry for Ethnic Communities (MEC). I was personally excited because this is what our Ethnic Communities always wanted and had been advocating for - for many years. I was one of the community advocates. I was also thrilled because I knew I was going to be part and parcel of this historic moment of establishing a new Ministry for Ethnic Communities in New Zealand.

After the appointment of a new Chief Executive, MEC was established on 1st July 2021. We had a huge historic celebration in the New Zealand Parliamentary Building. This was symbolic and significant for our NZ Ethnic Communities. By the end of September 2021, there was a minor organisational restructure. The only thing that changed in my role and those of my two colleagues was the job title from *Regional Manager – Community Engagement (Central Region)* to *Regional Manager – Community and Partnerships (Central Region).*

However, while enjoying my role, there was an unexpected announcement in early May 2022 that there was going to be another restructure. We were told that the final decision on the outcome of the redundancy process would be announced to individuals on the 29 June 2022. For sure in the morning of the 29th, I got a call from my Deputy Chief Executive and was informed that my job was disestablished and I was affected. In short, I had no job. That was on my birthday – 29th June. What a birthday present it was? As if it wasn't enough, after a few minutes, I received another international call from home; that my mother was seriously sick in Zimbabwe. I was devastated. Again, on the same day, we were eagerly awaiting a final call (settlement outcome) of the sale of one of our houses in Auckland – the settlement date. I got a third call from our real estate agent that the potential buyer was threatening to pull out of the settlement deal. What a coincidence? What a day it was on my birthday? The most affected and troubled person was my dear wife. She was feeling for me. She couldn't stomach all this torture. It was just too much for her. I really felt for her because I hate to see my love in such agony and pain. By end of August 2022, I had lost my dream job through this said redundancy. I was jobless and unemployed. This was devastating as I had thought that this was my chance to flourish in this role. I believe all things happen for a reason.

Employment Wilderness

In mid-August 2022, just before I left NZ for Zimbabwe to visit my sick mother, I got a call for a job interview for a very senior job with one of the public sector agencies. I was excited and hopeful because I had not applied for this particular role but it was a referral after failing to secure an interview for another senior role I had applied for. After a few days, they told me I had not made it. That was my 1st interview after my redundancy. While in Dubai, enroute to Zimbabwe, I received an email for another job interview (a week later) with another public sector agency. This was to be via Teams/Zoom at 6am Zimbabwe time (due to time differences). Unfortunately, exactly 20 minutes before the scheduled interview, power (electricity) 'disappeared'- this is known in Zimbabwe as load-shading, due to electricity shortages. I was devastated. I straight away emailed the hiring manager in NZ and we ended up doing the interviews through a phone call, which was not ideal as the communication-line would at time breakdown and made the conversations difficult. The interview lasted for one hour one minute. The hiring manager and the panel team were both professional and accommodative. However; I did not get the job. That was my 2nd interview. My 3rd interview was with the same public sector agency that gave me the 1st interview, but for a different senior role. I did not get the job. The 4th interview was with a crown entity for another exciting senior role, which I strongly felt I qualified for, but again, I was rejected. My 5th interview was with a professional private organisation that caters for chartered accountants. Again, I did not get the job. My 6th interview was with the same agency that gave me the 1st and 3rd interviews, but this time for a very junior position. In the interview, they threatened me not to give me the job as they felt that I was over-qualified and over-experienced. They openly told me that I would leave them soonest or get 'poached' by their national office for senior roles. However; I argued my case and told them if all prospective employers would treat me as such, then no one would employ me in this country. It looks like they finally got my message because after a week I got a call from them; giving me a verbal offer. My 7th interview was with an NGO for a junior managerial position. Two days after the interviews, I got a job offer. At least, I was grateful that I finally had two job offers. My 8th interview was with another public sector agency- for a senior advisory role. I am glad that I got all the last three smaller jobs and finally chose the one for my 8th and last interview. Although my current job pays far less than my Regional Manager role, I am very grateful that at least I now have a job.

Just before 2022 Christmas, I had applied for a total of 30 jobs. While it is not easy to get a managerial job in New Zealand, especially as a man of colour, I count myself as one of the blessed ones. As I stated before, one of my African Professors told me that I am one of the Africans in NZ who has been blessed to have good managerial jobs. I am very grateful for these opportunities.

This is the story of my life:
An African village-boy in Aotearoa New Zealand - navigating a
challenging managerial job market.

Chapter Eighteen:
Home Visits to Zimbabwe

My First Home Visit

My wife and children had their first visit to Zimbabwe in 2005 mainly because my wife had lost her elder sister, the one she comes after. My first visit back home was in 2007, after a long and painful 5-year period without seeing my mother, relatives and friends. I was really missing family, especially my mother, the woman who sacrificed so much for me. A few months before I visited home, my mother was in constant pain suffering from ulcers. My wife and I had to make financial arrangements for her to see her medical doctor. Once I arrived, and the moment she saw me, her ulcers disappeared. She was completely healed. It was one of the most significant and amazing reunions I have ever experienced.

Between 2007-2009, just before the Government of National Unity (GNU) in Zimbabwe, the economic situation had deteriorated to its lowest ebb. The worst of the inflation occurred in 2008, leading the country to abandon its own currency in favour of mostly the United Stated (US) dollar and to a lesser extent the South African Rand and the Botswana Pula. The peak month of hyperinflation occurred in mid-November 2008 with a rate estimated at 79,600,000,000% per month, with the year-over-year inflation rate reaching an astounding 89.7 sextillion percent. Around that time a loaf of bread was costing Z$10 million (Zimbabwe dollars). In addition, bread and other basic commodities such as cooking oil, mealie-meal and salt were scarce. People were on the verge of starving. I vividly remember during my first visit in 2007, I went to Ok Zimbabwe Supermarket, (in First Street Harare), which is one of the biggest chain-supermarket organisations in the country, there were only two items in the entire store, a withering cabbage and a one-plate electric stove. I was shocked. I had been told about the terrible state of the economy, but I could not believe what I was seeing - right there in front of me. When I left the country in 2002, the economy was not that bad. I never thought it would deteriorate to such a horrible and unbelievable state.

Since I knew the economic situation in Zimbabwe, I made arrangements and sent money (before I left New Zealand), to my young brother Nathan Tinashe Tuwe who was now working in South Africa to buy groceries for my mother and send them home. He did that. Upon my arrival in Zimbabwe, I collected the groceries in Harare and drove to my home-village in Sanyati, via KweKwe where my mother had come to welcome me. In KweKwe, my mother was staying with my young brother Tapiwa Ignatius Tuwe, his wife Nomusa and their only son Nyasha. I was given a car to use by my wife's younger sister Shinga (Shie) Gurupira, who apart from being my sister-in-law, we are best of friends.

The reunion with my mother in KweKwe, was indescribable. Although old as she was (73), I asked her to carry me on her back, just as most African mothers do to their toddlers. She did and I felt that profound connection and love from her. It was one of the greatest feelings I had ever felt in a long time. The following day we drove to my village in Sanyati, Jese, near Chiguvare Primary School and ARDA. It was good to see all my extended family members, friends and relatives in the village. After a few days in the village, I took off and visited my mother-in-law, gogo Mutema in Masvingo. I had a great time with her, getting all the attention, without the interference of her daughter (my wife) and grandchildren. I also visited many places in the country, seeing my friends and relatives.

Second Home Visit with the Whole Family in 2009

Since we went home separately with my family in 2005 and 2007, we decided to go together as a complete family in December 2009. I was fortunate that the organisation I was working for by then (NZAF), sponsored me to attend an international conference held in Randburg, Johannesburg, South Africa. After the conference, I met my wife and two children (who were coming from New Zealand) in South Africa at the Oliver Tambo International Airport and we proceeded home, (Zimbabwe) together.

Visiting the Village

When we arrived in Harare, Zimbabwe, we visited a number of our family members, relatives and friends. It was a great time to reunite, fellowship and laugh once again with our beloved ones. From Harare we visited my *amai* in the village in Sanyati. She slaughtered a goat and several home-grown free-range chickens for us. We had a good time. My two teenage children were excited to reunite with their gogo (grandma) and cousins. However, the children did not like the state of the main road from our district town of Kadoma to the village. It was in a terrible state. It was full of potholes and to make matter worse, it was raining such that while driving, I could not see the surface of the road hence 'falling' into these deep holes. A journey of 97 kms took us about four hours. At times I would stop the car - not knowing what to do and where to go as I could not see the surface of the road. It was frustrating, especially for our children who were not used to such dilapidated roads. Despite this road issue, the children were so excited that they didn't want to leave the village. Our daughter had an opportunity to cook on 'open' fire and go to the fields with her cousins.

Visiting My Mother-in-Law

From my village we visited my dear mother-in-law in Masvingo. Meeting my mother-in-law was great and exciting. We talked, ate, and laughed, a lot. It was also time to reconnect with Annette's friends and neighbours, especially mai Bobo and family who played a pivotal role in the early stages of our relationship. Masvingo has a lot of fond memories for both my wife and I, e.g., the '*ndizvozvo*' episode. This is where it all started and happened – when my wife accepted my proposal. After Masvingo, we visited other cities such as Bulawayo, KweKwe and Gweru, to see our friends and relatives. We also went to Chiredzi to visit mbuya VaChigumbu, who was in her late nineties and not feeling well. Mbuya VaChigumbu is Annette's paternal grandmother.

Get-together Christmas Party (2009)

Since it had been about a long 7-year hiatus, without having proper fellowship and comradeship with family, relatives and friends, we decided to have a Christmas get-together at our house in the city of Gweru. We were so blessed that my *amai* and mother-in-law and most of our close family members from both my side and that of my wife graced this special occasion. In addition, we invited our close friends, our pastors and neighbours. They all came, in one accord. Apart from fellowshipping and catching-up, there were lots of chatting and catching up, eating, drinking, laughing, and dancing. The majority of attendees were congregated at our house for about three days. It was a good and very special occasion to Annette, the children and I. Up to this day, we always talk about this

Christmas get-together as a very special occasion because little did we know that it was our very last good-byes to a number of people who attended. They passed on.

Soon after the Christmas party, my wife, my mother-in-law and I drove to Bulawayo, the second biggest city in Zimbabwe, to attend the 40th Wedding Anniversary of Annette's *sekuru* Cheda who is an elder brother to her mother. This uncle was a Judge in the Supreme Court of Zimbabwe. This event provided me with an opportunity to meet more relatives and some senior government officials such as the then Deputy Chief Justice of the Supreme Court and the then Vice Chancellor of the National University of Science and Technology (NUST).

Third Home Visit (2010)

In 2010 I was fortunate enough to be invited to speak at the 3rd Botswana International HIV Conference, in Gaborone, Botswana. They wanted someone qualified to talk about Human Rights Issues centred on HIV and Refugees. My role with the New Zealand AIDS Foundation as the National Programme Manager was also an added advantage to articulate and tackle the topic. I was so excited to be attending this conference, closer to my motherland. Zimbabwe shares its western-border with Botswana. After the conference, I took annual leave for about three weeks and visited my family in Zimbabwe. I was so grateful to the conference organisers for inviting me.

Fourth Home Visit (2012)

Based on my first presentation in 2010, I was again invited in 2012 at the 4th Botswana International HIV Conference, in Gaborone, Botswana. They hold these lovely and informative conferences bi-annually. It was good to meet and network with colleagues and professionals in the same sector. Again, after the conference, I took annual leave and flew to Zimbabwe to visit my family. Again, I was so grateful to the conference organisers for the invitation as it presented me with another opportunity to visit my home-country.

Fifth Home Visit (2013)

In July 2013, we suddenly lost my dear mother-in-law. I had to accompany my dear wife to Zimbabwe for the funeral. This was not a normal visit and as result, we did not have time to visit friends and relatives around the country.

Sixth Visit and Gogo Tuhwe's 80th Birthday Party (2014)

On the 9th September 2014, my dear *Amai* turned 80 years. Eighty years is a milestone and a divine blessing. As a way of thanking the Lord for a blessed long life, my wife and I decided to host a historic birthday party for her, a month later, in our village in Sanyati. In October 2014, I flew to Zimbabwe for the party. Due to other prior commitments, my wife and children could not make it. I went alone. My wife was fully represented by her two younger-twin sisters (Runyararo and Rose).

Before leaving New Zealand for Zimbabwe, we had made most of the arrangements and logistics for the party, such as invitations, food and etc. We were surprised by the overwhelming support and interest expressed by people to attend and grace this historic event. Despite the fact that the Kadoma-Sanyati road was in a terrible state (a 97-km trip lasted for 4 long-hours), there were many people who humbled me and my entire family by their gracious presence. From the family, we had people who travelled as far as from Gutu, Mhondoro, Harare, Bulawayo, KweKwe, Gweru, all over the country and South Africa. We will forever be profoundly grateful. Everyone who came, made a huge sacrifice and we are so indebted in thankfulness. Apart from my mother's younger sisters (Gogo Mai Para and gogo Mutero), other family and close relatives, I would like to mention the following few people for attending the party:

- **Rev Innocent & Mrs Agatha** (junior) **Mugumba** – they drove almost 800 kms from Victoria Falls. Rev Mugumba married my *amai*'s favourite niece (Agatha, junior) who is my mother's *sazita* (name-sake). Agatha, junior is daughter to my mother's elder and only brother. In my culture, she is my mother. As a result, Rev Mugumba was so close to *Amai*. He is the one who preached at the party. Sadly, he passed in 2021. *Amai* was devastated. Mrs Agatha Mugumba came with her mother (Mai Ridhi), her elder sister (the late Lydia) and her brother Paul Kanda.

- **Sekuru and Ambuya Aruan Nyatsambo and family** – they came from Chegutu. Sekuru Arun is a close cousin brother to my *Amai*. He spoke as a brother of my *amai*.

- **Timon Nyatsambo** - my uncle turned best life-friend, flew all the way from South Africa. He is my role model loves me to pieces. He is one person I am prepared to do anything for.

- **Apostle Pater Mabasa and Mai Beauty Mabasa** – they drove all the way from Harare. Mainini Beauty is a niece to my mother and a sister to uncle Timon Nyatsambo. I grew-up together with her in our village and we are very close. I was part of her bridal line-up (bridegroom). In our culture a son doesn't become part of the bridal procession, but in my case, I did because mainini Beauty insisted that I be there due to our friendship and closeness, for decades. We broke all traditional and cultural protocols.

- **Mr & Mrs Chirombe** – they came all the way from Harare. Mainini Bo Constance Chirombe represented my late mother-in-law. She is a daughter of my mother-in-law's brother, Justice Cheda, the former Suprem Court Judge. She gave a wonderful and humorous speech in her capacity as the *vaMukurungai* (the mother-in-law). What made her speech special and conspicuous is how she boldly told the party gatherers how good and loving I have been to their daughter (my wife) and how I have taken care of her. I was impressed. 🧡 😃

- **Mrs Anna-Mercy Mashingaidze** – she drove all the way from Harare. She did not only attend the party, but donated a beautiful and colourful Birthday Cake (photo below) and heaps of other groceries such as drinks. I vividly remember when I announced to all present, soon after her arrival and said, "*Ladies and gentlemen, comrades and friends, now the party can begin. Because the cake-lady and the cake have arrived. Since it's so hot she has also brought very cold drinks to cool us all*". There was a thunderous clapping of hands and stomping of feet from the happy and thirsty crowd. She received a standing ovation. She later officiated the cake-cutting ceremony. I have known Mai Mashingaidze for well over three decades (since 1989, when she was my boss). As a result of our strong family-friendship, my wife and I facilitated and assisted her first-born son to come and live in New Zealand. It was our joy-unspeakable when she visited us in NZ in 2015. My wife and I had an opportunity to take her places in NZ and we really enjoyed our time together.

- **Herbert (Herbie) Chingono** - my long-time brother in the Lord since we were youth, drove from Harare. When I told him about the birthday party while I was in NZ, he said he would come and I thought he was joking. Lo and behold, when he called me when he was in Kadoma (97 kms away), I couldn't believe it. He ended up picking up some of the family members in Kadoma to bring them to the party. After the party he offered a free ride to some of the party attendees who were Harare-bound.

On the evening of the party, people danced the whole night-away. No one slept. The tantalising African music was loud and melodious. For almost the whole week villagers were coming daily to our homestead to eat and drink. My wife and I had budgeted for this as we had anticipated it. No one had an issue about it since it's our culture to share food with neighbours, especially from the same village.

Seventh Home Visit (2016)

At the end of 2016, since we had spent almost three years without visiting home, my wife and I decided to do the unusual by celebrating our Christmas Day "in the air", thus, flying from New Zealand to Zimbabwe on a Christmas Day. We went via Sydney Australia. We had a stop-over in South Africa seeing my younger brother, Nathan Tinashe Tuwe and family and my sekuru Timon Nyatsambo and family. We departed NZ on the morning of Christmas Day and thanks to the global time-difference, we arrived in Johannesburg on the same day (Christmas Day) and joined in the festive celebrations. In 2016, we had two 'Christmases'. The other reason why we decided to fly on Christmas Day was the availability of cheaper tickets and lack of passenger congestion. Normally, the NZ-South Africa flights are fully booked, but on this trip, there was plenty of room on the seats to sleep comfortably. We were in the Economy-Class but it was as if we were in the First-Class because there was plenty of empty seats which we "converted into beds".

For clarity purposes, New Zealand is about 12 000 kms from South Africa by air which takes about 17 hours flight, via Sydney, Australia. We had a great time in South Africa with my younger brother. We had not seen each other for some time. It was indeed a great reunion. Later my dear sekuru turned my best friend Timon came to see us at my brother's place. These were the days when the quails (*zvihuta*) were very popular both in South Africa and Zimbabwe. Sekuru Timon brought heaps of *zvihuta* and we really enjoyed them. The catch-up and fellowship were great and memorable.

The following day, on Boxing Day we flew to Zimbabwe and landed at Joshua Mqabuko Nkomo International Airport in Bulawayo, the second biggest city and main commercial city in the country. This beautiful airport was named in honour of the late Vice President Joshua Mqabuko Nyongolo Nkomo, one of our well-respected national heroes in Zimbabwe. At the airport, we were gladly received by a jubilant battalion from my wife's side of the family – her elder brother (Nelson) and three younger beautiful sisters and their families. There was none from my side. 🤦‍♂️ 😃 The moment we landed, there was 'thunder' of joy and excitement from our family members. I physically lifted and threw (in the air) all of my three sisters-in-law, one-by-one. They all loved it. My wife's younger sisters were more excited to see me than their sister (💪 😃). We drove to Shie's house one of my sisters-in-law. When we got there, there was a big welcome-surprise party prepared for us. There was a small but beautifully decorated cake with a scripted message *"Welcome Mr & Mrs Tuwe"*. There was a braai (BBQ) plenty of food and drinks. We danced and celebrated – a few of the pictures below tell the entire story. Indeed, we felt loved and genuinely missed by these lovely and close family members. While in Bulawayo we visited our relatives including sekuru Justice Cheda and family.

Visiting the Village and Other Places Across the Country

After the great celebration in the city of "Kings" Bulawayo, we travelled to my village in Sanyati to see my dear *amai* and family. She slaughtered heaps of yummy and tasty traditional chickens. We had a good quality time to reconnect and fellowship, especially with my mother. Being in the village gives a certain sense and feeling of belonging and profound fulfilment. There is more fresh air and real life as compared to city-life. I felt more liberated and connected to mother-nature, than ever before. After a few days in the village, we drove across the country seeing our friends and relatives, as usual. We visited Masvingo, but we could not go to my wife's village in Gutu because it was raining and the roads were in a bad shape.

Eighth Home Visit (2022)

In April 2020, my wife and I had booked and paid for our flight tickets, hotel accommodation and travel insurance to celebrate our 27th Wedding Anniversary and my wife's birthday in Waikiki Resort, Honolulu, Hawaii. A month before we left New Zealand for Hawaii, international travel bans kicked in due to the COVID-19 (C-19). This meant that our historic trip we had planned for a number of months had to be cancelled. It was not easy. We had always wanted to visit Honolulu. We were lucky to be reimbursed all our payments, including insurance, which we later got told that it normally does not get refunded. I supposed we had a good travel agent we had used for a number of years.

When travel bans were suspended, around June 2022, we got an urgent message that my mother was seriously ill in Zimbabwe. When we spoke to her over the telephone, we were left shaking because she was extremely unwell, evidenced by her weak voice. We urgently arranged for her to see a medical doctor. We thank the Lord that she later recovered. We had no choice but to quickly start planning to visit our beloved motherland, so as to see my mother. I thank my dear wife for pushing that it was prudent to go home as soon as possible given *amai*'s health condition. She was turning 88 on the 9th September 2022. It could be five and a half years, without seeing my mother, our siblings, our in-laws, our relatives and our friends. In the absence of C-19, we were supposed to have visited home end of 2020. On Saturday 27th August 2022, we left New Zealand for Zimbabwe via Melbourne Australia, Dubai and Lusaka Zambia. It was a very long trip, a total of about 35 hours including waiting-time for connecting flights. It was our first time to go home via this route. We normally use the Australia-South Africa-Zimbabwe route, which is shorter- but this time there no flight on this route.

Due to time difference, we arrived in Harare, Zimbabwe on Sunday the 28 August 2022 around 5pm. At the airport, we had my lovely sisters-in-law (my wife's young sisters) and their families to welcome us home. My wife and her sisters are always teasing me that I don't have relatives who can welcome me at the airport. 😃

After resting for two days in Harare, we drove to KweKwe via Kadoma where we spent a night at Annette's brother, Pythias. We had a good catch-up with tsano Pythias and his wife, Vimbai. When we got to Redcliff, KweKwe, it was the greatest moment I have been waiting for, to set my eyes on my *amai*. She was equally overjoyed to see me and Annette. We hugged and embraced with *amai*. After a day in KweKwe, on Saturday 3 September 2022, we organised a family get-together (party) at Cactus gardens in Redcliff to celebrate *Amai*'s 88th. All my living-siblings save for my young brother Ignatius Tapiwa who is based in Durban, South Africa, were present. This naughty yougman of mine has not been home for a very time. It troubles me a lot. *Amai* was exceedingly excited to see her children, in-laws, and a multitude of grandchildren and great-grandchildren. Until this day, *Amai* and the entire family are still talking about this family get-together. This event acted as a conduit to reconnect and buttress family relations. To God be the glory for giving us this rare opportunity to celebrate our *Amai*'s 88th – because many of her friends have now passed on.

From KweKwe we drove to Bulawayo to see our relatives, including *sekuru* Justice Cheda, who is currently the only surviving sibling in my mother-in-law's household. From Bulawayo we went back to KweKwe where we spent three more days bidding farewell to my mother. It was one of the most difficult times in my life. After she laid her hands on my head and prayed for me and blessed me, I broke down and burst in tears. I had a strong feeling that it was the last time to see my *Amai* alive. I hope it's not true.

We left for Harare where my sisters-in-law had organised a welcome party for us on Saturday the 9 September 2022. Many people, mostly from my wife's side graced the event. We ate and danced to our Zimbabwe and African music. There was a lot of joy and excitement especially meeting some of the family members who had recently married. One of the highlights (at the party) was where the four of us (husbands to Annette's young sisters and I) had to squat down and traditionally greet a young boy who is a son to Annette's brother. The young people of his age were delighted and surprised at the same time that we (the older ones) were literally kneeling down to a young boy. In our culture, although he is a young boy, he is our father-in-law and he deserves all the respect.

The other highlight during this visit was that my wife and I were able to visit Mr G G Savanhu and his family in the affluent suburb of Chisipiti in Harare. As I stated before, Mr Savanhu was my first manager at Zimbank. It was our first time to meet after 36 years. The reunion was great and inspiring. We learnt a lot especially on how well the Savanhus have done in preparation for their retirement. Annette and I have been discussing and weighing retirement options, whether to retire in New Zealand or Zimbabwe. This is not an easy task for us because our children have grown up here in New Zealand and call this beautiful country their home. They have less and less connections in Zimbabwe. They have made it abundantly clear that they want to live here in New Zealand. They can only visit Zimbabwe. In any case, we brought them here, without their consent. There was no discussion when we brought them here. So, on the other hand if we decide to retire in Zimbabwe, is it not dumping our children and grandchildren here in New Zealand? I have recently discovered that the question of where to retire is in the minds of most diasporans who are mostly over the age of 50. In our discussions with my wife, we have established that despite economic challenges in Zimbabwe, people are happy and have fellowship with one another. They have a life. It was also great and refreshing to see my favourite couple, Apostle Peter Mabasa and Mai Beauty Mabasa. We reconnected and had a good time to catch-up and laugh. Manini Beauty and I had a wonderful time to 'gossip' and confide with each other. 😃

Exactly after three weeks we caught our New Zealand bound flight via Lusaka, Dubai, Kuala Lumpur, Auckland. We landed in New Zealand on Tuesday the 20 September 2022.

This is the story of my life:
An African village-boy in Aotearoa New Zealand
visiting his motherland - the home visits.

Chapter Nineteen:
Building A Decent Homestead
for My Mother

As I stated before, in 2012 I had an opportunity to visit my home-country (Zimbabwe) after attending an international conference in Gaborone, Botswana. As a result of attending the conference, I went home alone. A few years prior to this visit, my wife and I had already started building our *amai* a decent homestead, comprised of a 4-roomed main house, a round-thatched African traditional hut (*imba yekubikira*), a small flat and a toilet (see picture below). In 2012, my wife and I decided to add more comfort to our *amai* by installing a solar system to electrify her homestead. I went to Harare, the capital city and bought all the required material. Luckily, there was a brilliant and intelligent young man in the village who had good experience in solar-panel installation. Within three days, he had successfully completed the entire assignment. We fitted modern electrical equipment and gadgets such as plugs, switches and bulbs in all the rooms. There was no difference from a house in the city. My *amai* was profoundly grateful. This did not benefit my mother alone, but most of the members of my village as they could charge their mobile phones, for free. Before the solar installation, they used to walk a long distance to the growth-point (ARDA) to have this facility. We also bought our *amai* a brand new and powerful radio system. This meant she could listen to the global news as well as enjoy the music.

This is the story of my life:
An African village-boy in Aotearoa New Zealand,
building a decent homestead for his amai.

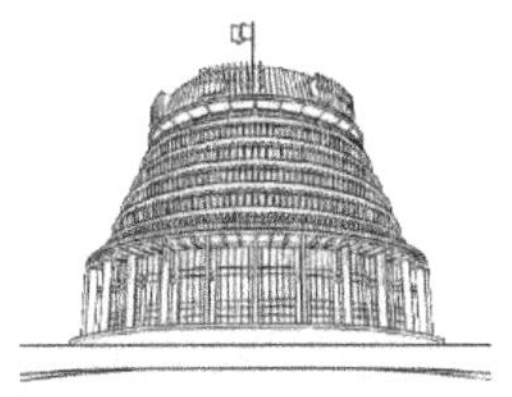

Chapter Twenty:
Celebrating My Surprise 50th

I had hosted, sponsored and performed as Master of Ceremony (MC) for many birthday parties, back home in Zimbabwe as well as in New Zealand. In fact, during my spare time, I invest or plough-back into my community (free of charge) as MC for many social events. Due to my poor background, I had never had a birthday party for myself in my entire life. My mother could not afford throwing birthday parties for us. In fact, our birthdays 'came and went' without anyone noticing or talking about them. It was not enshrined as an inherent part of our dominant culture. Celebrating a birthday was almost a foreign phenomenon.

However, sometime towards the end of 2015, a unique miracle happened. My dear wife Annette and our two lovely children Makanaka and Munashe decided to organise a big surprise birthday party for my belated 50th. While I was busy working and finalising my PhD thesis, these guys were full-on planning and organising my surprise birthday party. I never noticed anything. I had no clue. What I later learnt is that your wife and kids can easily arrange your 'funeral' and 'bury you' while you are alive, without you knowing. The only thing I remember was my wife telling me that she wanted to use a large sum of money on a special project of her own. Without thinking about it I simply said "it's okay honey". What made it easier for me to agree quickly is that in our home, she is the 'Finance

Manager'. We 'pool' our financial resources together. We use the same bank account and we both have equal access and say on our home finances. If my wife needs anything she does not have to consult me every time, especially on small and insignificant items. Honestly, I don't mind because I have discovered that over the last more than 30 years, my wife is the most prudent and sound person in financial management. When it comes to financial matters, she is fair and firm. As for me, I am too generous and to some extent, reckless. She has gained my trust over the years.

My wife and children hired a posh venue in one of the suburbs in Auckland City to provide everything, from food to drinks and other relevant facilities. In addition, they arranged all other necessities such as the cake, invitation cards and speakers. But as for the decorations, they decided to do it themselves (without any outside help), as a special way of acknowledging and appreciating me in their lives. They spent the whole day decorating the place. When they later told me, I was so humbled and at the same time proud of my beautiful wife and our lovely children. This memorable and dedicated commitment will stick with me for life.

A night before the party, my daughter Makanaka requested me to attend and give a brief speech at her function where she was launching one of her community projects. She had launched a number of these events before and I have had the honour of giving speeches. But this time around, I was under extreme pressure on finalising my PhD thesis. So, I politely turned down the offer. When I put my foot down, my daughter simply threatened to cancel her event but hold me responsible. I suggested other good speakers but she said she wanted her own father to do it. Due to my friendship and relationship with my daughter, I gave in but made it abundantly clear that I was going to leave as soon as I was done with my speech. When I insisted on the details of the event so as to align my speech, there was no clarity. I was categorically told that as a good and experienced speaker, I would simply welcome people, bless the event and declare it open. As my attention was on my thesis, I quickly agreed.

On the day, a sunny Saturday, I had a work-related function that took me away from home the whole day. Little did I know that my family took it as an advantage to visit the venue in order to do the said magnificent decorations. When I got home, there was no-one. When I called my wife, I was instructed to take a shower and smartly dress-up in my nice black suit (white shirt and a red neck-tie) and get ready for our daughter's event. In addition, I was told that we were running late so I needed to hurry up. The tone was a bit strong, so I complied without questioning.

By the time my wife and children got home, I was already smartly dressed, as instructed, and ready to go. They quickly showered and changed. My wife said we were going to use separate cars since her and I were coming back home earlier. The children used their own car and left home first. I saw some sense and concurred.

When we got to the event, my wife started talking to someone on the phone. I did not hear the whole conversation but I would tell that she was being given some instructions. When we got to the venue, she led the way into the main hall and suddenly stopped at the door. Before I asked why she was retarding her walking pace, she pushed me into the hall and there was a big shout of, "*Surprise! surprise! mdhara wakura manje*". Translated to, "*Surprise! surprise! You are now old, old man!!*" This was followed by a melodious "*Happy Birthday To You*" song. Red balloons and numerous bright colours of ribbons were flown in the air. I nearly froze before a cheerful and excited congregation of 50 guests, who were ready to dance the night away. Two Pastors gave brief speeches followed by my wife, children and then a few close friends. My wife testified about how blessed she was to have such an understanding and supportive husband. Speeches from my daughter and son touched me. My daughter said, "*If I have a husband who is 10% of my dad, I will be grateful to the Lord*". My son told the party revellers gathered, *"For others who want to see a role model they do so in books or movies, but as for me, I simply open his bedroom door and see this man, my dad"*. Speaker after speaker spoke a lot of good things about me. I was humbled and very grateful at the same time. It was so profound and powerful.

After food and speeches, we danced a lot to the sound of African beat-music. It was a day that I will never forget, especially that it was my very first-ever party in my entire life. A few days after the party, my wife bought me a special birthday present. It turned out to be the car of my dream, a Mercedes Benz (Merc). I have always wanted to drive a Merc. I am still driving this precious car - eight years down the line.

This is the story of my life:
A village-boy celebrating his 50th.

Chapter Twenty-One:
The Village-Boy Visits the
Nations of the World

Naturally, I love travelling and meeting new people, from diverse backgrounds and all walks of life. This presents an opportunity for me to learn from other cultures. While working for the New Zealand AIDS Foundation (NZAF), I am glad to say that I was blessed to have had opportunities to attend and present papers at conferences in some of the following great nations of this global-village: South Africa, Botswana, Eswatini (former Swaziland), Australia and Canada. I later visited the beautiful Island of Fiji on holiday with my wife.

These visits gave me an opportunity to learn and understand a bit more about the basic cultures of these countries and their people. In addition, I also learnt how we are wired as human-beings and how we operate and interact and treat visitors on our territorial grounds. I believe that if you want to understand how good or bad a nation is, just see how they treat their visitors. During my not-so-many visits to the aforementioned global-nations, I have learnt and gained some insights on some of the most crucial life-concepts such as diversity, equity, equality and inclusion. Often times these important issues are intentionally ignored in order to further relegate and do more harm to the already marginalised, oppressed and excluded minorities. Each time I engage on any of these abovementioned topical issues, I get fascinated, captivated and excited but at the same time saddened. Excited because I love and dream of a world where we respect, cherish and treat each other as equals. Saddened because most of the time the scale of equity and equality is too far unbalanced and unequal.

The Notion of Diversity, Equity and Inclusion

What Does Diversity Mean?

While I am aware that these concepts are fully-fledged subjects on their own, I feel it is important to briefly unpack these. Diversity is the range of human differences, including but not limited to race, ethnicity, cultural identity, age, creed, social class, gender, sexual orientation, religion, ethical values-system, physical ability or attributes, national origin, and political beliefs, political persuasions and political ideologies. Diversity is about representation or the make-up of an entity, our society.

In one of their position descriptions (PDs) for the role of *Diversity, Equity and Inclusion Manager - Inclusive Culture and Māori Sector Lead* (dated November 2022), the Chartered Accountants Australia and New Zealand (CAANZ) defines Diversity as '*the process of difference within a given setting including ethnicity, gender, gender-identity, sexuality, neurodiversity, culture, age, socioeconomic, class, disability, religion, education levels, veteran or parenting status, career break stage and many other individual factors*'. To make it clearer, neurodiversity refers to the idea that people experience and interact with the world around them in many different ways; there is no one 'right' way of thinking, learning, and behaving. Differences are not viewed as deficits but as diversity.

What is Inclusion?

Inclusion is about how well the contributions, presence and perspectives of different groups of people are valued and integrated into a system or society. Inclusion takes into account genuine involvement and honest empowerment of all stakeholders, where the inherent worth and dignity of all people are recognized. For example, an inclusive society genuinely promotes and authentically sustains a sense of belonging by valuing and respecting the talents, beliefs, backgrounds, and ways of living of all its members. CAANZ defines Inclusion as *'the practice of ensuring people feel a sense of belonging, safety and support, and are comfortable to be their authentic self'*. However, it is important to note that diversity and inclusion are two interconnected concepts, but they are far from interchangeable.

The Concept of Equity and Equality

Equity is the quality of being fair and impartial. Thus, 'equity of treatment'; meaning no favouritism. The term 'equity refers to fairness and justice and is different from equality. Equality means providing the same to all while equity is recognizing that we do not all start from the same place or level. Within the paradigm of equity, there is need to acknowledge the difference and maybe make fair and meaningful adjustments to address imbalances. This requires us to identify and overcome intentional and unintentional barriers arising from bias or systemic structures. CAANZ goes on to describe equity as *'the process of ensuring that processes and programs are impartial, fair and provide equal possible outcomes for every individual'*.

Why am I labouring on these concepts? My point is that in some of the said countries I visited, the divide between "the haves" and "the have-nots" is huge. The degree of diversity, equity, equality and inclusion, varies from country to country. For example, in one country, I was shocked to see a street literally dividing an affluent suburb and a sea of plastic shack-buildings, housing the poor. In my humble view, this is why this country has one of the highest rates of crime in the world. As someone who knows what material poverty is, I hold strong views that this should not happen at all. This is evil and wicked. My summary conclusion was: We live in an unfair and uncaring world. If we could share a bit more and be slightly generous, this world would be a better place to domicile. I will summarise my visits and experience per each nation as follows:

South Africa

I have now been to South Africa a few times. My first ever trip to that great rainbow-nation was in 1997. I had gone to attend a Christian Conference in Magaliesburg, which is about 54 kms northwest of

Johannesburg (about 40 minutes' drive). We passed through Johannesburg. Coming from a small city like Gweru in Zimbabwe, I found Johannesburg massive, gigantic and mesmerizing. The buildings were tall and numerous.

My second trip to South Africa was in 2001. I had gone to pick-up my car from the Port of Durban which I had bought from Japan for my wife's birthday present. I went by road using a Bus Coach and then drove my car back to Zimbabwe. This road-trip gave me an opportunity to see a bit of South Africa and her beauty. I had a night stop-over at my friend's house in Johannesburg where I got a higher degree of hospitality. This wonderful couple is Pastor Johana Luface and his wife Violet. I grew up with both Johana and Violet in Zimbabwe. We were youth "on fire" for the Lord. It's sad that Violet passed on in December 2021. MHSRIEP.

My third trip was towards the end of November 2009 when I attended a 4-day conference (*the 5th SAHARA International Conference on HIV and AIDS)* in Midrand, Gauteng Province (Johannesburg). This was hosted by the Human Sciences Research Council (HSRC). I was now working for the New Zealand AIDS Foundation. We had participants from most parts of the world. I was happy and surprised at the same time to meet a huge number of Zimbabwean medical professionals who were representing many other countries both as participants and presenters (some keynote speakers). I had actually worked with some of them back home in Zimbabwe.

Before and after the conference, I had an opportunity to visit my dear uncle, Timon Nyatsambo and his wife Pamhidzai (Pam) and family who were living in a posh suburb of Randpark Ridge, Johannesburg. Timon, Pam and their three children really looked after me so well. They took me places. The most outstanding highlight for me was seeing Timon's Insurance business empire and how well he was doing. Timon inspired me to join the insurance industry back then in Zimbabwe. Therefore, we both had a common interest and passion in this industry.

I later visited my young brother Tinashe Nathan Tuwe, who was then living and working in Vereeniging, which is about 68 kms south of Johannesburg. We had a great time with my brother and his family. The highlight was when we visited Soweto Township, the most popular African township in South Africa, on a sunny Sunday afternoon. I had a rare life-opportunity to visit House number 8115 Vilakazi Street Orlando Soweto, where the late and international icon President Nelson Rolihlahla Madiba Mandela lived, on and off for more than 14 years. He stayed there for 11 days after his release from prison. It's now a national museum. I don't know how we missed the other tourist attraction in the same famous Vilakazi Street - the house where the renowned Archbishop Desmond Mpilo Tutu once lived. I also visited the site where the apartheid regime killed around 176 young schoolchildren on 16 June 1976 which is now known as the Soweto Uprising. The Soweto Uprising site was emotional because I am aware of part of that history and its associated human brutalities.

As mentioned in the previous chapter, I also had another opportunity to visit South Africa where we had a stop-over at my younger brother's place in Springs, Johannesburg on a family trip to Zimbabwe in 2016.

Eswatini (former Swaziland)

Soon after the South African conference, I flew to the Kingdom of Eswatini (former Swaziland). The reason for visiting Eswatini was to check on the progress of McCorkindale Children's Village (Orphanage) in Manzini - one of the farm projects for orphans sponsored by an Auckland-based Rotary (in New Zealand). I was an active member of this Rotary Club. Our New Zealand-based Rotary Club was working in collaboration with the Manzini Catholic Church and the local Manzini Rotary Club to help the communities in Eswatini, in Manzini. After visiting the McCorkindale Children's Village farm project, I was taken to a number of other Catholic community projects such as Bee-making and Youth Centre around Manzini. I also visited their biggest city Mbabane where I had an opportunity to visit and catch-up with staff at the United Nations Programme on HIV/AIDS (UNAIDS) Office. On the night of visiting the McCorkindale farm, I was a guest speaker at the Manzini Rotary Club Christmas Party. The following day, I visited the amazing Lobamba Cultural Village, located between Manzini (commercial city) and Mbabane (the country's administrative and judicial capital city). We toured the Lobamba Cultural Village in Lobamba. Lobamba is the judicial capital which houses the country's Parliamentary Buildings, the official residence of the king, the offices of the Swazi National Council, the National Archives and Museum, and the National Stadium. The two most important cultural events of Eswatini, the sacred Incwala (National Ceremony) and the Umhlanga (Reed Dance), are held annually at Lobamba. Therefore, Lobamba is significant and historic hence my visit. In Eswatini, I was staying at a lovely and beautiful Esibayane Lodge, very close to the airport.

From the Kingdom of Eswatini, I met my wife and our two children (Makanaka and Munashe) at Oliver Tambo (OT) International Airport in Johannesburg, South Africa and we proceeded to Zimbabwe for our Christmas holiday.

Botswana

I have visited Botswana a couple of times, on business. The first time was around the year 2000, when I used to work in Zimbabwe within an insurance industry. We made good business in Botswana because of many Zimbabweans who had migrated there to work while they needed some investments back home. We visited many places such as Francistown,

Mahalapye, Palapye, Gaborone, Serowe, Lithahkane Village, Kanye, Jwaneng Mine and many others. I fell in love with Botswana and its beautiful people. Their economy was (and still is) one of the fastest growing in Africa and the globe.

As said before, towards the end of 2010 I was invited as a guest speaker at the 3rd Botswana International HIV Conference, Gaborone, Botswana. This was organised by the Botswana HIV Clinicians Society. It was indeed a blessing to be invited. It was good to meet a lot of people from countries of the globe. Again, I was happy to see a lot of Zimbabwean medical professionals representing other countries. In 2012, I was invited again to their 4th Botswana International HIV Conference. I miss this beautiful country and its people.

Australia

Apart from going via Australia on my way to Zimbabwe, I have been to a number of Australian cities, mostly on business. I have had opportunities to visit some of their following beautiful cities:

- **Sydney** – attended two conferences as a guest speaker in 2011.

- **Melbourne** – attended a number of conferences as a presenter, amongst others, the 20th International AIDS Conference at the Melbourne Convention Centre, in July 2014 and the African Studies Association of Australasia and the Pacific (AFSAAP) Conference in 2015.

- **Perth** - attended the AFSAAP conferences as a presenter in 2016.

- **Brisbane** - as reported before, I won the 2015 3-Minute Thesis (3MT) competition for my PhD thesis and represented my university (AUT) at the international final competitions at The University of Queensland in Brisbane, Australia.

- **Gold Coast** - After the 3MT competitions, I had the pleasure of taking my dear wife to the famous Gold Coast. As stated before, we have since code-named this Gold Coast trip "Our Second Honey-Moon."

Canada

In early 2011, I had an opportunity to attend a conference in Canada. I was one of the speakers on Health Promotion and Community Development. We first landed in the beautiful city of Vancouver and spent a day there. This was indeed a dream come-true because I vividly remember when I was a young boy in Form One, standing in front of my class and declaring that one day I shall be in Vancouver. Everybody in my class laughed at me and said I was daydreaming. Twenty-nine years later, the self-proclaimed prophecy was fulfilled. The Vancouver-dream was only inspired by Mr Salatiel Munedzimwe, a former Metalwork Teacher at Drake Secondary School who had bought me a nice watch while doing his studies in Vancouver. This was my first ever watch in my life. I treasured it so much. I had known Mr Munedzimwe for a while through Scripture Union circles as well as our Christian Youth Leader and role model in Karaga.

From Vancouver, I flew to Ottawa, the capital city of Canada, where the 4-day conference was held. After the main conference, I had another opportunity to share our New Zealand experiences with a small group of African community members in Ottawa. Though small, it was vibrant and interesting indeed. From Ottawa I flew to Toronto, the most populous and biggest city in Canada.

Toronto is an international centre of business, finance, arts, and culture, and is recognized as one of the most multicultural and cosmopolitan cities in the world. In Toronto, I visited a number of community-based organisations and exchanged some notes and ideas. I also had an opportunity to meet several people originally from Africa and we shared our diaspora challenges and experiences. One Sunday, I attended a church service at one of the Zimbabwean Churches in Toronto. What humbled me the most was the fact that when I called the Pastor from the airport to give me directions to his church, he offered and insisted to come and pick me. He did not send one of his many deacons and elders, but he chose to come himself. Until this day, we have remained friends with this pastor. From Toronto, I flew back to Ottawa to catch my connecting flight to New Zealand via Sydney, Australia. While flying between Canada and Australia, I got a message that I had been appointed by the Mayor of Auckland to the Ethnic Peoples Advisory Panel (EPAP) - details to follow later. In summary, apart from being a self-prophecy fulfilled, my Canadian trip was exciting, educative, informative and a great eye-opener for me. I met a lot of influential and inspiring people from all walks of life.

Fiji Trip

My wife and I had always wanted to visit the beautiful Island of Fiji. In October 2017 we were blessed to attend a wedding for our close friends' son at the First Landing Resort in the city of Nadi, Fiji. We were in Fiji for a week. We also visited the neighbouring towns and villages, historic and resort places. In summary, Fiji is about 2600 kms north of New Zealand and it takes about three hours by plane. Its capital is called Suva and the population is about 900,000 (Worldometer; 2019). It has more than 300 islands and is famed for rugged landscapes, palm-lined beaches and coral reefs with clear lagoons.

From my experience, Fiji is one of the best holiday destinations in the globe. The food was yummy, the weather is great, the people were kind and receptive to visitors. We also had a number of different entertainment activities each day, especially in the evenings, after dinner. The highlight was drinking the fresh traditional organic coconut and the daily live-music and dance performed by the local band and traditional dancers at our residence, The First Landing Resort. We all loved it.

This is the story of my life:
An African village-boy in Aotearoa New Zealand
visiting the Nations of the World.

Chapter Twenty-Two:
Community Development and Advocacy in New Zealand and Around the Globe

Each time I reflect, contemplate and introspectively examine my career life since I arrived in New Zealand in 2002, I am constantly reminded of the intense and deep discussions I once had with one of my learned and respected New Zealand academic supervisors. This academic is a polished university professor, originally from the beautiful and rich continent of Africa. We always talked about the employment challenges faced by people of colour in New Zealand. One day in the middle of a discussion, my professor looked at me straight into my eyes and told me to stop complaining. I responded in the affirmative and immediately kept quiet. In a respectful tone he said, *"Yes I agree with you Tuwe, that we have all had our share of poor employment outcomes for our people in this country, but as for you to complain, I don't think it's fair for both the system and the country"*. I was surprised by his comment as I thought he was going to support me and condemn the prejudicial and biased employment system because he had previously shared with me his employment struggles in this country. I asked him why I should not complain as well as for him to substantiate his arguments. He said, *"You should not complain because you are one of the few Africans in this country who have had an opportunity to be in good and meaningful managerial roles. I have seen you in your recent two managerial roles and both your employers have treated you with respect and looked after you so well. I saw all the support you were given as you and your teams engaged with our Ethnic communities. You made huge impact for our communities."* I concurred with him on the fact that, a few African people have had good jobs but not the majority.

It will be unfair for me not to mention one of my best employers, the New Zealand AIDS Foundation (NZAF) - where I worked for 11 years as the National Programme Manager – African Communities. My contributions were genuinely accepted and implemented, without any bias or prejudice. For that reason, I am grateful and thankful. Working for NZAF and other government departments gave me opportunities to be able to effectively engage and closely work with our NZ diversified communities. There was enough room to do advocacy work for our communities. I have included some photos to show a few community events and people I met in these roles. Inter alia, I was involved in the following community projects or organisations as a way of giving back to the communities that sacrificed so much for me:

Establishing Zimbabwe Association in Wellington (ZimDare) and Chairing the Immigration Sub-Committee

During our early days of settling in New Zealand, while living in the capital city of Wellington (before relocating to Auckland), I was instrumental, together with other community members originally from Zimbabwe, in establishing our community association which we named Zimbabwe Association in Wellington (ZimDare). In Shona, Dare means a gathering of elders who discuss community issues and advocate on behalf of the people, without fear and favour.

As new arrivals in the country, most Zimbabweans were experiencing immigration challenges. I was therefore appointed as the Sub-Committee Chair for the Immigration Portfolio under ZimDare. With the support of the then Office of Ethnic Affairs (now the new Ministry for Ethnic Communities), we were able to have intense discussions with the Immigration Department. We arranged one of the biggest community meetings in Lower Hutt, Wellington, where five senior officials from Immigration attended and addressed our community. A lot of questions and concerns were raised. The greatest concern raised by our community members was (a perception) that it was only the White Zimbabweans who were benefiting from Special Zimbabwe Immigration Policy (September 2003). In summary this policy stated that any Zimbabwean who had arrived in New Zealand, on a Zimbabwean passport, as of the 23 September 2003, automatically qualified for NZ Permanent Residency (PR). The outcome of this meeting was great because a lot of Zimbabweans got their PRs. The other highlight for the meeting was the fact that for some of the Immigration officials it was their first time to effectively engage, on one-on-one basis, with members of an African community. They also appreciated and 'confessed' that some of the officials did not know how smart and intelligent our Zimbabwe community members were. Some of them were accustomed to dealing with our brothers and sisters originally from African countries who did not use English language. It was indeed an interesting eye-opener for some of the officials. From this meeting, our relationship, as a community, with the NZ Immigration Department, improved.

Appointment to the New Zealand AIDS Foundation African Advisory Board (NZAF)

Before I became a staff member of NZAF, I was appointed as an Advisory Board Member of its African Programme. The appointment was necessitated and made possible by the active role I had played as the Sub-

Committee Chair for Immigration Portfolio under the ZimDare. Little did I know that the voluntary community work I was doing (together with my colleagues) was being noticed, nationally, especially by organisations such as NZAF, which had human rights and community advocacy at the centre of their operations.

The main function of this Advisory Board was to give strategic advice to the main NZAF Board especially on African cultures and other relevant matters such as health promotion. I really enjoyed this voluntary role. I used to fly to Auckland (biggest commercial city) from Wellington (capital city) every 2-3 months for the board meetings. However, the advisory role did not last long as I was appointed as a staff member of NZAF. My position was that of National Programme Manager–African Communities of NZAF.

Advisor to the Zimbabwe Association in New Zealand (ZANZ)

As a Zimbabwean, I automatically qualified to become a member of the Zimbabwe Association in New Zealand (ZANZ) when we relocated from Wellington to Auckland. It was fortunate that ZANZ was being led by a seasoned and competent Executive Committee comprising of people such as Titus Katiyo, Moses Chamboko, Charles Namba and Japhet Ncube. My role as the National Programme Manager–African Communities for NZAF, gave me an added advantage of closely working with all African communities, including ZANZ. It was indeed an honour and pleasure.

Closely Working with African Regional Organisations in New Zealand

{African Communities Forum Incorporated (ACOFI), The African Communities Council Wellington (ACCW) and the Canterbury African Council (CAC)}

I felt empowered and respected in my position at NZAF. I was in-charge of my team and budget. My decisions and contributions, both financially and strategically, were genuinely valued and respected by all in the organisation. I was sincerely embraced as a member of the management team. This created an environment where I was able to effectively engage with our communities, especially when it came to assisting them financially in their community projects. I would also travel a lot throughout the country closely working with regional African organisations such as ACOFI in Auckland (Northern Region), ACCW in Wellington (Central Region) and CAC in Christchurch (Southern Region) in New Zealand. I am grateful for the 11 years at NZAF.

Appointment to the Ethnic Peoples Advisory Panel (EPAP)

As I mentioned before, while I was flying from a conference in Canada to New Zealand, I received an email that I had been just appointed by the Mayor of Super City of Auckland to the Ethnic Peoples Advisory Panel (EPAP). This was the first-ever Ethnic Panel appointed by the Auckland Council. It was indeed an honour to be appointed to this high-profile panel. The EPAP panel represented more than 200 ethnic groups in NZ. The recruitment process was rigorous and intense. Only 12 members were finally appointed out of thousands of applications. This was a 3-year term. Our team of 12 met once a month, under the able leadership (chair) of Professor

Camille Nakhid. Apart from the EPAP, there were other panels representing other communities such as the Māori Panel, the Pacific Panel and the Disability Panel. There was talk of a youth Panel. As panel members we were fortunate to learn a lot and also blessed to have opportunities to meet a number of high-profile individuals and organisations from the globe. This also gave us an opportunity to create more relations with people and community organisations from both our ethnic communities and other ethnicities in NZ, and the globe. The Council also dedicated a councillor to each of the panels as the main contact person. During Council meetings, each dedicated Councillor would update the Council on what was happening within Ethnic communities and vice visa. This worked very well for both the EPAP and the Council.

President of the Waitakere Ethnic Board (WEB)

I was privileged and blessed to be nominated as the President of the Waitakere Ethnic Board (WEB) for a period of four years (2012 – 2016). WEB is an Incorporated Society established on 20th September 2003, as a result of calls from Waitakere's migrant and refugee communities for the creation of a multi-ethnic advisory body that would champion and advocate for ethnic communities, domiciled mainly in the Waitakere area. Apart from advocacy, WEB stands for, inter alia, the following:

- Provides a 'voice' for ethnic communities to influence what the Council and the Government do,

- Identifies the needs of the ethnic communities in West Auckland,

- Enables groups to share common interests and ideas while maintaining their own identity and helping ethnic communities in capacity building.

Appointment to the Waitemata Police Ethnic Board

Later around early 2017, I was appointed as a member of the Auckland-based Waitemata Police Ethnic Advisory Board. The chief purpose and objective of this Board was to give cultural and strategic advice to the Police in our geographic area. We used to meet once per month. I resigned in early 2019 when I relocated to the Paradise of Whakatane.

Zimbabwe Diaspora Nation Building Initiative (ZDNBI) & ZDNBI Advisory Council Member

In early 2019, I was approached to join the Zimbabwe Diaspora Nation Building Initiative (ZDNBI) to represent New Zealand. The purpose, vision and mission of ZDNBI are as follows:

- **The Purpose:** to provide a conduit and platform for the expression of a united global Zimbabwean Diaspora voice and network with the government, politicians, both public and private organizations for the benefit of the Zimbabwean community at large.

- **The Vision:** to have a society in which all individuals, including those of the Zimbabwe Diaspora, have equitable opportunities to realize their full potential and to participate meaningfully in Zimbabwe's Nation Building Enterprise.

- **The Mission Statement:** to contribute to the facilitation of the creation of a conducive environment where principal stakeholders in Zimbabwe can find each other as compatriots who work together to evolve a framework of national unity that achieves progressive socio-economic and political outcomes and to provide a community point of contact and a recognized group-voice for the global Zimbabwean Diaspora.

Due to work pressures and family commitments, I opted to resign from the ZDNBI Executive to become a member of its Advisory Council.

This is the story of my life:
An African village-boy in Aotearoa New Zealand,
contributing to Community Development and Advocacy.

Community Development Work in Pictures

Above: Dr Tuwe giving a speech at his friend's graduation ceremony in Auckland NZ (2007)

Below: Tuwe presenting prize - "Smartly Dressed Couple" at a Couples' Fellowship, in Auckland organised by the Zimbabwe Association in NZ (2008)

2010

Above: Dr Tuwe with Mr Michel Sidibé, Executive Director of UNAIDS in Auckland

Left: With Former Mayor of Christchurch City, Her Worship Lianne Dalziel (former Minister of Immigration) at a Community Event in Christchurch

Below: with former PM Hon Helen Clark at NZAF National Offices

2011

Top: Dr Tuwe with the 1st The Ethnic People Advisory Panel (EPAP) Team

Middle: Dr Tuwe & NZAF African Advisory Board Members

Left: Dr Tuwe speaking at a conference in Canada

2012
Top: - NZAF staff congratulating Miss Africa, Hamilton, NZ
Left: Dr Tuwe, former Zimbabwe Ambassador Jacqueline Zwambila, Mayor Len Brown & Vatican Ambassador

2014

(R) Dr Tuwe & Zimbabwe Minister of Health, Dr David Parirenyatwa
(L) Dr Tuwe & Zimbabwe Permanent Secretary of Health, Dr Gerald Gwinji – 2014 HIV UNAIDS International Conf in Melbourne, Australia

*Above: Dr Tuwe & members of NZ African Communities at
NZ Parliament (2014)*

*Below: Dr Tuwe and NZAF Team hosting a National Youth
Talent Show in Wellington (2014)*

2014

*Above: PhD Fellow Students (before graduation), Academic Writing Retreat
in Hillsborough, Auckland*
Below: *Tuwe with the New Papua Guinea (NPG) Traditional Performance Group
HIV UNAIDS International Conference in Melbourne, Australia*
Bottom: *Dr Tuwe, Botswana Minister of Foreign Affairs Hon Phandu Skelemani,
Mr Chris Jones, Honorary Consul of Botswana in NZ*

2015

Above: with Phil Goff,
Mayor of Auckland at WEB function

Left: Dr Tuwe
& Waitakere Councillor &
Deputy Mayor of Auckland Penny
Hulse - WEB AGM

Below: With former NZ Prime
Minister Hon John Key

Above: 2016 Dr Tuwe with WEB Executive Committee – as WEB President

*Dr Tuwe and son Munashe After a Speech
at the "Zimbabwe #thisflag Campaign" in
Auckland (2016)*

Above: Dr Tuwe as Guest Speaker at the Africa Day Celebration in Auckland
(May 2017)

Below: (L to R): Dr Tuwe, former NZ Prime Minister, Hon Jacinda Ardern (when she was MP), Dame Susan Devoy (former Race Relations Commissioner) and MP Hon Priyanca Radhakrishnan (now Minister for Ethnic Communities) at the Africa Day Celebration.

Above: Tuwe at Stats NZ Community Events in Auckland (2017)

Below: Dr Tuwe, Daughter Makanaka Tuwe and Professor Ngugi waThiong (International Author based in the USA) at his International Literature Presentation in Auckland, NZ (2018)

Chapter Twenty-Three:
"Ploughing Back into the Community"

As I mentioned before, when growing up, my *amai* always taught me and my siblings to be kind and helpful, especially to those in need. Materially poor, as she was, I saw my *amai* giving from her abject poverty. She taught us to generously give back to the community(s) that have sacrificed so much to be what we are today. When I look back, my *amai* was materially poor but very rich in cultural values and humane principles such as kindness, care, love and empathy. She always told us how blessed and spiritually gratifying it is to give than to receive. Especially helping and assisting orphans and widows. In accounting and community development terms, this principle is called '*Ploughing Back into the Community*'. This means giving back to the communities that once upon a time contributed (in one way or the other) to us to become what we are today. In the business world, it is known as '*Corporate Social Responsibility*'. This is where corporate organisations give back to communities in which they do business, for example, by building schools or constructing roads for local communities.

My Involvement with the Zimbabwe Rural Schools Library Trust (ZRSLT) in New Zealand

Around 2012, I had an interesting and empowering discussion with Mr Driden Kunaka, the founder and current Chair of Zimbabwe Rural Schools Library Trust (ZRSLT- The Trust) in NZ. We talked about the work the Trust was doing. He passionately articulated about the Trust and how the project would benefit and empower our disadvantaged rural schools and students, back home in Zimbabwe. The moment he mentioned about the disadvantaged rural learners, I had a strong flash-back and was taken aback in my old schooldays in the village where a class of 40 students could share 2-3 torn textbooks. Immediately, my life-history, poor family background and how I struggled to access education was resuscitated and became vividly alive within me. It resonated with my past education struggles. Based on my past experience, the love for education and the staunch belief in the emancipatory powers of education, I straightaway registered my keen interest to effectively participate in the Trust project. For a moment, I re-lived my challenging upbringing. It was laid bare before me. My heart yearned to help. I felt the pain. I felt empty. My heart bled. And I straightaway remembered what my *amai* had taught me and my siblings. To be kind to all humanity, but especially to the orphans and widows. I vividly remembered the famous quotation by Pope Francis which says: *"Rivers do not drink their own water; trees do not eat their own fruits; the sun does not shine on itself and flowers do not spread their fragrance for themselves. Living for others is a rule of nature. We are all born to help each other. No matter how difficult it is... Life is good when you are happy; but much better when others are happy because of you"*. I was in for the ZRSTL project. This was the genesis of an exciting journey with ZRSTL. Since then, I have never looked back. I am currently the Deputy Chair of the Trust in New Zealand. For the record, the Trust was registered in Zimbabwe on 27 January 2012 and officially launched publicly on 8 May

2012 in Zimbabwe. The New Zealand chapter was registered on 13 February 2013.

When I met Mr Kunaka, I was already working for the New Zealand AIDS Foundation as National Programme Manager - African Communities. This role gave me the opportunity to work with all African Communities in NZ. Through NZAF, we attended and supported every activity hosted by the Trust. For example, my wife and I have participated in all the annual Fundraising events, including the 3.8 kms-run, held at the scenic Rotorua Lake in the City of Hamilton, New Zealand. In 2019, I was one of the best sellers for the ZRSLT raffle tickets, raising funds to ship our third cargo of books to Zimbabwe, tentatively in early 2023.

Donating Books to Chiguvare Primary School, in Sanyati, Zimbabwe

In early 2016, the Trust sent its first ever cargo of books to Zimbabwe and 25 schools benefited. As someone who had played a significant role since the inception of the Trust, I was offered an opportunity to choose a school of my choice, one of the 25. I chose Chiguvare Primary School, in Sanyati, near ARDA. The school is about 2 kms from my newly founded homestead, in my village. Chiguvare received a total of 1016 brand new books. Thanks to ZRSLT. The books were handed over to the school on Parents' Day Celebration in 2016. I am told the teachers, parents and mostly students were so excited to have these books. Later on, in December 2016 my wife and I visited Zimbabwe to see family and friends. In mid-January 2017, we proceeded to Sanyati to see my dear *amai*. When word got to the 'ears' of the Chiguvare School Headmaster and school management that we were around, they secretly organised a surprise welcome party for us. A day before the party, the headmaster invited me to visit the school library so that I could see the donated books in the library. After the library tour, the headmaster requested one of the parents who was a Councillor to offer a prayer as thanksgiving to the Lord, for the books. Instead of being excited, I cried. At a glance, there was a clear demarcation of the old and new donated books. Although the school has beautiful buildings and infrastructure, it was heavily under-resourced in books. At that moment, the idea and dream I had carried for many years was birthed, thus, sponsoring a few orphans in their school fees. Again, my heart bled. I vividly remembered all the struggles and hardships I had faced when I was a village school-going boy. I 'heard' a silent and soft voice strongly urging me to urgently sponsor and help these orphan-children, in a small way.

After all this the headmaster persuaded us (my wife and I) to prolong our stay in the village by a day since he would be unable to attend the party the following day due to the call of duty in the nearby town of Kadoma. We couldn't because our schedule was tight. We were racing against time. We had a lot of friends and relatives to visit throughout the country. As a result, the party went ahead the following day on a Saturday, sadly without the headmaster. However, the headmaster was represented by his deputy. In addition, the headmaster's wife who was a teacher at Sanyati Government High School attended the party. Later the headmaster's wife approached my wife and I and kindly put a request for books for her high school - if another opportunity came-up. Although I did not promise anything, I took the request seriously.

On the party-day, firstly we were taken on a school tour. After the tour, we had wonderful and inspiring speeches delivered by some guests. I was also given an opportunity to say a few words. For me, although every speaker said good things, my heart was captured by a sermon by the local Pastor. His message was titled *'Ziva Kwawakabva/Yazi Odabuka Khona/Remember Your Roots.'* This simply means remembering, where one originally came from, 'the village' and the humble beginnings. This also calls for practical actions (not just words) to demonstrate one's commitment and love for one's village. His message was focused on '*Having a Heart for the Communities.*' He emphasised the importance of "*Remembering One's Roots*" thus, helping and assisting the communities that gave us so much, in order to be where we are today. He preached from the Book of Genesis on Joseph, the one who remembered and saved his entire family and the nation of Israel from starvation and later brought them over in the foreign land of Egypt, for a better life. His message resonated with me, my situation and the story of my life: *An African Village-Boy in Aotearoa New Zealand.*

The school slaughtered a goat for us. We ate as a community as we fellowshipped together. After the communal lunch, the school's Traditional Marimba School Band played their best songs. The songs were pregnant and packed with deep and powerful traditional stories - (photos attached). We joined in dancing with the students, to their delight. It took me back to my olden days, as a village-boy. It was so good and refreshing to see the innocent little children happy and taking to the dancing-floor. It was one of my happiest days in my entire life. I felt a deep sense of inner-fulfilment and joy unspeakable.

Sponsoring Orphans at Chiguvare Primary School

Soon after the Chiguvare Primary School party, both my wife and I had a burden to help a few orphans from this school, by paying their school fees. We talked and prayed about it. We both agreed to help. We asked the headmaster to choose five best students from each class (Grades 3-7) with effect from the 2017 academic year. The criteria were: first and foremost, they had to be orphans, and then last but not the least, good academic performers. We did not want to be involved in the selection process. We also wanted to remain completely anonymous to both the students and their guardians. We did exactly that. Unfortunately, or fortunately, after four years (in 2020), one of the staff members at Sanyati Government High school, whom we were dealing with, when paying the fees, was so touched when she discovered that our two children (the orphans) who were by then in Form 2 and 3, did not know who was paying their fees. She was further disturbed that we had not talked to any of the students since they were at primary school. Without asking us, she summoned the students in her office and called us in New Zealand. Initially, I was so excited to talk to them, for the first time in four years, but the moment they said, *"Thank you for paying fees for us,"* I could not stand it. My heart bled. My entire struggles as a village-boy, became so vivid and strong. I thought how my mother suffered and struggled to pay fees for me and my siblings. Deep down in my heart, I had one question that bothered me so much: *If my loving, caring and hard-working mother struggled that much to raise school fees for me and my siblings, then what about the plight of these orphans – no parents at all?* In my view, their plight was worse than mine. It was as if someone was shredding my heart into pieces. I felt the pain. That day I wished I could suddenly get rich. I would send all the orphans in this entire world to school. Again, I remembered the following cited quotation: *"I learned to give not because I have much but because I know exactly how it feels to have nothing"* (Author Unknown).

Our 'daughter' who was in grade 7 (in 2017), completed her "O" Levels in 2021. One of the two boys is completing his "A" Levels this year (2024). The other boy completed his "O" Level in 2023. We are hoping that the boys will do well and proceed with their education and achieve their life-dreams.

It is our humble wish and sincere prayer that the Lord gives us the grace and resources to be able to see these our lovely 'children' (students) up to university level and beyond. They deserve the best – just like anybody else. And they have the potential to make it in life. God willing and upon the provision of more resources, we would like to help more orphaned children.

As long as what we are doing brings a simple smile on the faces of these lovely and innocent children, my wife and I are the happiest creatures under the blue sky.

Donating Books to Sanyati Government High School (SGHS), in Sanyati, Zimbabwe

In 2018, ZRSLT sent a second cargo of books from New Zealand to Zimbabwe. A total of 46 schools were beneficiaries of this donation. Again, I was given an opportunity to choose a benefiting school. I chose Sanyati Government High School (SGHS) – in fulfilment of the request of the headmaster's wife. This is where some of our current sponsored children were learning. I thank the Lord for enabling us to keep the promise. On the day of the book hand-over ceremony, my elder brother Peter Tuwe represented me and ZRSLT. The then Headmistress, Mai Tinago presided over the event.

Future Initiatives

In the absence of the global epidemic COVID-19, the Trust had planned to send its third cargo of books to Zimbabwe in 2020. A lot of our planned activities such as fundraising were adversely affected by this epidemic. If all goes well, we are looking forward to sending this cargo later this year (2024). If I get another opportunity to choose a school, I plan to bless one in Mhondoro-Ngezi where I did most of my primary education, before relocating to Sanyati. We will partner with a Church-based organisation which is doing a great job in this area within the education space.

Interview with Studio 7 Voice of America (VOA) Zimbabwe

In October 2023, in my capacity as the Deputy Chair of the ZRSLT (New Zealand Chapter), I was given an opportunity to have a radio interview with a Washington DC, USA-based Studio 7 Voice of America

(VOA) Zimbabwe. The interviewer was Mr Jonga Kandemiri. I was given an opportunity to share our 10-year history and journey of shipping from New Zealand to Zimbabwe rural schools. The interview received wide coverage and good feedback especially from Zimbabweans who are dotted around the globe.

This is the story of my life:
An African village-boy in Aotearoa New Zealand -
'Ploughing Back into the Community.'

  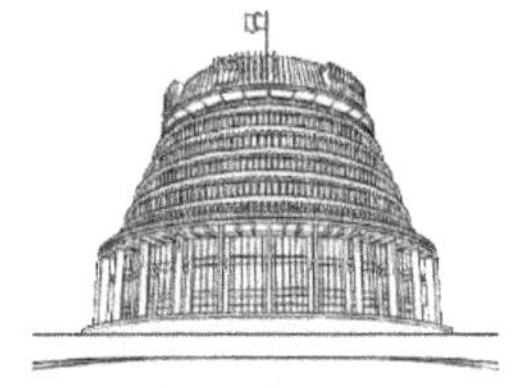

Epilogue

This is the story of my life,
from humble beginnings in the remote village of Mhondoro Ngezi
to where the Lord has taken me.

I believe that one's background does not determine one's destination. My humble and poor upbringing, no matter how bad it was, did not define my ultimate future. I have learnt that with hard work, focus and determination, coupled with the God-factor, all things are possible. In addition, I have discovered that no matter what life throws at you, keep pressing on and never give up. You can rise over and above the challenges and obstacles.

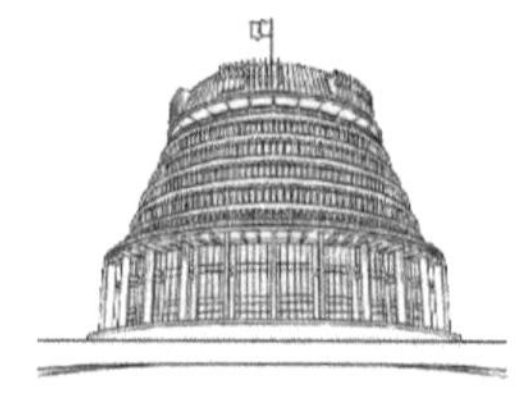

References

Achebe, C. (1959). *Things fall apart*. Greenwich, CT: Fawcett.

Carson, C. (1998). *The Autobiography of Martin Luther King, Jr.* New York, USA: Grand Central Publishing

Chavunduka, G. (1978). *Traditional Healers and the Shona Patient*. Gweru, Zimbabwe: Mambo Press.

Edward Riini, (2020). Verbal Communication 11 October 2020

DARE. (2021). Continuity & Novelty Amidst Challenges: COVID-19 & Natural Disasters. Holy Trinity Collage Journal Continuity Issue Number 13

Faal, C. (2009). The Partition of Africa.

International Convention on the Elimination of All Forms of Racial Discrimination (ICERD). (1969). *International Convention on the Elimination of All Forms of Racial Discrimination*. Switzerland, Geneva: ICERD. Retrieved from http://www.bing.com/search?q=International+Convention+on+the+Elimination+of+All+Forms+of+Racial+Discrimination,+(1969)&src=IE-SearchBox&FORM=IESR02

Johann, B. (2006, August, 24, 2015). *Ubuntu African life coping skills: theory and practice, in Recreation Linkages between Theory and Praxis in Educational Leadership*. Presented at the meeting of the The Commonwealth Council for Educational Administration and Management Conference, South Africa. Retrieved from

http://www.topkinisis.com/conference/CCEAM/wib/index/outli
ne/PDF/BROODRYK%20Johann

Lancaster House Agreement. (1979). *Lancaster House Agreement: Southern Rhodesia Constitution Conference Held At Lancaster House, Londom Sepember - December 1979 Report.* London, UK.

Mandela, N. (1994). *A Long Walk to Freedom: The Autobiography of Nelson Mandela.* Boston, USA: Little, Brown & Company

Morrison, S.(2015). Māori Made Easy. For everyday leanerns of the Māori langauige.

Morrison, S.(2019). Māori at Work. The Everyday guide to using te reo Māori lin the workplace.

Mubako, S. (1975). The Quest for Unity in the Zimbabwe Liberation Movement. *A Journal of Opinion, 5*(1), 5-17.

Mutasa, N. M. (1978). *Mapatya.* Harare, Zimbabwe: Longman.

New Zealand Beehive News (2004): Work permits for Zimbabwe nationals extended (https://www.beehive.govt.nz/release/work-permits-zimbabwe-nationals-extended*)*

Ngugi wa Thiong'o. (1964). Weep Not, Child. New York, USA: Penguin Group.

Ngugi wa Thiong'o. (1965). The River Between. New York, USA: Penguin Group.

Ngugi wa Thiong'o. (1967). A Grain of Wheat. London, United Kingdom: Penguin Classics.

Ngugi wa Thiong'o. (1982). Devil on the Cross (English translation of Caitaani mutharaba-Ini). Nairobi, Kenya: Heinemann Educational Books (East Africa) Ltd 1980.

Ngugi wa Thiong'o. (1986). Decolonising the Mind: The Politics of Language in African Literature. Nairobi, Kenya: East African educational Publishers.

Ngugi wa Thiong'o. (1998). The allegory of the cave: Language, democracy and a New World order! Black Renaissance/Renaissance Noire, 1(3), 25-46.

Ngugi wa Thiong'o. (2000). African Languages and Global Culture in the Twenty First Century in African Visions: Literary Images. Cheryl B. Mwari, Silvia Federici and Joseph McLaren. Presented at the meeting of the Political Change, and Social Change in Contemporary Africa,, Westport, Cape Town, South Africa

Nhemachena, A., & Warikandwa, T. V. (2019). *From African Peer Review Mechanisms to African Queer Review Mechanisms? Robert Gabriel Mugabe, Empire and the Decolonisation of African Orifices*

Sarkin, J., & Koenig, M. (2011). Developing the Right to Work: Intersecting and Dialoguing Human Rights and Economic Policy. The Johns Hopkins University Press. *Human Rights Quarterly, 33,* 1-42.

Sky City Auckland. (2021), .https://skycityauckland.co.nz/sky-tower/

Smith, I. D. (1997). *The Great Betrayal: The Memoirs of Ian Douglas Smith.* London, UK: John Blake Publishing.

Smith, R. K. M. (2003). *Textbook on International Human Rights Law.*

Tutu, D., & Tutu, M. (2014). *The Book of Forgiving* USA: William Collins.

Tuwe, K. (2012). *The challenges of health promotion within African communities in New Zealand* (A thesis submitted to Auckland University of Technology (AUT) in fulfilment of the requirements for the degree of Master of Philosophy). Auckland University of Technology (AUT) Auckland, New Zealand.

Tuwe, K. (2016). The African Oral Tradition Paradigm of Storytelling as a Methodological Framework: Employment Experiences for African communities in New Zealand: 21st Century Tensions and Transformation in Africa, Deakin University, 28th-30th October, 2015. *African Studies Association of Australasia and the Pacific (AFSAAP), Proceedings of the 38th AFSAAP Conference.*

Tuwe, K. (2018). *African Communities in New Zealand: An Investigation of their Employment Experiences and the Impact on their well-being.* (A thesis submitted to Auckland University of Technology (AUT) in the fulfillment of the degree of Doctor of Philosophy (PhD) in Social Sciences and Public Policy. Auckland University of Technology Auckland, New Zealand.

United Nations News. (2019): Global perspective Human stories. Zimbabwe 'facing worst hunger crisis in a decade'

Universal Declaration of Human Rights. (1948). Adopted 10 Dec. 1948, G.A. Res. 217A (III), U.N. GAOR, 3d Sess., art. 22, U.N. Doc. A/RES/3/217A (1948) [hereinafter UDHR]: Everyone, as a member of society, has the right to social security and is entitled to realization. *September 18, 2014.* Retrieved from http://www.bing.com/search?q=Universal+Declaration+of+Human+Rights+(1948).&src=IE-SearchBox&FORM=IESR02

University of Pennsylvania - African Studies Center. (1998).DRC: Zimbabwean, Angolan troops arrive to back Kabila 1998.8.21. (https://www.africa.upenn.edu/Hornet/irin_82198.html)

Whakarewarewa. (2021), https://whakarewarewa.com/experiences/maori-cultural-performance/

Worldometer (www.Worldometers.info) Elaboration of data by United Nations, Department of Economic and Social Affairs, Population Division. World Population Prospects: The 2019 Revision.

Zimbabwe Ministry of Primary and Secondary Education. (2018). *Government of Zimbabwe Ministry of Primary and Secondary Education:Program Document Application for the Variable Tranche Portion of the Zimbabwe GPE Program Implementation Grant and for the Approved Grant from the Multiplier Fund* Retrieved from https://www.globalpartnership.org/sites/default/files/program_document_final_rev_sept18.pdf